SETTING
NATIONAL
PRIORITIES
The 1982 Budget

JOSEPH A. PECHMAN *Editor*

SETTING NATIONAL PRIORITIES
The 1982 Budget

Barry P. Bosworth
Robert W. Hartman
William W. Kaufmann
Joseph A. Pechman
A. James Reichley

THE BROOKINGS INSTITUTION
Washington, D.C.

THE BROOKINGS INSTITUTION is an independent organization devoted to nonpartisan research, education, and publication in economics, government, foreign policy, and the social sciences generally. Its principal purposes are to aid in the development of sound public policies and to promote public understanding of issues of national importance.

The Institution was founded on December 8, 1927, to merge the activities of the Institute for Government Research, founded in 1916, the Institute of Economics, founded in 1922, and the Robert Brookings Graduate School of Economics and Government, founded in 1924.

The Board of Trustees is responsible for the general administration of the Institution, while the immediate direction of the policies, program, and staff is vested in the President, assisted by an advisory committee of the officers and staff. The by-laws of the Institution state: "It is the function of the Trustees to make possible the conduct of scientific research, and publication, under the most favorable conditions, and to safeguard the independence of the research staff in the pursuit of their studies and in the publication of the results of such studies. It is not a part of their function to determine, control, or influence the conduct of particular investigations or the conclusions reached."

The President bears final responsibility for the decision to publish a manuscript as a Brookings book. In reaching his judgment on the competence, accuracy, and objectivity of each study, the President is advised by the director of the appropriate research program and weighs the views of a panel of expert outside readers who report to him in confidence on the quality of the work. Publication of a work signifies that it is deemed a competent treatment worthy of public consideration but does not imply endorsement of conclusions or recommendations.

The Institution maintains its position of neutrality on issues of public policy in order to safeguard the intellectual freedom of the staff. Hence interpretations or conclusions in Brookings publications should be understood to be solely those of the authors and should not be attributed to the Institution, to its trustees, officers, or other staff members, or to the organizations that support its research.

Foreword

THE BUDGET for fiscal 1982 represents the beginning of a strong effort by the Reagan administration and Congress to slow the growth of federal spending and to lighten the tax burden on individuals and businesses. The proposed changes in outlays would affect many programs, large and small; the tax changes would reduce all marginal income tax rates and increase depreciation allowances for most business enterprises. The proposals are far-reaching and deserve serious consideration by the public as well as Congress.

This volume, the twelfth in an annual Brookings series published since 1970, explains the president's budget, examines alternative policies, and evaluates the implications of the various options for the short and long run. The original budget for fiscal 1982 was prepared by President Carter before he left office; it was thoroughly revised by President Reagan in two messages sent to Congress on February 18 and March 10, 1981. The revisions enabled the authors of this book to compare the choices made by the two presidents in dealing with the difficult budget and economic issues that confront the nation.

The book first describes recent budget developments that led to big increases in budget outlays and the deficit. It then examines the proposed budget for fiscal 1982 and the prospects for achieving the administration's budgetary and economic goals. Separate chapters devoted to the details of the nondefense and defense budgets are followed by a chapter that analyzes recent budget trends and evaluates the longer-run outlook. The final chapter traces the development of President Reagan's social and economic ideas and his efforts to implement a conservative philosophy. The first of two appendixes explains how the federal government finances private activities through loans and loan guarantees by off-budget agencies. The second deals with special income tax provisions, which are in many ways equivalent to direct federal expenditures in pursuing social and economic objectives—without, however, being subject to the same degree of congressional scrutiny.

This volume reflects collaboration among all three Brookings research programs. Joseph A. Pechman is director and Barry P. Bosworth and Robert W. Hartman are members of the staff of the Economic Studies program; William W. Kaufmann, a consultant to the Foreign Policy Studies program, is a member of the faculty of the Massachusetts Institute of Technology; and A. James Reichley is a member of the staff of the Governmental Studies program. The authors are grateful to other members of the Brookings staff, to Resources for the Future, and to ICF Incorporated for assistance in the preparation of their contributions.

The risk of factual error in this book was minimized by the work of Penelope Harpold, Ellen W. Smith, and Clifford A. Wright. Karen J. Wirt and Elizabeth H. Cross edited the manuscript.

The Brookings Institution is grateful to the Allie S. and Frances W. Freed Foundation, Inc., for providing funds to help support this volume.

The views expressed here are solely those of the authors and should not be ascribed to the Freed Foundation or to the trustees, officers, or other staff members of the Brookings Institution.

BRUCE K. MAC LAURY
President

April 1981
Washington, D.C.

Contents

1. Introduction and Summary 1
   Joseph A. Pechman
   Budget Policy *2*
   Economic Policy *3*
   The Nondefense Budget *6*
   The Defense Budget *8*
   The Budget Outlook *12*
   A Change in Ideological Direction *15*

2. The Federal Budget, Fiscal Years 1980–82 17
   Joseph A. Pechman and Barry P. Bosworth
   The Fiscal 1980 Budget *18*
   The Fiscal 1981 Budget *23*
   The Fiscal 1982 Budget *26*
   The Budget and the Economy *36*

3. The Nondefense Budget 45
   Joseph A. Pechman and others
   Social Security *48*
   Welfare *54*
   Employment and Training *60*
   Unemployment Compensation *64*
   Health *67*
   Education *72*
   Housing *77*
   Local Economic Development *82*

Energy *86*
Agriculture *92*
Transportation *97*
Natural Resources and the Environment *103*
Grants to State and Local Governments *108*
Pay and Benefits for Federal Workers *112*
Regulation *117*
Tax Expenditures *120*
Foreign Economic Assistance *124*
Summary *129*

4. The Defense Budget   133
   William W. Kaufmann

The Carter Defense Program *134*
The Reagan Amendments *136*
The U.S. Force Structure *138*
The Approach of the Carter Five-Year Defense Program *143*
Assessing the Future Military Balance *157*
The Range of Uncertainty *162*
Hedges against Uncertainty *171*
Summary *182*

5. The Budget Outlook   185
   Robert W. Hartman

Budget History, 1960–80   *185*
The Reagan Budget Plan *209*
The Reagan Plan in Historical Context *225*

6. A Change in Direction   229
   A. James Reichley

Taft and Goldwater Republicans *231*
The Making of a Conservative *233*
Supply-side Economics *236*
Avoiding an Economic Dunkirk *240*
The Old Federalism *246*
Conservative Nationalism *248*
The Moral Issue *255*
A Reagan Revolution? *259*

Appendix A. Fiscal Activities outside the Budget   261
Andrew S. Carron

Appendix B. Tax Expenditures   271
Joseph J. Minarik

Text Tables

2-1. The Federal Budget, Fiscal Years 1979–81   19

2-2. Chronology of the Estimates of Federal Budget Outlays for
Fiscal Years 1980 and 1981   20

2-3. Major Changes in Outlays and Receipts from Original Estimates,
Fiscal Years 1980 and 1981   22

2-4. Changes in Outlays and Receipts of the Current Services Budget,
Fiscal Years 1981–82   28

2-5. Current Services and the Carter and Reagan Budgets,
Fiscal Years 1980–82   30

2-6. Changes in Current Services Outlays in the Carter Budget,
Fiscal 1982   31

2-7. Changes in Current Services Receipts Proposed in the Carter
and Reagan Budgets, Fiscal 1982   32

2-8. Changes in Current Services Outlays in the Reagan Budget,
Fiscal 1982   34

2-9. Comparison of Carter and Reagan Economic Assumptions,
Calendar Years 1980–84   38

3-1. Federal Outlays for Welfare Programs, Fiscal Years 1980–82   55

3-2. Some Potential Savings in the Federal Transportation Budget,
Fiscal Years 1982–86   102

3-3. Federal Budget Outlays for Foreign Economic and Financial
Assistance, Fiscal Years 1961–82   127

4-1. The Carter Five-Year Defense Program, Fiscal Years 1981–86   134

4-2. Defense Outlays as a Percent of Gross National Product
and Federal Outlays, Selected Fiscal Years, 1944–82   135

4-3. Comparison of the Reagan Amendments and the Carter Five-Year
Defense Program, Fiscal Years 1981–86   137

4-4. Estimated Ten-Year Costs of Rapid Deployment Force Programs
in the Carter Defense Program   155

4-5. Potential U.S. Combat Deployments at M+40   175

4-6. Estimated Ten-Year Costs of First-Priority Increments to the
Carter Defense Program   176

4-7. Estimated Ten-Year Costs of Second-Priority Increments to the
Carter Defense Program   178

4-8. Estimated Ten-Year Costs of Third-Priority Increments to the
Carter Defense Program   180

4-9. Estimated Ten-Year Costs of Fourth-Priority Increments to the
Carter Defense Program   181

4-10. Summary of Estimated Ten-Year Costs of Priority Increments
to the Carter Defense Program   182

4-11. Estimated Five-Year Cost Impact of the Priority Increments
on the Carter Defense Program   183

5-1. Federal Budget Outlays, Receipts, and Surplus or Deficit as a
Percentage of Gross National Product, Selected Fiscal Years,
1960–80   186

5-2. Federal Budget Outlays by Major Category, Selected Fiscal
Years, 1970–80   188

5-3. Program Outlays as a Percentage of Gross National Product,
Fiscal Years 1970–80   189

5-4. Program Outlays in Constant 1972 Dollars, Fiscal Years
1970–80   190

5-5. Size and Growth of the Public Sector and Rates of Inflation
in Ten Industrial Countries, 1970–78   193

5-6. Federal and State and Local Receipts, Fiscal Years 1970–80   194

5-7. Estimated Marginal Tax Rates under 1980 Tax Law and under
1970 and 1975 Laws Indexed for Inflation, by Selected Income
Class, 1981   196

5-8. Federal Lending Activity, Fiscal Years 1978–80   199

5-9. Share of Funds Raised in Nonfinancial Credit Markets
by Borrowing Sector, Fiscal Years 1970–80   201

5-10. Public Debt and Loan Assets of the Federal Government,
End of Selected Fiscal Years, 1960–80   207

5-11. The Reagan Administration's Federal Budget Outlay Projections,
by Major Category, Fiscal Years 1980–84   210

5-12. The Reagan Administration's Program Outlays, by Major
Category, First-Stage Reductions Only, Fiscal Years 1981–84   211

5-13. Ratio of Federal Receipts under the Reagan Administration's
Budget to Outlays and Gross National Product, Fiscal Years
1980–84   218

5-14. Federal Borrowing, Reagan Budget Plan, under Alternate
Economic Assumptions, Fiscal Years 1980–84   221

5-15. Effects of Changed Economic Assumptions on the Reagan
Administration's Estimates of Outlays, Receipts, and Deficits,
Fiscal Years 1981–84   223

5-16. Federal Debt under the Reagan Administration's Budget,
Fiscal Years 1980–84   224

Appendix Tables

A-1. Outlays for the Budget, Off-Budget Federal Entities, and
Government-Sponsored Enterprises, Selected Fiscal Years,
1960–80   262

A-2. Net Change in Lending under Federal Auspices and Relation
to Total Funds Advanced in U.S. Credit Markets, Selected Years,
1965–82   264

B-1. Effect of Tax Expenditures on the Federal Current Services
Budget, Fiscal 1982   272

B-2. Major Tax Expenditures, Fiscal 1982   273

B-3. Estimated Federal Current Services Outlays and Tax Expenditures,
by Function, Fiscal 1982   275

Figures

4-1. U.S. ICBM Silo Survivability, 1979–85   145

4-2. U.S. Surviving Warheads after Soviet First Strike, 1979–89   146

CHAPTER ONE

Introduction and Summary

JOSEPH A. PECHMAN

PRESIDENT Ronald Reagan assumed office at a time when inflation was running at double-digit rates, unemployment was high, and
productivity growth was at a low ebb. He campaigned on a platform which emphasized that the major ills of the economy were
caused by excessive federal government spending and budget deficits.
Immediately upon inauguration, he set out to fulfill his campaign
promises to cut the size and scope of the federal government sharply
and to eliminate the deficit by the end of his term.

The major features of the Reagan budget policy are to reduce nondefense spending in the year beginning October 1, 1981, and ending
September 30, 1982 (fiscal 1982), by $48.6 billion below the level
proposed by his predecessor and to reduce taxes of individuals and
businesses by $53.9 billion. At the same time, defense spending is to
be greatly accelerated. If this program is enacted and the economic
assumptions of the administration are realized, fiscal 1982 outlays
will be cut from 23.0 percent of the gross national product to 21.8
percent, and receipts will be reduced from 22.1 percent to 20.4 percent. By 1984, outlays and receipts will be down to 19.3 percent of
the GNP and the budget will be balanced.

I thank Robert W. Hartman, William W. Kaufmann, and A. James Reichley for
their assistance in the preparation of this chapter; Katharine L. Bradbury, Lester B.
Lave, Joseph J. Minarik, Louise B. Russell, and Fred H. Sanderson for their comments; and Valerie J. Harris and Evelyn M. E. Taylor for their efficient secretarial
assistance.

The budget is only one element of a major reorientation of economic policy. In addition to spending and tax cuts, President Reagan also proposes to reduce the burden of federal regulations on the economy and to halve the rate of growth of the money supply. These proposals, he believes, will break the "cycle of negative expectations ... revitalize economic growth, renew optimism and confidence, and rekindle the Nation's entrepreneurial instincts and creativity." Thus the debate over the new policies is a debate about whether the Reagan program will produce a change in economic expectations and behavior and launch the U.S. economy on a new era of growth and stability.

Budget Policy

The background for the early decisions of the Reagan administration was a year of frustration in economic and budget policies. During 1980, interest rates soared to record levels; inflation remained at double-digit rates for the second consecutive year despite a brief but sharp recession; and the condition of the federal budget kept deteriorating. In his initial budget plans for fiscal 1980, which were transmitted to Congress in January 1979, President Carter proposed outlays of $531.6 billion and a deficit of $29 billion. Actual outlays were $48 billion higher than the original estimate, and the deficit rose $30.6 billion more than expected to $59.6 billion. About a fifth of the increase in outlays was attributable to increased defense spending, but the most important cause was the disappointing performance of the economy. Higher than expected inflation, unemployment, and interest rates raised social security and other federal benefits that are automatically adjusted for inflation and also increased unemployment benefits and interest payments on the national debt.

The estimates for fiscal 1981 suffered the same fate. The initial budget for that year, transmitted by President Carter in January 1980, called for outlays of $615.8 billion and a deficit of $15.8 billion. Again, defense spending increased and inflation, unemployment, and interest rates exceeded expectations as the year progressed. When the 1981 budget was reestimated a year later, budget outlays were raised by $46.9 billion and the deficit by $39.4 billion to

$55.2 billion. More recent estimates suggest that the final figures will be even higher.

The first version of the fiscal 1982 budget was completed by President Carter after he was defeated in the 1980 election. This budget, which was transmitted in January 1981, proposed another large increase in defense spending and significant cuts in nondefense spending; it also proposed a liberalization of depreciation allowances for business effective January 1, 1981, but cuts in individual income taxes were delayed until January 1, 1982. These policies would have resulted in 1982 outlays of $739.3 billion, receipts of $711.8 billion, and a deficit of $27.5 billion.

President Reagan revamped the 1982 budget completely in two messages delivered to Congress on February 18 and March 10, 1981. He raised defense outlays even more than President Carter had proposed, slashed nondefense outlays by $48.6 billion (including $8.2 billion of cuts proposed by President Carter), and proposed tax cuts of $53.9 billion for both individuals and businesses. His budget calls for outlays of $695.3 billion, receipts of $650.3 billion, and a deficit of $45.0 billion.

The tax changes recommended by President Reagan are virtually the same as the proposals he made during the presidential campaign. He recommends a modified version of the 10-5-3 depreciation proposal, which would permit tax write-offs over a period of ten years for structures, five years for equipment, and three years for vehicles. (The modification limits the ten-year write-off to industrial buildings, retail stores, and warehouses; other structures are given longer periods.) He also endorses the Kemp-Roth across-the-board cut of 30 percent in individual income tax rates, phased in over a period of three years. The depreciation proposal is to be made effective January 1, 1981 (to prevent delays in investment decisions while the tax bill is debated in Congress), and the cut in individual income tax rates is to begin on July 1, 1981.

Economic Policy

A considerable amount of rhetoric regarding the potentials of supply-side economics accompanied the unveiling of the Reagan budget. According to the supply-side school, cuts in marginal income tax rates will significantly stimulate work, saving, and investment incentives and generate large increases in productivity growth. A few enthusiasts even argue that large rate cuts quickly pay for themselves through the feedback of additional tax revenues from increased growth. The tax policies announced by President Reagan are almost identical to those that the supply-siders have been supporting. The Reagan budget does envisage more real growth and less inflation than the Carter budget, but not as much as some of the supply-siders have been predicting.

President Reagan expects his program to increase the nation's real growth rate by almost 1 percent over each of the next three years, accumulating to an increase of about 3 percent by 1984. Part of these gains (0.5 to 1.0 percentage point) would result from fuller use of existing resources; the remainder (2.0 to 2.5 percentage points) would be generated by improved incentives stimulated by the tax cuts. Supply-side gains of this magnitude are not outside the realm of possibilities, but they are not supported by the econometric evidence on past responses of investment, saving, and labor supply to increases in depreciation allowances and cuts in individual income tax rates of the kind proposed. The implicit increase in labor supply expected to result from the income tax cuts seems particularly high, since a large share of the cuts would simply offset the increase in effective tax rates as taxpayers are pushed up into higher tax brackets by inflation. Moreover, the proposed across-the-board cut in income taxes, much of which would increase consumption, would be less effective in stimulating productivity growth than tax adjustments that would increase investment and saving.

The novel aspect of the Reagan projections is the rapid decline in inflation expected during the next three years. The rate of increase in the consumer price index is to fall from 11.1 percent in calendar year 1981 to 5.5 percent in 1984. This improvement in inflation does not come about as a result of demand restraint to slow down the growth of economic activity—the traditional prescription. Rather, the administration's economists expect the improvement to occur because the new budget and tax policies, along with a restrictive monetary policy, will break inflationary expectations.

This interpretation of the inflation process and how it can be controlled differs markedly from the conventional view. Most economists believe that, in the absence of some policy to restrain wages and prices directly, a long period of economic slack will be needed to change inflationary expectations. By contrast, the Reagan team expects inflation to decelerate sharply even as the economy picks up steam. The mechanism that would bring about this optimistic combination of less inflation and more growth has not been convincingly explained.

Monetary policy is a key element of the Reagan economic plan, but the administration's monetary growth targets are difficult to reconcile with its other economic projections. The nominal GNP is expected to grow about 12 percent annually between 1980 and 1984, and real GNP by an average of almost 4 percent a year. The growth of nominal GNP must be financed by a combination of increases in the stock of money and its velocity (GNP per unit of money). The 1981 monetary growth target was set by the Federal Reserve at between 3.5 and 6 percent for M-1B; the Reagan program calls for a 50 percent reduction in monetary growth by 1986, with interest rates declining sharply during the period. The implied rise in velocity is outside the range of historical experience. If the velocity increase does not occur, interest rates will rise to bring the growth of monetary demand down to a level that is consistent with the monetary targets. The increase in interest rates will fall heavily on investment and retard the growth of the economy.

The fiscal policy objectives of the Reagan administration will be difficult to achieve. The Reagan budget projects a reduction of the deficit from $55 billion in fiscal 1981 to $45 billion in 1982 as a result of the higher economic growth assumptions. The budget proposes that the tax and spending cuts be linked so that the deficit will not be increased. If the spending cuts are shaved by Congress or if real growth is lower than expected, the deficit will be higher. For example, if real growth is one percentage point less than the forecast and inflation is one percentage point higher, the deficit would increase by $14 billion. Given the Federal Reserve's determination to restrain the growth in the money supply, the increase in the deficit would raise interest rates, which in turn would retard private spending, raise unemployment, and further increase the deficit. It would be risky, therefore, to act on the proposed income tax reduction of $44.2 billion for fiscal 1982 before action on the spending side of the budget has been completed.

The success of the Reagan budget and economic program hinges on the assumption that inflationary expectations can be changed without retarding growth. The supply-side effects of the tax cuts, even if they are significant, will be felt only gradually. In the meantime, the basic rate of inflation that is now at about 10 percent a year, reflecting the inertia of the wage-price cycle, may continue or worsen if energy, agriculture, or other shocks disturb the economy. Since the Reagan administration has eschewed any policy to moderate the growth of wages and prices through voluntary agreements, tax inducements, or direct controls, there is considerable danger that inflation will not be moderated and that the growth objectives of the program will not be achieved.

The Nondefense Budget

The reduction of $48.6 billion in nondefense outlays proposed by President Reagan extends into every corner of the nondefense budget, except for seven "safety net" programs that he promises to preserve. The safety net includes the basic social security benefits (retirement benefits and medicare); basic unemployment benefits; cash benefits for dependent families, the elderly and disabled veterans' pensions; Head Start; summer youth employment; and subsidized nutrition programs for low-income children and the elderly. By exempting the safety net programs, a reduction of one-sixth in other nondefense outlays is required to achieve the goal of cutting $48.6 billion.

The Reagan budget includes reductions of $4.6 billion in outlays for employment and training, $3.9 billion in energy programs, $3.5 billion in food stamps and other food and nutrition programs, $3.0 billion in social security benefits other than the basic benefits, $2.4 billion in health programs, $1.7 billion in transportation subsidies, $1.1 billion in support for elementary and secondary education, and numerous other cuts. In addition, substantial reductions are made in obligational authority for such programs as housing and foreign aid, which will appear in reduced outlays in future years. Particularly hard hit by these program reductions are grants-in-aid to state and local governments, which are cut by $13.4 billion, or 13 percent in nominal terms and 20 percent in real terms.

The idea of protecting some of the major social programs from the proposed budget cuts is appealing on humanitarian grounds (and understandable on political grounds), but there is no consistent rationale for the particular selections made by the Reagan administration. For example, some social security benefits are terminated and eligibility for disability is restricted. Yet the overadjustment for inflation that was made in the basic benefits during the past three years (because of a flaw in the price index) would not be corrected. The proposed budget cuts federal outlays for medicaid while medicare, which pays benefits to the aged regardless of income, is spared. It would be more consistent with the concept of the safety net to exempt only those programs that are heavily targeted on the poor and to concentrate the cuts in other programs. The two major possibilities are to correct the overadjustment of benefits for inflation and to introduce cost sharing in the medicare program.

Several of the specific proposals made by the Reagan administration are controversial in their impact on various segments of the population. It hardly seems possible to cut $5.5 billion in federal welfare outlays without hurting many truly needy people. Employment and training programs are being dismantled, even though unemployment remains high, particularly among youth. The proposed requirement that recipients of unemployment compensation accept minimum-wage jobs after thirteen weeks may accelerate job search by such workers, but it would force many of them to accept jobs below the level of their training and skills and would impose financial hardships. Housing subsidies for low-income families would be cut, but no effort is made to eliminate the tax benefits of homeowners with higher incomes that result in overinvestment in housing at the expense of industrial capital formation. Low pay raises for federal workers and a freeze on the salaries of top officials may reduce the quality and experience of federal officials; this is of particular concern in areas such as defense with rapidly rising spending and in agencies that will implement the administration's approach to regulatory reform. The proposed 10 percent cut in the real value of foreign aid for economic development would, if enacted, deny funds to millions of needy people in the developing countries and jeopardize the long-run security and economic interests of the United States.

President Reagan has asked Congress to decentralize government through a change in the system of federal aid to the states and local governments. He proposes the consolidation of numerous categorical grant programs into block grants, beginning with education, health and social services, and community development. The increased flexibility given to the state and local governments and the reduction in supervisory costs at the federal level should improve program efficiency, but the 20 percent real cut in total grants funds will place a heavy fiscal burden on many units of government. To prevent drastic reductions in services in the poorer localities, assistance under the new block grants could be targeted to the fiscally weak communities.

Many of the economies recommended by President Reagan are long overdue, although the steps taken are generally modest. Users of federal services and facilities should be required to pay for the costs of the benefits they receive; the proposed $2.1 billion increase is only a small fraction of the fees and charges that could be justified on efficiency grounds. Some uneconomical water projects are being phased out, but many more are not being touched. Transportation subsidies are being cut, but inefficient rail passenger service is still being retained and general aviation will continue to be heavily subsidized. The massive subsidies to support commercial production of synthetic fuels and gasohol are being reduced, but the extent to which these programs should be subsidized is not clear. Dairy price supports are being reduced, but other obsolete agricultural programs that impose costs on taxpayers as well as consumers are being continued with little change.

If cuts in outlays of the size proposed by President Reagan are approved by Congress and if no new programs are added, there will be room for modest reductions in effective income tax rates during the next few years. He must be given credit for a bold and comprehensive program of spending reductions designed to register a marked change in federal responsibilities. But he has not addressed some of the basic structural problems in major federal programs, such as social security, health, welfare, and intergovernmental relations. Consideration of the Reagan proposals will give Congress an opportunity to resolve some of these issues as well as to cut the growth of federal spending.

The Defense Budget

Regardless of the political party in power, there has been growing agreement in the last few years that expanding Soviet military capabilities, rising international turbulence, and the overseas interests of the United States require a strengthening of U.S. (and allied) defenses. With the support and indeed the insistence of Congress, the Carter administration submitted a defense program for fiscal 1981 that required $171.2 billion in obligational authority and proposed $157.6 billion in outlays. Before leaving office, President Carter submitted an even larger defense program that called for obligational authority of $196.4 billion and outlays of $180 billion in fiscal 1982.

Basically these two budgets were intended to support the now traditional U.S. defense policy of nuclear and nonnuclear deterrence. Strategic and theater nuclear deterrence is obtained through the continuing development and deployment of forces capable of covering a comprehensive target system in the Soviet Union and its satellites. Nonnuclear deterrence is provided by the maintenance of general purpose forces sufficient to respond simultaneously, in conjunction with allies, to one major and one lesser military contingency. These deterrent capabilities were to be enhanced by modernizing the strategic nuclear force, deploying intermediate-range ballistic and cruise missiles in Europe, increasing the readiness of the general purpose forces, improving the capabilities of the ground and tactical air forces to deploy to Europe and the Persian Gulf, and gradually modernizing the ground, naval, and tactical air forces.

The Reagan administration has proposed certain minor reductions in the two Carter defense budgets, but it has recommended adding budget authority of $6.8 billion to the original 1981 budget and $25.8 billion to the original 1982 budget. These increases will result in outlays of $158.6 billion in 1981 and $184.8 billion in 1982 —$1 billion and $4.8 billion more, respectively, than was planned in the two Carter budgets.

The additional funds requested by President Reagan for 1981 and 1982 would be used primarily to develop a new strategic bomber ($2.4 billion), raise military pay across the board ($2.3 billion), finance weapons and increasing fuel costs ($1.8 billion), raise major procurement for ground, naval and air force equipment ($12.6 billion), and increase minor procurement ($12 billion, of which $1 billion would be for the rapid deployment force).

All these increases are needed to maintain current defense policy. Even the reactivation of two battleships and a carrier are simply designed to support the navy's traditional goal of fifteen battle groups. It should be noted, however, that President Reagan has foreshadowed much larger increases in the 1983–86 defense budgets. These increases, which would be $169.6 billion higher (in 1982 dollars) than what was programmed by the Carter administration for the same years, would bring about major changes in policy.

Pending further knowledge about these projections and programs, it remains unclear whether the Carter program and the Reagan amendments fully address the U.S. security problems of the foreseeable future. There is a strong case for continued modernization, increased readiness, and greater force sustainability. It makes more sense to exploit the potential capability of current forces than to add partially effective and expensive force structure. Whether the right candidates are being chosen for attention is more debatable.

The strategic nuclear forces continue to warrant modernization. It is true that, despite the growing vulnerability of the Minuteman intercontinental ballistic missile force, the United States will retain a powerful second-strike capability through the 1980s. A new intercontinental ballistic missile (ICBM) will nonetheless be justified; and eventually so will a new bomber. Although questions remain about the appropriate basing mode for the new ICBM, the Carter program probably reflects the right scale and pace for upgrading the strategic force. A new interim bomber (such as the B-1 or the lengthened FB-111) does not seem worth its cost.

Much less certain is the case for additional airlift, large amounts of war matériel pre-positioned overseas, and the efforts to make U.S. conventional forces highly versatile. The most serious nonnuclear problem facing the United States and its allies in the years ahead is the possibility that military challenges could develop more or less simultaneously, following a period of observable enemy buildup, in three key theaters—Europe, the Persian Gulf, and northeast Asia. The current and programmed U.S. posture, even with the increased funding requested by the Reagan administration, will not be well suited to deal with this possibility.

Because of the constraints on acquiring additional military manpower and the difficulty of expanding the U.S. war production base in less than three years, adding to the existing force structure is the slowest and most expensive way to cope with the threat of multiple contingencies. Easier and cheaper alternatives would entail a greater reliance on the National Guard and Reserve forces, and on fast sea-lift rather than on airlift. War reserve stocks should also be increased, and selective pay raises should be provided to stabilize the present size and composition of military personnel on active duty.

This type of targeted approach might require net additional resources of about $42 billion (in 1982 dollars) over the next ten years. The Carter budget calls for the appropriation of about $1,085 billion (in 1982 dollars) from fiscal 1982 through 1986. Moderate hedging against multiple contingencies would raise that total by half of the $42 billion ten-year total, or $21 billion.

Less urgent but still important insurance against multiple contingencies and greater U.S. security against a massive Warsaw Pact attack would entail four main programs: additional amphibious ships for the marines and more frigates for the navy (to increase escort and convoy capabilities); more army and air force reserve units possessing modern equipment and brought to high states of readiness; full equipage of existing active-duty navy and air force wings with modern aircraft; and a further buildup of war reserve stocks. The ten-year costs of these programs would amount to more than $140 billion (in 1982 dollars). Over the period of the five-year defense plan, such insurance would increase the Carter totals by $70 billion.

The means could also be acquired to deter the more remote possibility of a large-scale surprise attack by the Warsaw Pact in Europe and prevent an eventual transfer of Soviet forces from the Far East to Central Europe. These contingencies might necessitate continuation (rather than cancellation) of a large program to acquire new military airlift aircraft (130 or more), more equipment and supplies pre-positioned in Europe, and as many as 7 additional wings of close air support aircraft for the air force. The ten-year costs of these programs could amount to $42 billion (in 1982 dollars), and raise the Carter five-year total by another $21 billion.

A final set of programs, at the lowest level of priority, would strengthen U.S. nuclear deterrent capabilities by increasing the day-to-day alert rate of the strategic bombers, substitute submarine-launched for ground-launched cruise missiles in Europe, begin a major program of constructing fallout shelters near U.S. military installations, and accelerate development of ballistic missile defenses for the protection of the ICBM forces. The ten-year costs of these low-priority programs would come to about $22 billion (in 1982 dollars), and would add about $11 billion to the Carter five-year totals.

If an orderly program of replacing older weapons systems were followed, these four successive increases would, over the five-year period, add another $60 billion in prospective capital costs to the defense budget.

With these additions to the Carter five-year plan, appropriations for fiscal years 1982–86 would amount to just under $1,270 billion (in 1982 dollars). According to the figures presented in the Reagan amendments, which constitute at best an outline of the five-year defense plan eventually to be developed by the new administration, total defense appropriations would increase to slightly more than $1,280 billion (in 1982 dollars) in 1982–86, an amount that is somewhat larger than the Carter five-year plan augmented by all four hedges fully financed. The annual outlays under the Reagan program range from $184.8 billion in 1982 to $263.3 billion in 1986 in 1982 dollars and $336 billion in current dollars.

With an adversary such as the Soviet Union, conservatism in defense planning and protection against even moderately plausible threats to vital U.S. interests can be justified. Whether additions of nearly $200 billion (in 1982 dollars) beyond the Carter five-year defense plan are warranted is much more open to debate. Of that total, at least $55 billion could be saved for other purposes over the five-year period, without any noticeable reduction in the security of the nation, by eliminating the appropriations for the two hedges with lowest priority and the capital funds associated with them.

The United States can afford whatever is necessary for a prudent defense. It cannot afford to overshoot the mark, especially if the effect becomes so threatening that it ratchets the adversary's military effort still higher. The United States may well be some distance from producing such an effect; judgments on that score no doubt will vary. Aside from the undesirability of provoking an even greater arms race, the expansion of defense spending must be tempered by budgetary and economic considerations.

The Budget Outlook

Planning the shape of the federal budget for several years ahead has become a deservedly important preoccupation of all presidents and congressional budget decisionmakers. The major elements of President Reagan's long-run program are a reduction in the growth of federal spending, a sharp change in the composition of the budget, cuts in individual and business taxes, and a balanced budget by fiscal 1984.

The increases in national defense spending and reductions in the nondefense budget already announced give a good indication of the administration's intentions as to the size and composition of government programs. The proposed real increase of 8 percent a year in defense spending will raise defense outlays from 25 percent of the budget in fiscal 1981 to 33 percent in fiscal 1984. The spending cuts will reduce real 1984 nondefense outlays 8 percent below the 1981 level on the average, but there are large variations among the different programs. After correction for inflation, programs designated as part of the social safety net rise by 4.1 percent; grants-in-aid to state and local governments decline by 37 percent, income-tested benefits by 11 percent, and all other programs (excluding interest and loans) by 19 percent. These dramatic reductions in nondefense spending became inevitable when the administration included in its budget plan the Kemp-Roth 30 percent reductions in tax rates designed to reverse the trend of rising taxes and decided to protect the social safety net programs from the kinds of cuts that were made in other programs.

The spending reductions already announced account for only about two-thirds of the cuts in outlays intended by the Reagan administration for fiscal 1984. If just the proposed $81 billion in cuts were put into effect, real federal spending in fiscal 1984 would be only slightly larger than it is estimated to be in 1981. If the additional $44 billion promised for later submission were made, the real level of spending in 1984 would be about 5 percent lower than in 1981. By contrast, the real growth in the three years ending in 1981 was about 4 percent.

The proposed cuts in individual and business taxes would amount to $148 billion in fiscal 1984. Of this total, $30 billion would go to business through liberalized depreciation allowances; the remaining $118 billion would go to individuals through across-the-board cuts in marginal tax rates. If enacted, these cuts would reduce taxes in 1984 from 22.9 percent of the GNP under presently scheduled tax rates to 19.3 percent. This would bring the tax ratio down to about the level reached in 1978, which is still equal to or higher than any previous post-World War II year except for 1969 and 1970 when the Vietnam War surtax was in effect.

The Reagan budget devotes a great deal of attention to opening up capital markets to business investment. Large reductions are proposed in government lending activities that rose rapidly in the 1970s and favored nonindustrial borrowing such as mortgages and student loans. At the same time, the reduced deficits projected in the program would lessen the federal government's role as a borrower in credit markets. It remains to be seen whether these changes will result in enhanced productive investment or whether the 1970s diversion of capital to housing and mortgage-financed consumption will be repeated.

The long-run economic assumptions that were incorporated in the administration's budget plan—high rates of real economic growth and large reductions in inflation and interest rates—are as optimistic as the short-run assumptions. If the growth rate is lower and inflation is higher than what has been forecast, federal outlays in fiscal years 1983 and 1984 would exceed the projected amounts and the budget would remain in deficit unless the tax reductions were cut back drastically. A significant part of the higher outlays would stem from the higher rates of interest the government would have to pay on the public debt.

If the economic scenario becomes less favorable than the Reagan administration has projected, borrowing to finance the deficits may crowd out some business investment. If primacy is given to increasing private investment even under conditions of slower growth, the shift of resources away from consumption may be even more painful.

The abrupt shift toward using a larger fraction of the national output for private business investment and national defense and the consequent reduction in federal benefit, grant, and operating programs called for in the Reagan budget raise issues of size and of timing. There is little doubt that public and expert opinion support a redirection toward productivity-enhancing activities and toward strengthening defense capabilities. But because the payoffs from these shifts are realizable only after a period of years and because the economic assumptions underlying the budget projections seem particularly optimistic, there is a serious question whether the nation should risk tax cuts extending to fiscal years 1983 and 1984 until the magnitude of the spending cuts and the performance of the economy become better known.

A Change in Ideological Direction

The Reagan administration's approaches to current national and international problems are based on a broadly consistent conservative ideology. Ronald Reagan now holds more political leverage than any president since Lyndon Johnson in 1965. If conservatism fails, the conservatives will not find it easy to argue that it has not been given a fair chance.

In his inaugural address, the president emphasized many of the themes for which Barry Goldwater campaigned in 1964: reduction of federal taxes and regulations, elimination of the deficit in the federal budget, return of power to the states, renewal of national pride, and a tougher attitude toward potential adversaries overseas. There have, however, been some changes in the conservative program since 1964, reflecting both adjustments to meet altered conditions and developments in conservative thought.

In economic policy, the administration takes its direction from the traditional free-market doctrine that the least possible government intervention, consistent with a stable currency and protection of public health and safety, will produce the most desirable levels of economic efficiency and growth. Supply-side economists, and their political allies like Congressman Jack Kemp, have persuaded the president to propose a sharp cut in tax rates on personal incomes and a substantial liberalization of depreciation allowances as a means of stimulating work, saving, and investment incentives. To reduce the danger of inflation, President Reagan has followed the advice of more orthodox economic conservatives in calling for large cuts in federal spending simultaneously with the tax cuts. Both supply-siders and orthodox conservatives agree on the need for tight restraint on the growth of the money supply.

Beside aiming to reduce the size of government, the administration has set out to decentralize control of government services. This effort is motivated in part by the belief that decentralization will make it easier to hold down government spending. Also, however, President Reagan and his associates regard decentralization as a means to strengthen control of public services at the state and local level and to make government programs more responsive to the realities of local needs and conditions.

The new administration also believes that federal regulation of the economy has imposed heavy burdens on U.S. industry. The Carter administration promoted deregulation of a number of industries (airlines, railroads, and finance); the Reagan administration will speed up the process in other industries and intends to make the remaining regulations more effective and less intrusive into business activities.

In foreign policy, the administration is forthrightly nationalistic, apparently sharing Irving Kristol's view that the American people want "rather more Theodore Roosevelt, and a lot less of Woodrow Wilson" in the conduct of international affairs. This nationalism is based not only on pursuit of direct economic and security interests, but also on the conviction that the United States has a special responsibility to uphold Western values. Where the Carter administration sought to put the United States on the side of change toward a more liberal world order, the Reagan administration takes the view that resistance against terrorism and communist aggression are the nation's most important international objectives.

The administration's conservative ideology is carried over into social issues not directly related to the budget, such as abortion and school prayer. On these issues, the administration has staked out a position as defender of traditional moral values against what President Reagan has called "perhaps the most serious challenge in our nation's history." How far the administration will go in promoting legislation on such controversial issues remains to be seen.

President Reagan's record as governor of California indicates that he is a pragmatic rather than an autocratic conservative. But he goes well beyond his recent Republican predecessors, Richard Nixon and Gerald Ford, in his commitment to change the direction of national government. He seeks not merely to modify existing trends, but to shift policies into a fundamentally altered ideological framework. History will decide whether he will succeed, but there is little question that the President is asking the nation to pursue new directions in both domestic and international policy.

CHAPTER TWO

The Federal Budget, Fiscal Years 1980–82

JOSEPH A. PECHMAN *and* BARRY P. BOSWORTH

FEDERAL budget outlays and the federal deficit reached post-World War II peaks in relation to the size of the economy in fiscal 1976. In that year, outlays amounted to $366.4 billion, or 22.3 percent of the gross national product; the deficit was $66.4 billion, or 4.0 percent of the gross national product. President Jimmy Carter came into office promising that he would reduce federal spending to 21 percent of the GNP and wipe out the deficit by fiscal 1981. He made what appeared to be good progress in the first three years of his term. Although federal outlays grew to $493.6 billion by fiscal 1979, they rose at a slower rate than the rest of the economy and ended the three-year period at 20.9 percent of the GNP; the deficit, which was reduced to $27.7 billion, declined to 1.2 percent of the GNP in the same year.

But the improving trend in the budget was sharply reversed in 1980. In that year, outlays increased 17 percent to $579.6 billion, or 22.6 percent of the GNP, and the deficit increased to $59.6 billion, or 2.3 percent of the GNP. Moreover, the budget outlook for the future remained grim. Despite considerable efforts by the administration and Congress, estimates of outlays and of the deficit for both fiscal years 1980 and 1981 continued to rise—by substantial amounts

The authors are grateful to Henry Aaron, Ralph C. Bryant, Robert W. Hartman, and Darwin G. Johnson for their advice and comments. Michael K. Kuehlwein and J. Edward Shepherd provided research assistance, and the manuscript was typed by Evelyn M. E. Taylor.

—as the fiscal years progressed. Thus, when the Reagan administration took office, it also placed the highest priority on reducing the growth of federal spending and balancing the budget.

On January 15, 1981, President Carter submitted his last budget for fiscal 1982, which called for outlays of $739.3 billion, receipts of $711.8 billion, and a deficit of $27.5 billion. Within a month the new president had identified the broad outline and many of the details of his budget plan and within two months he had transmitted his detailed budget to Congress. Although this is customary when a new president takes office, the scope of the proposed changes was unusually great. Proposed outlays and receipts for 1982 were both lower in the revised budget, but the deficit was higher. President Ronald Reagan requests outlays of $695.3 billion and receipts of $650.3 billion, which leaves a deficit of $45.0 billion.

To evaluate future budget prospects, it is necessary to understand why expenditures in 1980 and 1981 seemed to have gotten out of hand. The first two sections of this chapter are concerned with budget developments in these two fiscal years. In the third section the budget proposals of the outgoing Carter administration and the incoming Reagan administration are examined for fiscal 1982. The final section discusses the impact of the 1982 budget plans on the economy.

The Fiscal 1980 Budget

President Carter's initial budget plans for fiscal 1980 were transmitted to Congress in January 1979, when the economy was expanding rapidly, the inflation rate was rising, and Washington was reacting to the approval of property tax limitations in California and other states. Carter's response to these developments was to recommend what he called a "lean and austere" budget, one that would sharply reduce the rate of growth of federal spending. His budget proposed outlays of $531.6 billion (7.7 percent above the 1979 level) and a deficit of $29.0 billion. As table 2-1 shows, actual outlays were $579.6 billion, receipts were $520.0 billion, and the deficit was $59.6 billion. The increase in outlays is the largest that has ever occurred between the time a budget is proposed and its actual outcome when the fiscal year ends.

The federal budget in any particular period is only partly under the control of the administration and Congress. Each year in January

Table 2-1. **The Federal Budget, Fiscal Years 1979–81**

Billions of dollars

		1980		1981	
Item	1979 actual	January 1979 estimate	Actual	January 1980 estimate	January 1981 estimate
Outlays	493.6	531.6	579.6	615.8	662.7
Receipts	465.9	502.6	520.0	600.0	607.5
Deficit	− 27.7	− 29.0	− 59.6	− 15.8	− 55.2

Sources: *The Budget of the United States Government, Fiscal Year 1980*, p. 576; *The Budget of the United States Government, Fiscal Year 1981*, p. 614; and *The Budget of the United States Government, Fiscal Year 1982*, p. 613.

the president submits his estimates of what federal outlays and receipts will be under the program he proposes in the fiscal year that
begins nine months later, but many events intervene to alter the estimated totals. The laws governing some of the programs—like social
security, unemployment insurance, food stamps, medicare and medicaid—stipulate rules that determine who is "entitled" to benefits and
how much a recipient will receive. Many of these benefits are automatically increased as consumer prices rise, so that inflation automatically generates higher outlays. Entitlement programs can be
changed, but only through legislative action by Congress, which must
be approved by the president. Inflation also increases the costs of
other ongoing federal programs, such as defense procurement, highway construction, and health care services. Increases in interest rates
boost budget outlays for servicing the federal debt. Receipts also increase during inflation, but in 1979 and 1980 the rise in federal outlays brought about by inflation exceeded the rise in receipts even
though real income tax rates increase as taxpayers are pushed into
higher brackets. When unemployment increases, outlays for unemployment benefits increase automatically and tax receipts rise less
than expected or even fall. In addition, foreign and domestic developments often require changes in policies that were not foreseen when
the budget was originally put together. The demand for more defense
spending has increased in response to a continuing Soviet military
buildup and developments in Afghanistan and in the Persian Gulf;
as a result defense outlays have risen much faster than the initial
budget estimates anticipated. Finally, the budget is a fiscal *plan* proposed by the president, but every detail is subject to the approval of

Table 2-2. Chronology of the Estimates of Federal Budget Outlays for Fiscal Years 1980 and 1981

Billions of dollars

Item	Outlays	Receipts	Deficit (−) or surplus
		Fiscal 1980	
January 1979 budget	531.6	502.6	−29.0
July 1979 midsession review	542.4	513.8	−28.7
January 1980 budget	563.6	523.8	−39.8
March 1980 budget revision	568.9	532.4	−36.5
September 1980 actual outcome	579.6	520.0	−59.6
		Fiscal 1981	
January 1980 budget	615.8	600.0	−15.8
March 1980 budget revision	611.5	628.0	16.5
July 1980 midsession review	633.8	604.0	−29.8
January 1981 budget	662.7	607.5	−55.2

Sources: *The Budget of the United States Government, Fiscal Year 1980*, p. 579; and *The Budget of the United States Government, Fiscal Year 1982*, p. 613; Office of Management and Budget, *Midsession Review of the 1980 Budget*, p. 2, and *Midsession Review of the 1981 Budget*, p. 3.

Congress. The modifications in the president's budget plans made by Congress are frequently significant.

A chronology of the increases in outlays in the budget for fiscal 1980 between the time it was transmitted to Congress in January 1979 and the end of fiscal 1980, twenty months later, shows how many changes occur in the history of the budget for a single year and why spending is so difficult to control (table 2-2). By the time the midyear review of the budget was prepared in July 1979, estimated outlays had already increased by $10.8 billion, largely as a result of increases in spending on income security benefits (social security, and so on) and of higher interest payments on the debt because of a higher rate of inflation than expected. This effect was even more pronounced than usual because of a defect in the consumer price index that results in excessive weight being given to mortgage interest rates.[1] When the budget was reestimated in January 1980 (three months after the beginning of the fiscal year), the outlay estimates soared another $21.2 billion because of the continued increase in the inflation rate and the failure of Congress to enact most of the cost-

1. See chapter 3 for a discussion of this problem.

saving proposals recommended by President Carter (particularly containment of hospital costs). Nine months later, when the fiscal year ended, outlays jumped another $16.0 billion, this time because of the sharp drop in business activity in the spring of 1980, which increased unemployment benefits, and the continued high rate of inflation. Moreover, defense spending estimates were raised every time the budget estimates were revised. In total, actual outlays for the year exceeded the original estimates by $48.0 billion, or 9.0 percent.

The major factors contributing to the $48.0 billion rise in outlays during fiscal 1980 are summarized in table 2-3. Defense accounted for $9.8 billion of the increase; other major policy changes in a wide variety of federal activities (for example, increased outlays on dairy price supports, low-income energy assistance, mortgage-credit programs, and the Soviet grain embargo) and lack of action by Congress on the administration's cost-saving proposals raised outlays by $9.3 billion; and changes in estimates for particular programs and unforeseen events (mainly the Mount Saint Helens' eruption, which increased spending for disaster relief and for small business loans) added $8.5 billion. But the largest source of the higher spending was the disappointing economic performance, which raised non-defense outlays by $20.4 billion. Of this total, the effect on entitlements of the higher-than-expected rate of inflation accounted for $5.3 billion; higher unemployment, $6.5 billion; higher interest rates and increased borrowing, $6.8 billion; and outlays to support the mortgage market and financial institutions during the period of high interest rates and credit stringency, $1.8 billion.

Unanticipated inflation explains most of the unpredicted rise in receipts in fiscal 1980. The higher inflation rate increased income and payroll tax receipts by $13.5 billion. In addition, the windfall profit tax on oil, which was proposed after the original 1980 budget was submitted and went into effect three months before the fiscal year ended, raised receipts by $3.9 billion. On the other hand, a real-wage insurance program proposed by President Carter was rejected by Congress; because this insurance was to be provided through tax credits that would have reduced receipts, the failure of the proposal to be approved raised receipts by $2.3 billion. Other tax legislation proposed by Carter was not enacted (mainly acceleration of state and local government deposits of social security taxes), and this re-

Table 2-3. Major Changes in Outlays and Receipts from Original Estimates, Fiscal Years 1980 and 1981

Billions of dollars

Item	1980[a]	1981[b]
Outlays		
Defense	9.8	14.9
Nondefense	38.2	32.0
Major nondefense policy changes	9.3[c]	1.5[d]
Unforeseen events	1.8[e]	5.1[f]
Other differences	6.7[g]	−2.9[h]
Changes in economic conditions	20.4	28.3
Inflation	5.3	6.2
Unemployment	6.5	6.7
Interest rates and increased borrowing	6.8	12.7
Support for financial institutions	1.8	2.7
Total increase above original estimate	48.0	46.9
Receipts		
Changes in economic conditions	13.5	9.5
Total legislative changes	3.9	−2.0
Windfall profit tax	3.9	−1.4
Real wage insurance (not enacted)	2.3	...
Other (net)	−2.3	−0.6
Total increase above original estimate	17.4	7.5

Sources: *The Budget of the United States Government, Fiscal Year 1980*, p. 75; *The Budget of the United States Government, Fiscal Year 1981*, p. 71; *The Budget of the United States Government, Fiscal Year 1982*, p. 83; Office of Management and Budget, "Why 1980 Outlays Increased by $47 Billion"; and authors' estimates. Figures are rounded.

a. The original estimate was made in January 1979.

b. The original estimate was made in January 1980.

c. Includes dairy price supports ($0.6 billion), low-income energy assistance ($1.7 billion), mortgage-credit programs ($2.9 billion), the effect of the Soviet grain embargo ($1.5 billion), and congressional inaction on cost-saving legislative proposals like hospital cost containment ($3.0 billion), minus net reductions in other programs ($0.1 billion).

d. This is a net figure of increases and reductions in a large number of programs.

e. Includes outlays for disaster assistance and loans ($1.6 billion), refugee assistance ($0.3 billion), emergency construction ($0.2 billion) and claims and judgments against the United States ($0.2 billion), minus a reduction in the allowance for contingencies of $0.5 billion.

f. Includes the payment of the Penn-Central settlement ($2.1 billion) and increased disaster relief and refugee assistance ($3.0 billion).

g. Major items include increases in highway outlays ($1.8 billion), Export-Import Bank loans ($1.3 billion), foreign military outlays ($1.0 billion), minus a reduction in outlays for the strategic petroleum reserve ($1.5 billion), and increased receipts from leases of the offshore continental shelf ($2.0 billion), which count as reduction in outlays.

h. Mainly differences in estimates. A major item is increased receipts from leases of the offshore continental shelf ($1.8 billion).

duced receipts by $2.3 billion. Together, these changes increased receipts by $17.4 billion, or 3.5 percent.

By the end of fiscal 1980, outlays rose much more than receipts, which increased the deficit to $59.6 billion, more than twice the initial estimate. Since inflation was unacceptably high, fiscal policy was almost universally regarded as excessively expansionary.

The Fiscal 1981 Budget

When President Carter transmitted his budget for fiscal 1981 to Congress in January 1980, the economy was still expanding rapidly and the rate of inflation was accelerating. Although growth was expected to be slow in 1980, concern about inflation predominated both inside and outside the administration, and it was generally agreed that slow growth of the economy was a prerequisite to the control of inflation. Under the circumstances, the president was expected to submit an extremely tight budget for fiscal 1981, especially because he had promised "balance" in that year.

To the surprise of almost everyone, President Carter's fiscal 1981 budget kept outlays at the same level in real terms as they were in 1980, which meant a 9.0 percent increase in outlays, or $615.8 billion in current dollars. The proposed budget was, in fact, rather tight in the nondefense area because the president had previously promised the NATO allies that real defense spending would rise by at least 3.0 percent. Thus, to keep total real spending level, the budget projected a reduction of 1.0 percent in real nondefense spending. But the expansion in real defense spending made total outlays appear less lean and austere than had been expected. Moreover, although the budget projected a greatly reduced deficit of $15.8 billion, the eagerly awaited balance was delayed. Finally, the proposed reduction in the deficit was to be accomplished by $21.0 billion of proposed tax increases (including a new windfall profit tax for oil, withholding on interest and dividends, and acceleration of individual and corporate tax payments), which were widely viewed as unlikely to be enacted.

Congress and the business and financial community were critical of the budget. Almost immediately, short-term interest rates rose sharply and stock and bond prices declined. Reflecting in part the large rise in mortgage rates, which lagged only slightly behind other interest rates, the rate of increase of the consumer price index—which had risen at an annual rate of 13 to 14 percent in the last quarter of 1979—shot up to an annual rate of 18 percent in the first quarter of 1980. Borrowing of all types surged—by consumers as well as by businesses. Depositors began withdrawing money from savings institutions, which left those institutions in a precarious position. It was clear that the budget deepened fears of accelerating inflation and that drastic action was needed to avoid panic.

On March 14, 1980, the administration responded by taking the unprecedented action of withdrawing its budget and announcing that it would work with Congress to reduce federal outlays sufficiently to balance the fiscal 1981 budget. It also requested the Federal Reserve to adopt a program of selective controls on credit. These controls included increases in bank reserve requirements, a surcharge of 3 percentage points on frequent borrowing by large banks from the Federal Reserve, and special new deposit requirements for increases in credit card lending, consumer installment credit, department store charge accounts, and money-market mutual fund assets.

The response to this program was sharp and swift. Business and consumer spending declined; total economic activity fell sharply in the second quarter of the year; unemployment rose; interest rates dropped; and the rise in the consumer price index fell to an annual rate of less than 4 percent in July and August. As it turned out, the recession was short-lived. Business activity rose in the last half of the year; interest rates rose to the peaks of the early months of the year; and the rise in the consumer price index quickened to an annual rate of more than 13 percent in the last quarter.

As these developments unfolded, the administration and Congress worked hard to restrain the growth in federal spending and to balance the budget. In March 1980 the president resubmitted his budget, with sharp reductions in outlays (estimates of which had already increased sharply as a result of the higher inflation and interest rates) and proposed additional tax increases. The revised budget called for outlays of $611.5 billion and receipts of $628.0 billion, which if realized would yield a surplus of $16.5 billion (table 2-2).

But economic developments again intervened to thwart the attempt to reduce the growth in outlays and to achieve a balanced budget. By July, when the midsession review of the budget was released, estimated outlays had already increased by $22.3 billion more than the March estimates and receipts had been reduced $24.0 billion, thus converting the planned surplus of $16.5 billion to a deficit of $29.8 billion.

During the following six months, Congress tried to reach agreement on the outlay reductions and tax increases proposed by President Carter in his March revisions of the fiscal 1981 budget. An untried legislative vehicle—called reconciliation—was used to implement the budget changes. The first congressional resolution on the budget, which in previous years had set guidelines for the appropriations and tax committees with weak enforcement provisions, was strengthened by including a reconciliation provision that stipulated the outlay savings and tax increases to be achieved. After the operating committees reported their proposals to the budget committees, they were packaged together in a single reconciliation bill that was subject to the approval or disapproval of both houses in toto.

Despite the good intentions, the final reconciliation bill, which cleared Congress on December 3, 1980, fell considerably short of the president's proposals. Instead of the reductions of $15.0 billion in outlays and the increases of $16.0 billion in receipts in fiscal 1981 (from withholding on interest and dividends and a new tax on gasoline production), Congress reduced outlays by only $4.6 billion and did not enact either of the new tax changes. However, the law did make small, permanent changes in some programs, approved a previously recommended speedup of the payment of corporation income taxes, and restricted the use of tax-exempt bonds for home mortgages. These decisions reduced permanent outlays by about $1.0 billion a year and increased receipts in fiscal 1981 by $3.4 billion.

This experience underscored the obstacles to restraining the budget even when there is agreement in principle on the need for restraint. At least part of the difficulty was the novelty of the legislative procedure used and the tight time constraints imposed. But the basic problem was that the reconciliation approach implied a shift in congressional power to the budget committees, power which the operating committees were not prepared to relinquish. Today the Reagan administration once again is attempting to use the reconciliation device to obtain congressional approval of its programs.

The last revision of the fiscal 1981 estimates by President Carter was contained in the budget he transmitted to Congress in January 1981. This revision raised estimated outlays for 1981 by another $28.9 billion above the July 1980 figure, while estimated receipts were increased by only $3.5 billion. Thus the budget, which in January 1980 called for outlays of $615.8 billion, receipts of $600.0 billion, and a deficit of $15.8 billion, was expected a year later to produce outlays of $662.7 billion, receipts of $607.5 billion, and a deficit of $55.2 billion (table 2-2).

The factors accounting for the rise in estimated outlays in fiscal

1981 are similar to those that contributed to the disappointing performance of the fiscal 1980 budget, though the amounts are different (see table 2-3). The defense program accounts for $14.9 billion, changed economic conditions for $28.3 billion (including $12.7 billion of higher interest payments), and program changes for $3.7 billion, or a total increase of $46.9 billion in estimated outlays. The rise of $7.5 billion in estimated receipts above the original estimate is the net effect of reduced receipts of $2.0 billion from new legislation and increased receipts of $9.5 billion from higher incomes resulting from inflation. The $39.4 billion increase in the deficit is due primarily to the rise in outlays, which in turn reflects the difficulty of containing total spending when defense commitments are increasing and when entitlement benefits and interest payments are rising sharply as a result of inflation.

The Fiscal 1982 Budget

Against this background, it is not surprising that one of the main issues of the 1980 campaign for the presidency was the growth of federal spending. Even as the campaign progressed, the estimates of outlays were being revised upward by substantial amounts. Both major presidential candidates promised to gain control of total spending and at the same time to increase defense outlays and cut taxes. President Carter proposed an income tax credit of 8 percent for social security taxes paid by employers and employees and a liberalization of the depreciation allowances used for tax purposes. Governor Reagan endorsed a proposal introduced by Representative Jack F. Kemp of New York and Senator William V. Roth of Delaware that would cut individual income tax rates by 30 percent over three years and also supported more generous depreciation allowances than those proposed by President Carter. Both candidates committed themselves to reducing the deficit quickly and to balancing the budget by the end of the following presidential term.

President Carter completed the budget for fiscal 1982 after he was defeated in the 1980 election. He could have submitted a budget that simply adjusted outlays for inflation and continued taxes at levels called for under existing law—the "current services" budget —and have allowed his successor to suggest changes he thought necessary. Instead, he proposed a large real increase in defense spending and significant cuts in nondefense spending and delayed most of the tax cuts he had proposed during the campaign.

President Reagan's budget plans are the centerpiece of his program to solve the serious problems of the U.S. economy.[2] In his budget proposal he argues that the growth in federal spending is the major cause of the high rate of inflation, and that large spending and tax cuts are needed to reduce inflation and raise the rate of productivity growth. Thus he recommends much larger spending cuts than President Carter's and urges that the Kemp-Roth tax plan for cutting personal income taxes be implemented. The nature of these proposals and their effect on the budget can be better understood by first examining the current services budget for fiscal 1982.[3]

The Current Services Budget

The current services estimates show outlays and receipts on the assumption that policy would remain unchanged. They allow for anticipated changes of a relatively uncontrollable nature (such as increases in the number of social security retirees), but they omit all proposed or pending new initiatives either by the president or by Congress. Clearly temporary programs are assumed to expire, but those that are routinely renewed are assumed to be renewed. The estimates reflect the effect of inflation on virtually all budget accounts, so as to provide a constant real program base against which the president's budget can be measured. The receipt estimates are based on current law, including any scheduled tax changes for the future, under the economic assumptions made by the administration.

In January 1981 the current services estimate of outlays in fiscal 1981 was $660.5 billion. To continue ongoing federal programs and activities at the 1981 levels, total outlays would have to reach $736.2 billion in 1982—$75.7 billion, or 11.5 percent, above the 1981 level, as shown in table 2-4. Most of this increase is accounted for by increases in outlays for income security, national defense, interest on

2. In addition to budget policy, Reagan proposes reforms in federal regulatory procedures and a gradually slowing rate of growth of the money supply. See the section on the budget and the economy for an analysis of the program.

3. The official "unified" budget does not include the activities of a number of federal agencies, called "off-budget entities"; and numerous tax subsidies, called "tax expenditures," are reflected in the budget in lower tax receipts rather than outlays. Outlays of off-budget entities and tax expenditures have been rising rapidly in recent years. Appendix A analyzes the activities of off-budget entities and how they should be treated in the budget; appendix B explains tax expenditures and their effect on the budget.

Table 2-4. Changes in Outlays and Receipts of the Current Services Budget, Fiscal Years 1981–82

Item	Billions of dollars
Outlays	
1981 current services estimate	660.5
1981–82 changes	75.7
Income security	27.7
Social security	21.4
Federal employee retirement	2.9
Food stamps and nutrition assistance	2.1
Housing assistance	1.6
Unemployment compensation	−2.0
Other	1.7
National defense	18.6
Military and civilian pay raises	7.2
Procurement	3.4
Operations and maintenance	3.4
Military retiree pay	2.2
Other	2.4
Health	9.3
Medicare and medicaid	8.7
Other	0.6
Net interest	8.3
Civilian agency pay raises	3.2
Energy programs	3.0
Farm income stabilization	3.5
Other (net)	2.1
1982 current services estimate	736.2
Receipts	
1981 current services estimate	605.0
1981–82 changes	101.5
Payroll tax	12.3
Windfall profit tax	7.4
Other legislation[a]	−4.1
Effect of inflation and growth	85.9
1982 current services estimate	706.5

Source: *Special Analyses, The Budget of the United States Government, Fiscal Year 1982*, pp. 10, 11, 14, and *The Budget of the United States Government, Fiscal Year 1982*, pp. 71–83.

a. Includes interest and dividend exclusion in the Crude Oil Windfall Profit Tax Act of 1980 (−$2.0 billion), acceleration of employer deposits of withheld income and FICA taxes (−$0.5 billion), the Omnibus Reconciliation Act of 1980 (−$0.2 billion), and other legislation (−$1.4 billion).

the debt, and health programs, largely as a result of the effect of continued inflation and higher interest rates.

Current services receipts are projected to increase from $605.0 billion in fiscal 1981 to $706.5 billion in fiscal 1982, a rise of $101.5 billion. Of this total, $12.3 billion comes from scheduled increases in the payroll tax for social security and $7.4 billion from the windfall profit tax; other legislation enacted in 1980 reduces receipts by $4.1 billion. The remaining $85.9 billion reflects tax increases resulting from inflation and some real growth.

With receipts rising by $101.5 billion and outlays by $75.7 billion, the current services deficit is expected to fall from $55.4 billion in fiscal 1981 to $29.7 billion in fiscal 1982, or a decline of $25.7 billion. Thus, even if federal spending programs were adjusted for inflation, revenues would rise more than outlays because of the automatic and scheduled tax increases. The reduction in the current services deficit, it should be emphasized, assumes no policy changes in existing outlay programs and the continuation of the tax system as it was in January 1981. New outlay initiatives and tax cuts would, of course, change the budget picture significantly.

The Carter Budget

President Carter proposed numerous increases and decreases in specific outlays and receipts in the current services budget, but the net changes in the aggregate figures were small. His recommendations would have resulted in 1982 outlays of $739.3 billion, $3.1 billion above the current services level, and receipts of $711.8 billion, $5.3 billion higher than the current services level. Thus the $27.5 billion deficit he recommended was only $2.2 billion lower than the current services level, as shown in table 2-5. But this relatively minor change in the deficit does not give a true picture of the many changes he would have made in both the outlay and receipt sides of the budget.

OUTLAYS. The increases in the Carter budget above the level of the 1982 current services outlays total $19.1 billion, as shown in table 2-6. Of this total, the largest single item is a $10.8 billion increase in defense outlays. The reductions total $15.9 billion, of which the largest ($5.8 billion) is from a proposal to reduce the federal pay increase of October 1981 to 5.5 percent for civilian employees and 9.1 percent for military personnel, instead of the 13.5

Table 2-5. Current Services and the Carter and Reagan Budgets, Fiscal Years 1980–82
Billions of dollars

		1981 estimate		1982 estimate	
Item	1980 actual	Carter budget	Reagan budget	Carter budget	Reagan budget
Outlays					
Current services	579.6	660.5	658.0	736.2	736.5
Proposed reductions	...	−1.4	−6.4	−15.9	−48.6
Proposed increases	...	3.7	3.6	19.1	7.4
Budget outlays	579.6	662.7	655.2	739.3	695.3
Receipts					
Current services	520.0	605.0	608.7	706.5	701.6
Proposed reductions	...	−3.1	−8.9	−18.3	−53.9
Proposed increases	...	5.6	0.2	23.6	2.6
Budget receipts	520.0	607.5	600.3	711.8	650.3
Deficit					
Current services	−59.6	−55.4	−49.3	−29.7	−34.9
Proposed deficits	−59.6	−55.2	−54.9	−27.5	−45.0

Sources: *The Budget of the United States Government, Fiscal Year 1982*, p. 8; and *Fiscal Year 1982 Budget Revisions*, pp. 3, 15.

percent raise called for by the comparability standard under existing legislation.[4] A $1.1 billion reduction in outlays results from a shift from twice yearly to annual cost-of-living adjustments for federal employee retirement programs. Other savings include reductions in the public assistance and food and nutrition programs of $0.5 billion each; $0.6 billion from reduction of subsidies under the college student loan program; and $0.4 billion each from assistance to railroads, the post office, and local school districts.

RECEIPTS. The major features of President Carter's tax program were business tax cuts to stimulate investment[5] and income tax relief

4. Another major saving of $2.2 billion in the Carter budget was to have come from a revised assumption about the unemployment rate that triggers extended unemployment compensation benefits, but this saving would not be realized if 1982 unemployment turns out to be significantly higher or lower than was assumed.

5. The proposed investment stimulus consisted of three features. First, a new system of depreciation would be established to simplify depreciation accounting for tax purposes and to increase allowable depreciation by about 40 percent. Second, the 10 percent investment tax credit would be made available in full for all machinery and equipment lasting more than one year. (Under present law, reduced credits are provided for assets with a useful life of less than seven years.) Third, 30 percent of any unused investment tax credits (that is, credits that cannot be offset against the tax on profits) would be made refundable. The refundable tax credit would benefit new and growing firms that do not have enough earnings to use up the credit and assist older firms and industries such as automobiles and steel that experience structural adjustment problems.

Table 2-6. Changes in Current Services Outlays in the Carter Budget, Fiscal 1982

Item	Billions of dollars
Current services outlays	736.2
Proposed increases	19.1
Defense purchases, excluding pay	10.8
Refundable tax credits	4.2
Student financial assistance	0.4
Foreign economic assistance	0.3
Science and space programs	0.3
Other	3.1
Proposed reductions	−15.9
Federal pay	−5.8
Federal retirement indexation	−1.1
Food and nutrition assistance	−0.5
Public assistance	−0.5
College student loans	−0.6
Railroads	−0.4
Post Office	−0.4
Federal impact aid	−0.4
Unemployment compensation	−2.2[a]
Proposed budget outlays	739.3

Source: *The Budget of the United States Government, Fiscal Year 1982*, pp. 9, 11.
a. Most of this reduction relates to the national trigger for extended benefits, which would be modified in the Carter budget. If the unemployment rate were only 0.25 percentage point higher for 1982 than the rate projected in the budget, the outlay savings from this proposal would be relatively small.

to families in which there are two earners, social security taxpayers, low-income earners, and Americans working abroad (table 2-7). He specifically rejected the Kemp-Roth approach of cutting income tax rates across the board. The cuts, which would cost $18.3 billion in fiscal 1982, were to be more than offset by increases totaling $23.6 billion from taxes on new motor fuels and highway use and taxes for the airport and airway trust fund, withholding on interest and dividends, and restrictions on the use of various tax devices that are used to avoid taxes. To minimize the effect on the fiscal 1981 deficit, which, it will be recalled, was estimated at $55.2 billion without any tax cut, President Carter proposed that only the tax cuts that were intended to stimulate investment should be effective for the entire calendar year 1981, but all the personal tax changes should become effective on January 1, 1982 (with a phase-in of the relief for two-earner families over a period of two years beginning on that date).

Table 2-7. Changes in Current Services Receipts Proposed in the Carter and Reagan Budgets, Fiscal 1982

Billions of dollars

Item	Carter budget	Reagan budget
Current services	706.5	701.6
Proposed increases	23.6	2.6
Motor fuels and highway use taxes	14.6	...
Airport and airway trust funds	1.4	1.9
Withholding on interest and dividends	3.9	...
Other	3.7[a]	0.7[b]
Proposed reductions	−18.3	−53.9
Reductions in individual income tax rates	...	−44.2
Revised depreciation allowances	−9.0	−9.7
Refundable investment credit	*	...
Social security tax credit	−8.5	...
Marriage tax penalty relief	−0.4	...
Exclusions for Americans working abroad	−0.3	...
Earned income credit	*	...
Proposed receipts	711.8	650.3

Sources: *The Budget of the United States Government, Fiscal Year 1982*, pp. 8 and 81, *Fiscal Year 1982 Budget Revisions*, p. 15.
* Less than $50 million.
a. Includes increased receipts from tax revisions relating to commodity straddles ($1.3 billion), independent contractors ($0.7 billion), foreign tax credits ($0.5 billion), tax-exempt bonds ($0.5 billion), railroad retirement taxes ($0.3 billion), and other proposals ($0.4 billion).
b. Includes increased user charges ($2.1 billion), savings from federal employee injury compensation reform ($0.1 billion), and other proposals ($0.1 billion).

The Reagan Budget

President Reagan goes far beyond President Carter in cutting both nondefense outlays and receipts, and beyond Carter's proposed increases in defense spending. Although some of Reagan's supporters urged him to cut taxes quickly even without a firm commitment from Congress to cut spending, he recommends large simultaneous cuts in both spending and taxes. Starting from a fiscal 1982 current services estimate of $736.5 billion for outlays and $701.6 billion for receipts,[6]

6. The Reagan current services estimate is a modification of the current services estimates in the Carter budget. It includes the defense purchases and foreign aid recommended in the Carter budget and is based on the Reagan economic assumptions, which show lower inflation, lower interest rates, and lower unemployment. The revised economic assumptions reduce estimated receipts and outlays. Overall, the Reagan current services estimates are higher than the Carter estimates by $0.3 billion in outlays and lower by $4.9 billion in receipts.

Reagan recommends increases of $6.2 billion in defense outlays and in a few nondefense programs of $1.2 billion, but then proposes reductions totaling $48.6 billion. The proposed tax cuts would reduce receipts by $53.9 billion, but this is to be offset by increases in user charges and other receipts of $2.6 billion, leaving a net reduction in receipts of $51.3 billion. With these changes, outlays in 1982 are to be reduced to $695.5 billion and receipts to $650.3 billion, leaving a deficit of $45.0 billion (table 2-5), which would be eliminated by 1984 if the economic assumptions of the Reagan administration are realized.[7]

OUTLAYS. The $48.6 billion cut in outlays proposed by President Reagan includes $8.2 billion of cuts proposed by President Carter. In addition, reductions are made in practically every major category of federal spending except what President Reagan calls the "social safety net," which he promises to preserve. The safety net programs include the basic social security benefits (retirement and disability benefits and medicare); unemployment benefits other than trade adjustment assistance; cash benefits for dependent families, the elderly, and the disabled;[8] and income support and medical benefits for veterans. In addition, he recommends that outlays for Head Start, summer youth employment, and subsidized nutrition programs for low-income children and for the elderly be maintained at the previously authorized levels. Outlays for these seven programs are expected to amount to $266 billion in fiscal 1982.

Except for these programs, no other part of the budget is to be immune from cutting. As table 2-8 indicates, Reagan proposes reductions of $7.2 billion in direct payments to individuals; $7.8 billion in farm, business, and other subsidies; $11.6 billion in grants to state and local governments (other than for subsidies); $0.8 billion in veterans' services; and $0.5 billion in foreign aid. These proposed reductions would cut nondefense outlays that are outside the social safety net by 16 percent.

The major thrusts of these budget cuts are as follows:

1. The entitlements would be revised to eliminate what the Reagan administration regards as unintended benefits. These include cuts in

---

7. For a discussion of the long-run budget outlook, see chapter 5.

8. These cash benefits are aid to families with dependent children and supplemental security income for the aged and disabled.

Table 2-8. Changes in Current Services Outlays in the Reagan Budget, Fiscal 1982

Item	Billions of dollars
Current services	736.5
Added defense funds	6.2
Current services with added defense	742.7
Proposed increases	1.2
Proposed reductions	−48.6
Savings included in Carter budget	−8.2[a]
Direct payments to individuals	−7.2
Social security	−3.0[b]
Food stamps	−2.3
Trade adjustment assistance	−1.2
Unemployment insurance	−0.3
Medicare	−0.8
Farm, business, and other subsidies	−7.8
Energy	−3.9
Transportation	−1.7
Natural resources and environment	−1.8
Agriculture	−0.4
Other grants to state and local governments	−11.6
Employment and training	−4.6
Social services	−1.2
Child nutrition	−1.2
Elementary and secondary education	−1.1
Medicaid	−0.9
Aid to families with dependent children	−0.7
Community and economic development	−0.8
Hardship assistance block grant	−0.4
Other (net)	−0.7
Other	−13.3
Withdrawal of proposed payments relating to taxes	−4.2[c]
Veterans' services	−0.8
Foreign aid for economic development	−0.5
All other	−5.4[d]
Proposed outlays	659.3

Source: *Fiscal Year 1982 Budget Revisions.*

a. Includes reductions in unemployment compensation ($2.2 billion), impact aid ($0.5 billion), federal pay and retirement benefits ($5.0 billion), and aid to families with dependent children ($0.5 billion net).

b. This reduction would be offset by an increase in supplementary security income payments of $0.3 billion.

c. Includes withdrawal of proposals in the Carter budget to refund businesses for unused investment tax credits ($3.5 billion) and to provide energy tax credits for state and local governments ($0.5 billion).

d. Major items include reduction of outlays by the National Aeronautics and Space Administration ($0.5 billion), cuts in defense outlays ($0.8 billion), reduction of outlays for the national defense stockpile ($0.5 billion), and increased receipts from mineral leases on the outer continental shelf ($0.7 billion).

the minimum and student social security benefits and tightening of eligibility requirements for disability benefits ($3.0 billion), lowering the family income eligibility level for food stamps from $14,000 a year to $11,000 ($2.3 billion), cutting the unemployment compensation benefits for people who are unemployed more than thirteen weeks and limiting the assistance to workers who are laid off in industries affected by exports under the trade-adjustment assistance program ($1.5 billion).

2. The basic structure of the welfare system would not be altered, but reductions of $5.5 billion would be made in outlays for medicaid, aid to families with dependent children, food stamps, and school lunches.

3. Major cuts would be made in the grants-in-aid to the states and local governments, and numerous categorical grants would be combined into block grant programs to give the states and localities more flexibility in deciding on how the funds should be spent. The public service employment programs, which are scheduled to provide jobs for 340,000 workers in fiscal 1982, would be phased out by the end of 1983; this would reduce outlays by $4.6 billion in 1982. The block grant for social services would be reduced by $1.2 billion, and the block grant for elementary and secondary education would be reduced by $1.1 billion. In total, grants to state and local governments would be reduced by $13.4 billion, or 13 percent below the level proposed by President Carter.

4. A wide variety of subsidies would be cut, including those provided for agriculture ($0.4 billion), energy ($3.9 billion), transportation ($1.7 million), and natural resources and the environment ($1.8 billion). New direct loan obligations by off-budget and on-budget federal entities would be reduced by $2.6 billion, and loan guarantee commitments by $18.4 billion.

5. In addition to the reduction of $5.8 billion in federal pay increases recommended by President Carter, the method by which federal civilian pay rates are kept comparable to private sector rates would be revised, and federal civilian employment would be cut by 83,000 positions.

The only major category of federal spending slated for an increase in the Reagan budget is the defense program. President Carter proposed national defense outlays of $200.3 billion for fiscal 1982, with increases that would bring total spending to $324.1 billion in 1986. President Reagan raises the 1982 level by $6.2 billion to $207.5 billion and the 1986 level by $63.1 billion to $387.2. The Reagan plan raises real defense spending from 5 percent to 8 percent a year in the 1981–86 period if the rate of inflation he projected materializes.

RECEIPTS. The tax changes proposed by President Reagan are virtually identical with those he promised during the campaign. He recommends the Kemp-Roth across-the-board cut of 30 percent in individual income tax rates over a period of three years beginning July 1, 1981.[9] He also proposes a modified version of the depreciation changes he supported during the campaign, to be made retroactively to January 1, 1981 (to prevent delays in business investment decisions while the tax bill moves through Congress).[10] The income tax cut is estimated to reduce receipts by $44.2 billion in fiscal 1982 and $162.4 billion in 1986, while the depreciation change is to reduce receipts by $9.7 billion in 1982 and $59.3 billion in 1986. These proposals would reduce receipts from 23 percent of GNP to 21.8 percent in 1982 and to 19.3 percent in 1984–85. To expedite congressional action, the president urges that the income tax cuts and depreciation proposals be acted on immediately and that other tax changes, such as the reduction of the marriage penalty, be included in a second tax bill to be enacted later.

The Budget and the Economy

There is considerable agreement with President Reagan that the U.S. economy is in serious trouble. Disruptions in major international markets and erratic economic policies have driven the inflation rate

9. According to estimates by the Department of the Treasury, the average reduction in tax rates actually amounts to about 27 percent. This occurs because the maximum tax rate of 50 percent on earned income remains unchanged. See "The President's Proposal for Tax Reduction," in Office of Management and Budget, *America's New Beginning: A Program for Economic Recovery* (OMB, February 18, 1981), table 7, p. 17.

10. During the campaign President Reagan endorsed the so-called 10-5-3 proposal, which would have permitted tax write-offs over a period of ten years for structures, five years for equipment, and three years for vehicles. The proposal submitted to Congress in February 1981 retains the original five- and three-year periods for equipment and vehicles, but limits the ten-year write-off to industrial buildings, retail stores, and warehouses used by their owners. Other nonresidential structures and low-income rental housing would be written off over a fifteen-year period and the remaining residential structures (mainly apartment buildings) over eighteen years. The Carter administration opposed the 10-5-3 proposal mainly because of the generous treatment of depreciation for structures.

to double-digit levels. Despite three recessions in ten years, the rate of increase in domestic wages and prices is about 10 percent a year, and future disruptions could push inflation even higher.

The collapse of productivity growth from the postwar annual trend of 3 percent to less than 1 percent over the past five years (and to a negative figure in the past three years) has sharply limited gains in real incomes. Paradoxically, real family income has continued to rise, despite the small gains in output per worker, because the number of workers per family has grown and social security benefits and other transfer payments, financed by reducing defense outlays rather than by higher taxes, have increased. These trends cannot be sustained in the 1980s. Concern with inflation in the conduct of fiscal and monetary policy threatens to limit the growth of aggregate demand and job opportunities; and demographic trends suggest that the rate of expansion of the labor force will slow. Defense expenditures are expected to claim a larger share of gross output. Thus the depressing effect of slow productivity growth on real incomes will be more evident in future years.

If there were no change in policy, there would be no reason to expect inflation to slow, growth to accelerate, or unemployment to decline. Unexpected events, such as disruption of petroleum supplies from abroad or a drought, could worsen already discouraging prospects. The unsatisfactory results of the old policies and the changing nature of the economic problems call for a shift in economic policy. At the beginning of the 1960s there was a heavy emphasis on such problems as high unemployment, a stagnant economy, and the need to stimulate full use of capital and labor. In the 1980s the situation has been greatly complicated by severe inflation, slow growth in productivity, and the failure of the capital stock and industrial capacity to expand in line with the rapid growth of the labor force.

President Reagan has identified the growth of government as the chief culprit in this unhappy story of the U.S. economy. To break with the past, he proposes a program of substantial budget cuts and tax reductions, reform and elimination of regulations, and a steady reduction in the rate of growth of the money supply.

Much of the Reagan program poses issues that are as much political as economic in nature. Whether government should be large or small or whether the distribution of income should be altered are matters requiring primarily political decisions. The Reagan administration believes, however, that the tax and spending cuts will have a major beneficial effect both in speeding economic growth and in reducing inflation, and that such cuts will therefore benefit all income groups. How does the Reagan program propose to increase productivity growth? Will the program reduce inflation and unemployment?

Supply-side Projections

Table 2-9 compares the economic projections of the Reagan and Carter administrations. The projections of nominal GNP in the next four years are roughly the same, but the Reagan projections envisage more real growth and less inflation.

Despite the rhetoric and controversy surrounding the discussion of

Table 2-9. Comparison of Carter and Reagan Economic Assumptions, Calendar Years 1980–84

Billions of dollars unless otherwise specified

Assumption	Actual 1980	Estimated			
		1981	1982	1983	1984
		Growth rates[a]			
Gross national product, current dollars					
Reagan	9.8	11.0	13.3	11.8	10.1
Carter	9.8	12.3	12.6	12.2	11.5
Gross national product, constant 1972 dollars					
Reagan	−0.0	1.4	5.2	4.9	4.2
Carter	−0.0	1.7	3.5	3.7	3.7
Gross national product deflator					
Reagan	9.9	9.5	7.7	6.6	5.7
Carter	9.9	10.4	8.8	8.2	7.5
Consumer price index					
Reagan	12.6	10.5	7.2	6.0	5.1
Carter	12.6	12.6	9.6	8.2	7.5
		Annual averages			
Gross national product, 1972 dollars					
Reagan	1,482	1,497	1,560	1,638	1,711
Carter	1,482	1,493	1,545	1,600	1,659
Unemployment rate, percent					
Reagan	7.2	7.8	7.2	6.6	6.4
Carter	7.2	7.8	7.5	7.1	6.7
Treasury bill rate, percent					
Reagan	11.5	11.1	8.9	7.8	7.0
Carter	11.5	13.5	11.0	9.4	8.5

Sources: *The Budget of the United States Government, Fiscal Year 1982*, pp. 3, 5, and *Fiscal Year 1982 Budget Revisions*, p. 13.

a. Fourth quarter of one year to that of the next.

the supply side of the program, the growth and employment projections of the Reagan administration, while higher than most private forecasts, are clearly within the range that might be predicted by conventional economic analysis. The level of real output is projected to exceed that assumed by the Carter administration by 1.0 percent in 1982, 2.4 percent in 1983, and 3.1 percent in 1984. Part of these gains results from better use of existing resources. In 1984, for example, from 0.5 to 1.0 percentage point of the 3.1 percent increment in output is attributable to a lower unemployment rate, leaving from 2.0 to 2.5 percentage points to be accounted for by the supply-side factors of larger gains in output per worker and a larger labor force.

On the investment side, President Reagan proposes a variation of the 10-5-3 proposal. The major criticism of the early proposal was that it treated structures too favorably and equipment in such industries as automobile and steel manufacturing not favorably enough. The revised 10-5-3 proposal reduces the advantage of structures but retains the original allowances for equipment and vehicles.[11] There are competing proposals for liberalizing depreciation that might be more evenhanded in the treatment of short- and long-lived assets, but none of them responds to the fundamental problem of the distortion of investment incentives caused by the failure to adjust depreciation and other determinants of taxable income for the effects of inflation.[12] Nevertheless, any increase in depreciation allowances would raise rates of return in many industries and stimulate investment. The effect on productivity and growth is likely to be small, however. Even if all the money saved from the business tax cut were used for investment, the annual rate of growth of productivity would be increased by only 0.1 to 0.3 percentage point.[13]

11. See note 10.

12. It is possible to accomplish this objective by permitting businesses to deduct the present value of future economic depreciation in the same year the investment is made. See Alan J. Auerbach and Dale W. Jorgenson, "Inflation-Proof Depreciation of Assets," *Harvard Business Review*, September–October 1980, pp. 113–18. Another method would be to allow full deductions for investment outlays in the years they are made and eliminate the deduction of interest payments. See Robert E. Hall, "Tax Treatment of Depreciation, Capital Gains, and Interest in an Inflationary Economy" (Urban Institute, 1980). These and other similar proposals are not being given serious consideration by the administration or by Congress, however.

13. The tax cut for business would amount to about 1 percent of GNP in 1985. According to the most recent evidence, this would raise productivity growth by only 0.1 to 0.3 percentage point. For the low estimate, see Edward F. Denison, "The Contribution of Capital to Economic Growth," *American Economic Review*, vol. 70 (May 1980, *Papers and Proceedings, December 1979*), p. 222; for the high estimate, see *Economic Report of the President, January 1981*, p. 79.

Some advocates of cuts in the individual income tax maintain that the reduction of marginal tax rates will increase work and saving by large amounts. Few economists will disagree that incentives are important and that tax policy can play a role in promoting them. However, there is considerable controversy about the magnitudes of the responses; the reactions to tax changes are complex, and it is impossible to undertake controlled laboratory experiments to measure them.[14] Given the diversity of individual responses, the net effect of the cut in tax rates for all taxpayers is not easy to determine. The discussion of these issues has generated very different estimates; the numerical projections in the Reagan budget are based on response estimates that are moderately optimistic but not extreme.[15]

In fact, the proposed cuts are much smaller than they seem and the supply response is therefore likely to be modest. A major tax reduction would be required simply to prevent an increase in effective tax rates in the years ahead. Continuation of current tax rates would lead to a rise in tax burdens as inflation and real growth push taxpayers into higher tax brackets. About three-quarters of the proposed rate reductions will be necessary to offset this effect during the next three years, and if inflation proceeds more rapidly than the administration projects, that fraction will be even larger.[16] To a con-

14. A simple illustration can be provided by speculating about the response to a tax cut by physicians earning $100,000 a year who take time off one afternoon a week to play golf. In responding to a lower tax rate, will they give up their day of golf because another day of work yields a larger gain in after-tax income? Or will they feel more affluent and better able to indulge their tastes for leisure sports? Similarly, the reduced tax on income from capital will enable them to have higher incomes and consumption in the future by saving less today, but they may be encouraged to build more assets because of the increased return and therefore might increase their saving.

15. For a review of the evidence on the supply responses to changes in taxation, see Henry J. Aaron and Joseph A. Pechman, eds., *How Taxes Affect Economic Behavior* (Brookings Institution, 1981).

16. This is an estimate based on a comparison of individual income tax receipts in fiscal years 1979 and 1984. (The recession year of 1980 was omitted.) Individual income tax receipts averaged 11.5 percent of personal income in fiscal 1979 and would be 14.3 percent of personal income in fiscal 1984 if tax rates were unchanged (using the Reagan economic assumptions). The proposed tax rates would reduce individual income tax receipts to 10.6 percent of personal income. Thus 76 percent of the tax cut would offset the rise in the average effective individual income rate between 1979 and 1984.

The 76 percent offset is an average for all taxpayers, and the exact percentage will differ among income brackets. In general, the proposed rate reductions would not offset the effective rate increases for the lower income brackets (because no adjustment is made for the reduction in the real value of the personal exemptions and standard deduction), and would more than offset the effective rate increases in the higher income brackets.

siderable degree, therefore, the Reagan proposal is similar to the periodic changes made by Congress during the 1970s to keep tax rates from rising. The major change from this past policy is the commitment to a specific set of tax cuts for several years to come.

Inflation

The novel and controversial aspect of the Reagan program lies in the projection of a rapid decline of inflation in future years. The rate of consumer price increase is to fall from 12.6 percent in 1980 to 5.1 percent in 1984. Beginning in 1981, the inflation rate is to be 2.0 to 2.4 percentage points below the rates assumed in the Carter budget, which were generally viewed as optimistic. A continuation of relatively restrictive demand policies might have been expected gradually to reduce domestic wage and price increases. But the Reagan projection incorporates sharply lower inflation rates while output growth accelerates and unemployment declines.

The new administration's perspective on inflation does not evolve from the traditional emphasis on excess demand and the need to restrain the growth of demand relative to that of supply. Today's inflation is seen, instead, as the product of expectations of future inflation. Until now, those expectations are believed to have been fueled by perceptions that the federal government would continue to finance excessive future spending through its fiscal and monetary policies. Administration economists have declared that a firm government commitment to more restrictive fiscal and monetary policies in the future can change these expectations. The first evidence would be a decline in interest rates. Wage and price decisions may respond with a lag, but they may also be affected by the new expectations. In the official Reagan projections, all the inflation benefits are realized by the end of 1981, after which the inflation rate is predicted to follow a path that is lower but parallel to the path assumed by the Carter administration.

This view is controversial both in its emphasis on expectations as the driving force in the current inflation and in the assertion that expectations of future inflation can be reduced without first reducing inflation in the current period. While expectations of future developments are undoubtedly a critical element in the behavior of financial markets, much of the inertia of the wage-price cycle is more backward- than forward-looking as the participants try to catch up with past price and cost increases or to maintain parity with competing groups. Even if expectations about future inflation and government policy have played a key role in generating the current inflation, it is questionable whether those expectations can be altered unless the economy actually experiences a sustained period of demand restraint. Most economists believe that a good deal of economic slack will be needed for a relatively long period of time to break inflation expectations. But the Reagan program does not envisage a long period of slow economic growth. In this respect, it differs significantly from that of the Thatcher government in the United Kingdom, which regards a rise in unemployment as an unavoidable part of the effort to lower inflation expectations and inflation.

Some supply-side advocates have argued that the tax cuts will encourage capital formation, improve productivity growth, and thereby drive a wedge between increasing wage costs and prices that will contribute to an unwinding of inflation. The improvements in real income that would be associated with greater productivity growth and the direct benefits of lower taxes would moderate pressures for wage increases. However, this is clearly not the mechanism envisaged by the Reagan administration because its projections do not imply a large acceleration of productivity growth in the early years.

Integration with Monetary Policy

The inflation projections are critical to the consistency of the fiscal and monetary policy goals set forth in the Reagan economic plan. The assumed growth in nominal GNP is nearly equal to that of the previous administration—about 12 percent annually between 1980 and 1984—but the projected sharp decline in inflation makes room for an accelerated expansion in real output. This growth must be financed by a combination of increases in the stock of money and its velocity (GNP per unit of money). The 1981 monetary growth objective for the M-1B definition of the money supply was set at 3.5 to 6.0 percent by the Federal Reserve Board.[17] In the last five years the velocity of money according to this definition has also shown a trend increase of about 4 percent annually. Thus the upper range of the

17. The M-1B definition of the money supply includes currency, demand deposits, and other checkable deposits in thrift institutions and commercial banks. The range of 3.5 to 6.0 percent for 1981 is adjusted for changes among types of deposits attributable to regulatory changes mandated by the Deposit Deregulation and Monetary Control Act of 1980. Without such adjustment, the range for M-1B is stated as 6.0 to 8.5 percent.

1981 Federal Reserve goals for money growth, if sustained, would be insufficient to finance the expected growth of GNP in future years. However, the program also calls for a reduction of 50 percent in monetary growth by 1986, with interest rates declining sharply during the period. Such a lower path for the money supply could be consistent with the projected growth of GNP *only* if there were an unprecedented acceleration of velocity. The causes of this projected flight from money are difficult to understand because the forecast of declining inflation and lower interest rates should increase rather than decrease the public's demand for money balances.

If the projected decline in inflation should not occur, the fiscal policy objectives of the Reagan program are clearly on a collision course with the monetary targets. Since the implied increase in money velocity is outside the range of historical experience, a rise in interest rates would be required to scale back the growth in demand if the monetary targets are to be met. Such a policy of monetary restraint would fall heavily on investment, negate much of the effort to stimulate capital formation, and result in sluggish growth.

Comparison with the 1960s

The Reagan program of tax reductions is, as its advocates maintain, strikingly similar to the fiscal policy proposals of the Kennedy administration in the early 1960s. In fact, the similarities are even greater than most realize. Both the Kennedy economic advisers and the supply-side advocates of today anticipated a large rise in aggregate demand and supply (productivity growth). Yet most of those who advised President Kennedy oppose the Reagan program today. It is interesting to ask what has precipitated such a reversal of opinion.

The changing views on economic policy reflect the experience with supply-side policies in the 1960s and the differences in the economic situation of that decade and the 1980s. First, in the 1960s it proved to be more difficult than anticipated to accelerate the growth of productivity through government policy actions. Productivity expanded rapidly in the first half of the 1960s under the impetus of a sharp rise in the use of existing resources; but its growth slowed after the 1964 tax cut despite rapid rates of capital accumulation. The experience gave rise to a greater appreciation of the complexity of the growth process and of the importance of many factors besides private capital formation in determining economic growth, and left some early advocates of the use of government policies to spur growth skeptical about the magnitude of the impact of fiscal actions.

More important, the 1960s program was initiated when prices were stable, workers unemployed, and capital underutilized. As a result, fiscal and monetary policies could work together to finance the expansion of demand and output with stable credit costs. Today, high inflation makes the monetary authorities unwilling to finance a rapid economic expansion in the presence of high rates of inflation. A reduction in taxes, if it is not offset by expenditure reductions, will add to credit demands and thereby boost interest rates and squeeze capital formation. Hence the success of the Reagan program hinges crucially on its record in lowering inflation and on its effectiveness in improving supply.

The Outlook

The interaction of inflation and slow growth greatly complicates the problem of designing an effective economic program. Continuing disputes over the causes and cures of inflation have repeatedly frustrated efforts to develop a consensus on economic policy during the past decade, and opinion has swung wildly from one extreme to another. The Reagan program attempts to avoid the conflict between growth and price stability by relying on a theory of inflation in which expectations play the primary role.

The administration is surely correct in its belief that a return to a high rate of economic growth would prevent a sharp increase in social conflict over distributional issues. The development of effective means of improving productivity growth is the key element of such an effort. Yet the success of the program depends on the assumption that it can break inflationary expectations without retarding growth.

If inflation declines rapidly, an accelerated growth of real output can be financed within the current goals of 4 to 6 percent for monetary growth only if velocity continues to rise. But if the program does not alter expectations and the inflation response is less than anticipated, monetary policy and high interest rates will restrain rather than stimulate overall growth. In such circumstances the Reagan policies will not be very different in effect from those that have been followed in the United Kingdom since 1979.

CHAPTER THREE

The Nondefense Budget

JOSEPH A. PECHMAN *and others*

THE nondefense part of the budget has been rising rapidly in recent years in real as well as in nominal terms and as a percentage of total outlays. In fiscal 1967, nondefense outlays amounted to just over $90 billion, or about 57 percent of total outlays; in the budget prepared by President Carter for fiscal 1982, these outlays were expected to reach $554.9 billion, or 75 percent of the total. In the five years ending in fiscal 1972, real nondefense spending rose at an annual rate of 5.3 percent; it continued to rise at a rate of 5.7 percent between 1972 and 1978, but slowed to an annual rate of 0.3 percent between 1978 and 1982 as a result of the considerable efforts of the Carter administration and Congress to restrain federal nondefense spending (see chapter 2). Because defense outlays will rise rapidly in real terms in the next several years (see chapter 4), the growth of nondefense spending must be drastically curtailed to make room in the budget for tax cuts or for debt retirement.

A large share of the nondefense budget for the years immediately ahead is determined by decisions made in previous years. Such outlays have been considered relatively "uncontrollable" because they can be altered only if the basic legislation authorizing such spending

The authors are grateful to Robert W. Crandall, John L. Palmer, Robert D. Reischauer, and Milton B. Russell for their advice and comments. Gregory D. Call, J. Elizabeth Callison, Thomas C. Hier, Michael K. Kuehlwein, Thea M. Lee, and Therese E. Windt provided research assistance, and the manuscript was typed by Evelyn M. E. Taylor, Vickie L. Corey, Charlotte Kaiser, Lisa F. Saunders, Darlene M. Webber, Anita G. Whitlock, and Susan F. Woollen.

is changed. Uncontrollable outlays have increased from slightly less than 60 percent of total outlays in fiscal 1967 to 76.6 percent in fiscal 1982.[1]

The largest category of uncontrollable spending is for the "entitlement" programs that provide benefits to retired, disabled, unemployed, sick, and poor people (including social security and other retirement programs, unemployment compensation, medicare and medicaid, housing assistance, food stamps, public assistance, and supplemental security income). These open-end programs have grown from about 27 percent of the budget in fiscal 1967 to an estimated 48 percent in fiscal 1982, or from 5.5 percent of the gross national product to 11.0 percent.[2]

Although the entitlement programs generally have public support, the growth in outlays has far exceeded expectations. Outlays keep rising because the number of eligible persons or average benefit levels continue to rise, the latter to provide higher real benefits as prescribed by law, and in all cases, except for public assistance, to adjust for inflation. Social security is one example of this type of program. The number of eligible social security recipients grows by almost 500,000 a year. Their average benefits would automatically rise gradually even without inflation because the average earnings on which benefits are based increase over time. Inflation increases social security outlays even more because the law requires adjustments in benefits for current recipients to keep pace with the cost of living.

Of the 24.3 percent of the budget that goes for the so-called "controllable" programs, two-thirds—15.7 percent of the budget—is for the defense program, and this percentage is now rising sharply (see chapter 4). The remaining 8.6 percent is for such civilian programs as energy development, education, transportation, agriculture, and manpower training, which are not necessarily any easier to cut than the uncontrollable programs.

Although most federal programs have a constituency that will

1. These include uncontrollable outlays in the defense program, but the amount is small relative to the total (less than 10 percent in 1982).

2. Other open-end programs, which would have accounted for 12.5 percent of the 1982 Carter budget, include interest payments on the national debt (which have more than doubled in the last four years as interest rates and the debt have risen), farm price supports, and more than half the grants to state and local governments (both of which have declined in recent years). In addition, 16.1 percent of the proposed 1982 outlays were required to pay for contracts and commitments of previous years for construction, procurement, and similar obligations.

strongly defend them, there is a growing recognition that all outlays —whether controllable or uncontrollable—will need to be scrutinized carefully because total budget costs exceed the amount that taxpayers appear to be willing to pay. Federal outlays have jumped from 20.9 percent of GNP in fiscal 1979 to an estimated 23.3 percent in 1981 and 23.0 percent in the Carter budget for fiscal 1982 (see chapter 2). Budget receipts, which amounted to 19.8 percent of GNP in fiscal 1979, are expected to rise to 22.1 percent in fiscal 1982 and will have to reach 23.0 percent if the proposed budget were to be balanced in that year. The increase of 3 percentage points would amount to $96 billion of additional taxes at 1982 income levels. There is widespread agreement that spending should be reduced to avoid increasing the tax burden to such an extent.

President Reagan's proposed budget for fiscal 1982 would cut federal outlays by $48.6 billion below the levels authorized under present laws and would increase receipts through the imposition of higher user charges and fees by $2.1 billion. If enacted along with the proposed tax cuts, these changes would reduce 1982 outlays from 23.0 percent of GNP to 21.8 percent and receipts from 22.1 percent to 20.4 percent. The budget would be balanced by 1984, when outlays and receipts would be reduced to 19.3 percent of GNP.

When he submitted his budget amendments, President Reagan announced that he would "preserve and maintain the social safety net programs that represent the accrued permanent consensus of the American people over the five past decades." The social safety net includes four basic programs with estimated outlays of $262.6 billion in fiscal 1982: social insurance benefits for the elderly and disabled (including old age, survivors' and disability insurance and medicare); basic unemployment benefits; cash benefits for dependent families, the elderly, and the disabled; and some veterans' benefits. In addition, three other programs—Head Start, summer youth employment, and nutrition programs for children and the elderly— would be maintained at their previously estimated levels totaling $3.7 billion.

President Reagan developed the following nine criteria to be used to trim the federal budget:

1. Maintain the social safety net.
2. Revise entitlements to eliminate unintended benefits.

3. Reduce middle- and upper-income benefits.

4. Recover clearly allocable costs from users.[3]

5. Develop sound criteria for economic subsidy programs.

6. Stretch out and retarget public sector capital improvement programs.

7. Impose fiscal restraint on other national interest programs.

8. Consolidate categorical grant programs into block grants.

9. Reduce overhead and personnel costs of the federal government.

This chapter is not intended to provide a detailed list of budget cuts that would be justified on the basis of these criteria. Rather, the purpose is to present the issues in the major programs of the non-defense budget, evaluate the reductions proposed by President Reagan on the basis of his criteria, and discuss alternative methods of accomplishing these objectives. The programs to be considered are social security, welfare, employment and training, unemployment compensation, health, education, housing, local economic development, energy, agriculture, transportation, natural resources, grants-in-aid to state and local governments, compensation of federal employees, the regulatory programs, tax expenditures, and foreign economic assistance. It is hoped that this analysis will provide readers with enough information to make up their own minds about the budget issues that were raised by President Reagan and are now being considered by Congress.

Social Security

Social security today is the largest single federal program; more than 90 percent of the working population participates, and benefits are paid to more than 95 percent of people aged sixty-five or older. Outlays for this program under present laws would amount to $160 billion in fiscal 1982, or 21.6 percent of total outlays. Social security is included in the group of programs designated by President Reagan as the social safety net provided by the federal government. However, the system is receiving considerable attention because the trust funds are at low levels and could become exhausted; the index

3. Some of these costs would increase receipts, while others would appear in the budget as negative outlays.

used for adjusting benefits to keep pace with inflation is acknowledged to be defective; and the cost of the program will rise sharply
when the baby-boom generation of the 1950s and 1960s begins to
retire in the twenty-first century.

Short-run Financing

Social security benefits are financed out of current payroll taxes.
In normal times, the trust funds should have enough accumulated
assets so that taxes need not be increased even if revenues fall short
of projections temporarily (during a recession, for example). But
when the economy is sluggish for a long period, receipts do not rise
fast enough to keep up with benefit payments, and the trust fund
balances can run down quickly. The problem is exacerbated when,
as in recent years, the rate of inflation exceeds the rate of wage
increases.

Current projections indicate that the total payroll taxes to be
collected under present law will be sufficient to finance the social
security benefits that are expected to be paid out over the next fifty
years. But the program will be in difficulty in the shorter run, particularly if the high inflation rates persist and unemployment remains
at a high level. If the Reagan administration's economic assumptions
turn out to be correct, the short-run financing problem can be solved
without reducing benefits or raising taxes. But according to the projections of the Congressional Budget Office, the largest fund—which
pays the old age and survivors' benefits—will be exhausted in two or
three years. The disability and hospital insurance funds, which are
the other two trust funds, seem to be sufficient for a number of years
to come. This short-run problem can be remedied by some combination of reducing benefits, increasing taxes, and permitting the three
trust funds to borrow from one another and, when needed, from the
general fund of the federal government.

A number of marginal changes in the benefit structure, which
have been recommended by task forces and commissions, could hold
down outlays without cutting the basic social security benefits. First,
the benefits paid to students over the age of eighteen could be eliminated and assistance provided through existing federal grant and
loan programs specifically designed to help finance needy students.
Second, the $122 a month minimum benefit could be eliminated and
reliance placed on the benefit formula, which is based entirely on the

amount of social security earnings credited to an individual's account. The minimum benefit was designed to help the lowest paid workers, but in practice it is used frequently by federal, state, and local government employees who work for the minimum period of four years under social security (the "double-dippers"). This change would respond to the criticism that the minimum benefit is a windfall for those who are not solely dependent on social security coverage for their retirement income. The supplemental security income program would protect retirees and disabled persons with no other resources. Third, disability benefits are now paid to people who have worked in employment providing coverage during five of the last ten years. In addition, a "recency of work" test could be imposed, limiting benefits to applicants who have worked in at least six of the thirteen quarters before becoming disabled. Fourth, the $255 lump-sum death benefit, which has remained the same for almost thirty years, is now insufficient to pay for a funeral and goes to many surviving relatives who do not need it. The value of the benefit has been eroded by the passage of time, and its purpose could be served by creating a death benefit under the supplemental security income program that is confined to the needy who are aged and disabled.

Although these changes would not alter the basic structure of the social security program, they are fiercely opposed by representatives of the aged and disabled and government employees. These groups believe that such changes would violate the implicit contract between the government and the workers who previously paid taxes into the system and are concerned that such changes could be a prelude to deeper cuts in the basic benefits. The total saving from the enactment of these changes would amount to $3.0 billion in fiscal 1982 and much more in subsequent years. Modifications in the student, minimum, and death benefits were recommended by the Carter administration in 1979 but were rejected by Congress. The Reagan administration supports all four modifications.[4]

In addition to changes in benefits, the financial arrangements for the trust funds need to be reconsidered. Of the three funds, two (disability insurance and hospital insurance) are now in surplus; the

4. One major difference between the two sets of recommendations is that the Carter administration proposed to eliminate the student and minimum benefits for new beneficiaries only; the Reagan administration would also phase down benefits now being received by students by 25 percent a year and would recalculate benefits of current beneficiaries to eliminate the minimum benefit alternative.

third (old-age and survivors' insurance) is almost depleted. Permitting the old-age and survivors' insurance fund to borrow from the disability and hospital insurance funds or redirecting some of their payroll taxes to it would be a helpful expedient, but it would be only a temporary stopgap.

The major possibilities for providing additional revenue to the social security system are to (1) give the trust funds the authority to borrow from the general fund; (2) finance part or all of the hospital insurance program with general revenues and reallocate the payroll taxes that go to this fund to the old age and survivors' fund; and (3) raise the payroll tax by increasing the rates or by accelerating legislated increases now scheduled for 1985 and 1990. The first two proposals would depart from the tradition of financing the social security system with a payroll tax. However, the present retirement and disability system is a compromise between the views that social security should be a wage-related annuity program, with benefits geared strictly to past contributions, or a transfer program to provide a minimum income for the retired and disabled and their families. Supplementing the payroll tax with general revenues would serve to make people recognize that the retirement and disability benefits are not strictly wage-related, an approach that is particularly relevant for hospital insurance, which provides benefits that bear no relation to past wages. The third alternative—raising the payroll tax rates—will doubtless be resisted by Congress, since it received considerable criticism when the payroll tax was increased sharply over the 1978–81 period.

The Indexation Problem

Since 1975, social security benefits of current beneficiaries have been adjusted for inflation on the basis of the official consumer price index published monthly by the U.S. Bureau of Labor Statistics. The current consumer price index significantly overstates the importance of owner-occupied housing and gives too much weight to changes in mortgage interest rates, both of which cause the index to overstate inflation when interest rates rise, as they have in recent years. The Bureau of Labor Statistics currently publishes an index that bases the housing component on changes in rents paid for housing of all types. This index, referred to as the rental equivalence index (X-1), is a better measure of changes in the cost of living.

Substitution of this index for the previous one was recommended by the Carter administration.

The adjustment of social security benefits due on July 1, 1981, will be based on changes in the current index for the year ending March 31, 1981—an increase of over 11 percent. Because interest rates on home mortgages have risen, the index will probably over-state the true change in the cost of living in 1981 as it did in the two previous years. For the three-year period ending in December 1980, the official consumer price index rose almost 5 percent faster than the rental equivalence index. Neither the Carter nor the Reagan budget addressed this problem. As a result, the overadjustment for inflation is automatically included in the safety net programs that were declared off limits for the Reagan budget cutters.

Budget costs for fiscal 1982 could be reduced by revising the inflation adjustment before it goes into effect for social security benefits on July 1, 1981. Two alternatives are available: an arbitrary reduction of the adjustment might be made to take the recent overstatement into account; or the law could be revised to provide inflation adjustments by using either the official price index or the index of earnings, whichever is lower. Yet another alternative is to delay the adjustment from July 1 to October 1 of each year, but continue to base it on price changes through the first quarter of the year. Each reduction of one percentage point in the inflation adjustment for a full year would reduce fiscal 1982 outlays for social security and other federal programs by $2 billion. Whether or not such an adjustment is made, it is appropriate to revise the official price index so that it will more accurately reflect changes in the cost of living.[5]

The Long-run Financing Problem

Social security outlays will rise sharply as a percentage of taxable payrolls beginning in about the year 2005. This increase is attributable to the changing demographic structure of the population. Today there are about thirty beneficiaries per one hundred workers; in 2055, there will be almost fifty per one hundred workers. This increase in the ratio of beneficiaries to workers inevitably implies that

5. A change in the official consumer price index to the rental equivalence index mentioned above could increase social security outlays in the next year or two if interest rates decline. The change in the index should be made regardless of the short-run consequences, however.

the cost of the social security program will rise. Legislated increases in payroll taxes are projected to keep the system in surplus until the year 2010, and accumulated reserves will assure benefits until 2030. Again, the problem can be resolved either by scheduling a larger increase in taxes than is provided under current law or by reducing benefits.

According to official estimates, the shortfall begins in the year 2015 and, by 2035, the payroll tax would have to be increased by 4.2 percentage points to eliminate it (2.1 percentage points each for employers and employees). If payroll taxes are increased beginning at an earlier date and accumulated with interest in the trust funds, the eventual increase in the payroll tax could be moderated.

If the reduced benefits approach is taken, one possibility is to increase the age at which the usual benefits are paid from sixty-five to sixty-eight years (phased in over a period of years to prevent hardship and to permit workers to make plans for their retirement under the new rules). This proposal is justified by its supporters on the ground that life expectancy has increased and is expected to increase further in the future; at the same time, the proportion of jobs requiring limited physical effort is increasing. A second method of bringing down long-run benefit costs would be to modify the formula for calculating benefits. Under the current law the formula is adjusted annually to take account of the increases in wages. An alternative method is to adjust the formula on the basis of prices. Wages generally grow 1 to 2 percent a year faster than prices. The use of a wage index therefore results in a faster rise in initial benefits than would occur if the benefit formula were adjusted by prices. Wage indexing automatically assures that workers at the same *relative* position in the earnings distribution will receive benefits equal to the same proportion of earnings whenever they work. Price indexing of the benefit formula would assure workers with the same *real* earnings the same benefits. In 1977 Congress chose to adjust benefits by the wage index; changing to price indexing would represent a decision not to commit the nation to as generous a formula as that enacted in 1977 and would leave to future Congresses the question of whether to incorporate the benefits of productivity growth in the social security benefit formula. Neither the Carter nor the Reagan administration expressed any views about which course of action to take.

Welfare
Prepared by Michael C. Barth of ICF Incorporated

Five programs are generally associated with welfare spending at the federal level. These are the means-tested programs that provide benefits to people in need: medicaid; aid to families with dependent children; supplemental security income for the aged, blind, and disabled; food and nutrition assistance; and low-income energy assistance.[6] The supplemental security income and food stamp programs are operated directly by the federal government; the remainder of the programs are under the auspices of state and local governments, with financial assistance from the federal government. Federal outlays for the five programs under current law and regulations would be $54.3 billion in fiscal 1982, or 7.4 percent of total federal outlays for that year.

In the aggregate, federal outlays for these programs have been growing at about the same rate as that of inflation, but there are significant differences among the trends of the individual programs. Medicaid has become increasingly expensive because of the rapid growth of per capita medical expenditures generally and the growth in the number of people over age sixty-five. (Medicaid pays about 35 to 40 percent of its benefits to people in this age bracket.) Food and nutrition programs have grown dramatically because of increases in the number of families eligible for food stamps and in the number eligible for a special high-protein program for low-income women, for infants and children, and for school lunches. The costs of these programs also rise as the price of food goes up. Outlays for low-income energy assistance have risen only slightly since the inception of the program in 1979. The increases in outlays for the cash assistance programs (aid to families with dependent children and supplemental security income) cannot be attributed either to the greater number of case loads or to the rising levels of real benefits. Benefits under the supplemental security income program are adjusted annually according to the rise in the consumer price index. Aid to families with dependent children is not indexed and real benefits under this program have been declining as prices have risen.

6. Not included in this list is housing assistance to low-income households, which is provided through subsidies to owners of rental housing units and public housing agencies. For a discussion of these programs, see the section on housing below.

Although the share of the budget allocated to welfare has not been rising, there is considerable dissatisfaction with these programs because of their complexity and the widespread feeling that there is a good deal of waste and fraud. Presidents Nixon and Carter each recommended a comprehensive program of cash assistance (called a negative income tax by economists), but these recommendations were rejected by Congress. Instead, Congress adds new categorical programs from time to time, like low-income energy assistance, to help the poor purchase specific items that are considered essential for their survival. Legislation to tighten requirements for determining eligibility in one or another of these programs is passed practically every year, but the dissatisfaction continues. President Carter recommended reductions of $1.1 billion in these programs in fiscal 1982, and President Reagan added $5.5 billion of additional cuts for the same year, as shown in table 3-1.

Medicaid

The Carter administration's approach to reducing outlays for medicaid was to try to hold down the costs of providers of medical care. The major proposal, debated in the last two Congresses, was to put a cap on payments to hospitals—whose rapidly rising charges are the primary factor in rising health expenditures—through a hos-

Table 3-1. Federal Outlays for Welfare Programs, Fiscal Years 1980–82
Billions of dollars

Program	1980 actual	1981 current services estimate[a]	1982 Current services estimate[a]	1982 Carter budget	1982 Reagan budget
Medicaid	14.0	16.6	18.3	18.2	17.3
Aid to families with dependent children	7.3	7.8	8.2	7.7	7.0
Supplemental security income	6.4	7.3	8.0	8.0	8.0
Food and nutrition assistance[b]	14.0	15.9	18.0	17.5	14.0
Energy assistance	1.6	1.8	1.8	1.8	1.4
Total	43.3	49.4	54.3	53.2	47.7

Sources: *Special Analyses, Budget of the United States Government, Fiscal Year 1982*, pp. 37–39; and *Budget Revisions, Fiscal Year 1982*, pp. 69, 73.
a. Based on laws and regulations in effect January 1, 1981.
b. Includes food stamps, food supplements for low-income women, infants and children, and school lunches.

pital cost-containment program. Another proposal was to deny reimbursement of hospitals' outlays for equipment that was not approved by various area planning groups. There were also attempts
to limit payments to certain medical specialties, to encourage health
maintenance organizations to provide for more regional planning in
medicaid, and to encourage cooperation among hospitals. None of
these plans was approved by Congress, nor would they have greatly
reduced the rapid growth in federal medicaid outlays.

Several other proposals to cut medicaid were made by President
Carter in the fiscal 1982 budget, the largest being an attempt to
collect state outlays for unapproved expenditures, which would reduce federal outlays by $100 million a year. President Reagan rec-
ommended as an interim measure that a limit be placed on federal
outlays for medicaid. The specific limit he proposed was to allow
federal outlays to increase by 5 percent in fiscal 1982 (about 4 percentage points below the projected rate of inflation for that year)
and by the rate of inflation thereafter. The cost saving would amount
to $0.9 billion in fiscal 1982 and $6.2 billion in fiscal 1986. This
proposal would probably lead to a reduction of medicaid benefits
because many states would not be willing or able to substitute their
own funds for the reduction in the federal share. It would also place
a larger burden on public hospitals, which must serve the indigent
population.

One possibility for reducing medicaid outlays that was not endorsed by either the Carter or the Reagan administration is to introduce more cost sharing into the medicaid program. Currently, cost
sharing is limited to the "medically needy" component of the program (those in the welfare categories whose medical bills pull their
income below the state welfare standard). For recipients of cash
assistance, cost sharing can only be imposed for optional services, of
which there are relatively few. The likely impact of cost sharing on
medicaid outlays is difficult to assess; however, it may not be very
large because a large fraction of medicaid outlays (about 40 percent) goes to nursing homes for long-term care.

Aid to Families with Dependent Children

The Carter administration proposed cuts of approximately $500
million in fiscal 1982 outlays for the program providing aid to families with dependent children. These include reductions and standard-

ization of allowable work expenses (which has the effect of increasing the marginal tax rate on income earned by the participants in the program) and a provision to allow states to count the income of stepparents in determining program eligibility and benefits. They also proposed that all families be assumed to receive the earned income tax credit for which they are eligible. The Reagan administration accepts these proposals and adds $700 million of additional cuts to be obtained from unspecified changes that would improve program administration, determine welfare needs more accurately, and reduce fraud and abuse. It also proposes that able-bodied parents should work for their welfare grants in specially created public jobs ("workfare").

These proposals provide some insight into the attitudes toward federal spending for the poor. Because the welfare program remains unpopular, there is a continuous demand for restraining outlays. While the changes actually proposed would not alter the basic structure of the program, they would have the effect of reducing benefits for selected groups of the eligible population, but there is little room for cutting further without depriving needy people of assistance. Workfare requirements have been tried in several states, but there is no evidence that they improve the skills of the welfare population or greatly reduce the program rolls. The major potential for reducing costs further, in medicaid as in aid to families with dependent children, would appear to be in better management. In particular, computerization of payment and claim systems would prevent needless overpayment. But the effect on outlays would not be large.

Supplemental Security Income

Little can be done to modify outlays for this program other than to reduce the rate of adjustment of the benefits to inflation or to cut benefits directly. Neither the Carter nor the Reagan administration recommended any changes in this essential program.

Food and Nutrition Assistance

Total expenditures on food programs, which include food stamps, direct food distribution, supplemental food programs for women, infants and children, and child nutrition, have more than doubled during the past five years—from $8.5 billion in fiscal 1977 to an estimated $18 billion in fiscal 1982 under present legislation. The food stamp program accounts for most of this growth in the 1977–82 period: it more than doubled in size, after allowing for inflation in food prices. Participation in this program doubled from 10 million in fiscal 1971 to 21 million in fiscal 1980; the average real benefits per person increased by about 50 percent. The growth of the program is due in part to the liberalization of the eligibility criteria and to the elimination (in 1979) of the requirement to purchase a portion of the food stamp allocation. Another important factor is cyclical unemployment, which caused a bulge in both participation and benefits per person during the 1974–75 recession and again in the 1979–80 period. Outlays for the supplemental food program have also increased sharply—from $14 million in fiscal 1974 to $717 million in fiscal 1980.

Attempts were made in 1979 and 1980 to improve the administration of the food stamp program and to reduce waste and fraud. The major change was to restrict student participation. In addition, recipients were required to repay the costs of fraudulently recovered stamps before being recertified for eligibility, and states were made liable for a portion of erroneously issued benefits if they do not reduce high error rates.

The Carter administration recommended legislation for fiscal 1982 that would retain the present method for annual (rather than semiannual) indexing of food stamp allotments and school lunches, which was approved by the Congress only for fiscal 1981. In addition, it proposed that food stamp benefits be based on income during the previous month rather than on an estimate of income for the following month. The Reagan administration endorses these proposals and also suggests lowering the income eligibility ceiling for food stamps to families with incomes below 130 percent of the poverty level and reducing food stamp benefits by taking into account free school lunches. Eligibility for school lunch subsidies would be limited to children from poor households and outlays would be cut for the supplemental nutrition programs for infants and low-income pregnant women. In total, these proposals would reduce outlays below the proposed Carter budget by $3.5 billion and below the amounts that would be spent under present legislation in fiscal 1982 by $4.0 billion, or 22 percent—a cut that would impose hardships on many low-income families.

Low-income Energy Assistance

Rising fuel costs resulting from the Carter administration's decision to decontrol oil prices and the increases in the price of oil charged by the Organisation of Petroleum Exporting Countries have adversely affected all domestic consumers. Those particularly hard hit have been the poor, because they spend a larger proportion of their budgets on fuel and utilities relative to other income groups. To mitigate the added burden of rising energy costs on low-income families the federal government has provided such households with energy-related assistance since 1979. Currently these funds are administered by state governments through block grants from the Department of Health and Human Services—a system of disbursement favored by the Reagan administration.[7] Despite some administrative difficulties that are inevitable in a relatively new program, the assistance has been vital to the economic and physical well-being of many low-income families.

The Carter administration recommended $1.85 billion of outlays for low-income energy assistance in fiscal 1982. The Reagan administration proposes a consolidation of low-income energy assistance with other emergency assistance currently provided to needy households into one "hardship assistance" block grant to the states. A total outlay of $1.4 billion is requested for the proposed program. This level of support would reduce energy-related benefits despite the continued difficulties the poor will have in paying for heat for their homes. Moreover, since the states will be allowed to make the hardship assistance available for nonenergy-related contingencies, there will inevitably be a reduction of coverage of the energy needs of low-income households.

Effects of Reducing Welfare Outlays

Given the tightening and management changes of the past few years it will be difficult to reduce further the costs of the basic welfare programs by significant amounts through administrative improvements alone. Thus, to cut welfare outlays significantly, eligibility of some low-income recipients must be eliminated and benefits

7. A portion of the funds for low-income energy assistance is allocated by the Community Services Administration for the provision of aid to low-income families with unforeseen energy-related needs.

that in most cases help people in real need must be cut. Furthermore, cuts in federal funds for welfare programs, particularly medicaid and aid to families with dependent children, would shift costs to the states, many of which will not or cannot assume the additional fiscal burdens necessary to maintain benefits at current levels.

Assuming that it is desirable to economize on outlays for transfers as well as other programs, the question is whether the appropriate programs are scheduled to be cut. In 1979 the benefit from supplemental security income for an individual with no other income was $199 a month, and the average pension for veterans without a disability connected with military service was $175 a month; by contrast, the benefit from aid to families with dependent children averaged $88 a month throughout the country. Even taking into account that many recipients in the latter program are children, this difference is still large. There seems to be little basis for cutting this program and medicaid outlays while leaving supplemental security income and veterans' benefits unchanged. The present welfare system does not seem to have any internal logic, and the system that would remain after the proposed cuts are made would not be an improvement.

Employment and Training
Prepared by Marvin M. Smith

Most federal employment and training programs are authorized under the Comprehensive Employment and Training Act and administered locally by a network of prime sponsors. In 1978 Congress consolidated the adult employment programs into two titles—one focusing on structural unemployment (II-D) and the other on cyclical unemployment (VI). The public service jobs provided under these two titles were specifically restricted to workers who are economically disadvantaged (those who are unemployed for fifteen weeks under title II-D and ten weeks under title VI). Titles II-A, II-B, and II-C provide training programs and work experience for workers of all ages, with II-B being designated for those who are economically disadvantaged and unemployed (or underemployed) or in school. Title III includes a set of nationally administered programs for such groups as migrant farm workers and native Americans. Title IV provides a variety of work experience projects for unemployed youth. The job corps, a special program under this title, concentrates on economically disadvantaged youth (aged fourteen to twenty-one) through intensive training provided in residential centers. Finally, title VIII established the young adult conservation corps, which provides work experience in conservation work on public lands and waters.

A major feature of the economic stimulus package adopted during President Carter's first year in office was an increase of 70 percent in outlays for programs under the Comprehensive Employment and Training Act—from $5.6 billion in fiscal 1977 to $9.5 billion in fiscal 1978. They have remained between $8 billion and $9 billion since then. Most of the increase in outlays is accounted for by the expansion in public service employment and the introduction of a number of programs to provide employment and training for young workers.

The Carter budget for fiscal 1982 retained the majority of the employment and training programs at the same number of jobs as in 1981,[8] while pinpointing the young adult conservation corps as the only program to be phased out by the end of the fiscal year. In addition, the Carter budget included two new proposals that would have added almost $300 million to the fiscal 1982 budget: a consolidation and expansion of the youth employment and training program,[9] and a positive adjustment assistance program supporting approximately ten pilot projects to test alternative methods of finding employment for workers who are displaced as a result of unfavorable changes in economic conditions (such as competition from imports). President Reagan rejects these new initiatives and recommends that federal support for public service employment be phased out by the end of fiscal 1981 along with the youth conservation corps. He also proposes phasing out the young adult conser-

8. The number of jobs for title VI in 1982 did not equal its level in fiscal 1981, but instead the reduced number of 100,000 jobs were maintained as mandated by Congress in its 1981 continuing budget resolution. This action by Congress resulted in a $500 million cut in funding for the program in fiscal 1981.

9. The Carter youth initiative was composed of two titles. Title I called for a consolidation of several youth programs into one program serving all youth aged sixteen to twenty-one from families with incomes at or below 85 percent of the Bureau of Labor Statistics lower living standard. Title II provided for a formula-based grant program to secondary schools in school districts with a large proportion of low-income students to develop programs that stress the acquisition of basic education skills and good employment habits.

vation corps by the end of 1982. These actions are to reduce outlays in fiscal 1982 for employment and training programs by $4.6 billion.

Public Service Employment

As mentioned above, the original intent of title VI was to address cyclical unemployment problems while title II-D was to deal with structural unemployment problems. In practice, the two public service employment programs function in much the same manner and, since 1978, both programs have become increasingly targeted on disadvantaged groups. There is a case, therefore, for consolidating the two programs to eliminate duplication.

The arguments for entirely eliminating federal support for public service employment are that the output produced by many of these workers is of questionable social value and that most of the jobs provide little if any training that could serve as a bridge from employment in the public sector to that in the private sector. The contention is also made that the title VI funds are simply supplanting state and local expenditures—that is, they provide "fiscal substitution" rather than add to their ability to finance employment and training programs. Those who support continued federal assistance for public service employment maintain that the elimination of titles VI and II-D will deprive members of disadvantaged groups who urgently need such assistance of job opportunities and training. They also point out that reduction of outlays for this assistance would bring about an increase in outlays for such federal programs as welfare, food stamps, and unemployment compensation and reduce social security and income tax receipts.

Youth Employment Programs

After much experimentation and evaluation, the prevailing view is that youth employment and training programs should be focused on young people with the most severe employment handicaps. Two youth employment programs, the young adult conservation corps and the youth conservation corps, do not meet that criterion. In fact, in fiscal 1979 only 33.5 percent of the program participants in the young adult conservation corps were considered economically disadvantaged. Thus these programs are regarded by many as prime candidates for budgetary savings.

Although the Carter budget did in fact propose phasing out the young adult conservation corps by the end of 1982, it maintained the youth conservation corps at a cost of $60 million a year. Given that the only major difference between the two programs is that the former is a year-round program while the latter is in operation only during the summer, the same rationale—that is, lack of focus on the severely disadvantaged—would justify phasing out the youth conservation corps as well. The work performed by participants in the two programs, if deemed useful, could be supported with funds from the relevant state or federal agencies.

Instead of a separate youth initiative, the Reagan administration proposes to consolidate two youth programs (the youth community conservation and improvement projects and the youth employment and training programs) with the employment and training programs under titles II-B and II-C.[10] Budget authority requested for titles II-B and II-C will be increased to accommodate the proposed consolidation, but will be $0.9 billion below the total amount requested for the three programs in the Carter budget. According to the new administration, the reduction in spending on youth programs will be more than offset by the administrative savings resulting from the consolidation of employment and training programs into one grant. Whether or not the savings are realized as anticipated, the Reagan administration will clearly rely on the private sector to provide the jobs and much of the training needed for disadvantaged youths. One possibility is to reduce the minimum wage for youths in order to encourage employers to hire them. Another is to design effective subsidies to encourage private businesses to employ young people.[11] Given that the unemployment rates for youth (particularly black youth in urban areas) are expected to remain high and the proposed single block grant for employment and training programs will have limited funds, some initiative on the part of the new administration is needed to increase private sector involvement in youth employment.

10. In 1983 the summer youth employment program is scheduled to be included in the consolidated grant for employment and training programs.

11. Current knowledge of the potential effectiveness of wage subsidies, however, is limited. For instance, little is known about the size of the subsidy necessary to induce employers to hire targeted workers. For an analysis of the likely economic effects and administrative problem of federal wage subsidies, see Robert H. Haveman and John L. Palmer, eds., *Categorical Wage Subsidies* (Brookings Institution, forthcoming).

Consequences of Budget Cutting

It is not difficult to identify those who would be hurt most by reductions in outlays for the employment and training programs— the unskilled, uneducated, and unemployed, especially among members of minority groups. If the hardships that they are bound to suffer from federal budget cuts are not alleviated, many fear that the result will be an increase in crime and urban civil disorder.

The elimination of federal support for public service jobs will also have a significant impact on the budgets of state and local governments, particularly those in the northeast region having large programs under the Comprehensive Employment and Training Act. For many, federal funds for public service employment have the same effect as general revenue-sharing grants. The large net cut in federal grants-in-aid recommended by the Reagan administration (see below) may impair the fiscal capacity of many of the nation's cities, and even some of the states.

Unemployment Compensation
Prepared by Marvin M. Smith

Unemployment insurance is available to approximately 97 percent of all U.S. wage and salaried workers and provides support to those who experience temporary spells of joblessness and are searching for other employment. During fiscal 1981 an estimated 4.1 million workers a week received unemployment benefits; the figure for fiscal 1982 is likely to remain about 4 million workers a week.

Under current law, an insured individual can receive basic unemployment compensation for twenty-six weeks. The payments are extended, however, for an additional thirteen weeks when a state's insured unemployment rate reaches 4 percent or more for thirteen consecutive weeks and is at least 20 percent above the rate for the same period in each of the previous two years. Moreover, states have the option of continuing the extended benefits for thirteen weeks if their insured unemployment rate reaches 5 percent, regardless of its level in the previous two years. Also, the extended payments are made for thirteen consecutive weeks in all states when the national rate of unemployment among insured workers reaches 4.5 percent— which is referred to as the "national trigger" rate.

Ever since its enactment in 1935, controversy has centered on the unemployment compensation program's conflicting aims of providing sufficient income support to those who are involuntarily unemployed and of encouraging individuals who are out of work to find other employment. Although this point of contention remains, various changes in certain features of the program are under consideration because of the potential savings to be gained. Another program that is being scrutinized carefully is the controversial trade adjustment assistance program, which provides workers displaced as a result of foreign competition with benefit payments that are more generous and of longer duration than the regular unemployment insurance.

Under the current system, the existence of a national trigger and the inclusion of those claiming such benefits in the calculation of the insured unemployment rates have given rise to a number of anomalies that the Carter administration proposed to eliminate.[12] The Reagan administration accepted the Carter proposal and added the following: (1) the state trigger for unemployment rates should be increased from 4 to 5 percent and 120 percent of the rate in the previous two years; (2) the state optional trigger rates should be increased from 5 to 6 percent and without regard to the insured unemployment rates in previous years; and (3) the national trigger for extended benefits should be eliminated.

In addition to supporting the technical proposals for extended benefits, the Reagan administration intends to enforce the rule—adopted by Congress in 1980—that extended benefits be denied to workers who refuse to take other jobs paying wages that are at least equal to their unemployment benefits or the minimum wage, whichever is higher. The administration proposes legislation to apply the same rule to claimants who have collected at least thirteen weeks of regular benefits and eliminates unemployment compensation for

12. The insured unemployment rate is equal to the number of people claiming regular or extended benefits divided by the number of people in covered employment in the base period. The anomalies are (1) delays may occur in extended benefit payments in some states when unemployment rises; (2) one state may pay extended benefits while another with an identical unemployment rate does not; (3) payment of extended benefits continues after the overall unemployment rate falls below the trigger levels; and (4) payments of extended benefits are offered in states with very low insured unemployment rates when the national trigger is activated. To correct these anomalies, the Carter administration proposed that those claiming extended benefits be eliminated in the calculation of the insured employment rates.

people who quit the military services voluntarily. It also proposes to provide trade-adjustment assistance benefits to eligible workers only after they exhaust their regular unemployment benefits and to limit payments to the same amount as the worker's weekly unemployment insurance payments for up to fifty-two weeks. Taken together, the Reagan and Carter proposals would reduce fiscal 1982 outlays by $2.6 billion.

The elimination of unemployment benefits to persons who leave the military voluntarily and refuse reenlistment offers is intended to place them in the same position as civilian employees who are denied benefits after they quit their jobs and refuse employment offers in their customary occupation. However, this change would actually place the people who left the military at a disadvantage relative to their civilian counterparts because in practice most civilian workers receive unemployment compensation even if they leave their jobs voluntarily.[13]

The proposed modifications of the trade-adjustment assistance program would reverse a decision that was made by Congress as recently as 1979. One argument advanced in favor of the proposed changes is that workers in industries affected by foreign competition should not receive greater benefits than those paid under regular unemployment insurance merely because of the circumstance giving rise to their unemployment. Another is that the generous payments under the trade-adjustment assistance program serve as a disincentive for workers to develop new skills and seek new employment. Those opposed to the changes contend that the failure of the government to protect domestic industry from foreign competition results in significant injury to the workers attached to those industries. Payments under the trade adjustment program which, as mentioned above, are more generous than regular unemployment insurance, are justified as compensation to the recipients for bearing the burden of the government's policy decisions. Although the merits of the program will be vigorously debated, the larger issue that should be addressed is the government's inability to deal adequately with those who experience long-term unemployment.

---

13. Currently states may temporarily disqualify civilian workers who quit their jobs from receiving unemployment compensation benefits. However, most of these workers actually receive benefits because the states recognize a "good personal cause" as an explanation for leaving their jobs.

The proposal to require unemployment insurance claimants to seek and accept jobs outside of their customary occupation after the allotted time for job search in their occupational areas is also controversial. Several studies have found that workers' job search intensifies as the date when their benefits will be exhausted draws near. Thus the more restrictive job-search requirement would probably lower the average duration of unemployment, although the magnitude of the reduction cannot be estimated. Another objective of the proposed revision is to increase the interindustry mobility of the labor force. But career decisions are unlikely to be made on the basis of forced job search or by encouraging workers to accept jobs paying minimum wages. Structural shifts in the labor force are generated by recurrent unemployment in declining industries and changes in relative wages.

The proposed modification would amount to the abandonment of a fundamental tenet of the unemployment insurance program—that workers should not be forced to accept jobs that clearly require lesser skills. It would impose financial hardships on many unemployed middle-income workers with major financial obligations (such as mortgages, car payments, and college bills) and require them to accept jobs that they would regard as demeaning. In addition, forcing workers to accept jobs outside their occupation prematurely could mean a waste of the previous investment made in their job training.

Overall, the purpose of the proposed changes in unemployment insurance and trade-adjustment assistance are to improve the assistance to workers who are involuntarily unemployed for long periods and to encourage unemployed workers to seek other employment sooner. While the new administration's proposals might improve the functioning of labor markets, they would adversely affect the welfare of many workers who have come to rely on the unemployment compensation system for support during periods when they cannot find work in their chosen occupations.

Health
Prepared by Louise B. Russell

Payments for medical services make up the overwhelming majority of federal outlays for health, and two programs in particular, medicare and medicaid, are largely responsible for the rapid growth in health outlays. Under present law these two programs would cost $65 billion in fiscal 1982 out of a total of $75 billion for all programs classified under health in the budget—$47 billion for medicare and $18 billion for medicaid, the latter to be matched by $14 billion from the states. Another $20 billion of health-related outlays, mostly for medical care services for veterans, members of the military services, and federal employees, are reported elsewhere in the budget.

Both medicare and medicaid were created by legislation passed in 1965. Medicare offers benefits to people aged sixty-five or older. About 95 percent of the aged are currently enrolled in the hospital insurance part of the program, and most of them also choose to enroll in the medical insurance part, which pays doctors' bills and charges a monthly premium to help cover its costs. Medicare was extended in 1973 to cover people with end-stage kidney disease and beneficiaries of the social security disability insurance program.

Medicaid pays for medical services for the welfare population. To qualify, applicants must meet two criteria. First, they must be in one of the "categorical" groups for which welfare is intended—the aged, the blind, the disabled, or certain kinds of families with dependent children. Second, the applicant's income must be less than the welfare standard set by the state. For the aged, blind, and disabled, that standard can be no less than the cash assistance payment made by the federal supplemental security income program, which took over income payments for these three groups in 1974. For recipients of aid to families with dependent children, the standard for a family of four in 1979 ranged from $148 a month in Alabama to $525 a month in Oregon; it was less than 55 percent of the federal poverty line (about $340 monthly) in twenty-three states. Thirty states also offer medicaid to the medically needy, people in the welfare categories whose medical bills are so high that their remaining income is less than the state standard.

Most people who receive medicaid services (over half) are members of families with dependent children, but they account for only about one-fourth of the program's outlays. It is not widely recognized that medicaid spends a great deal for the aged to fill gaps left by medicare. Between 35 and 40 percent of medicaid's outlays are for the aged poor: to pay for coinsurance, deductibles, and premiums under medicare; and, most important, to pay for services medicare does not cover—especially nursing-home care, which accounts for three-fourths of the medicaid payments made on behalf of the aged. Medicare's original objective was to pay for skilled nursing-home care after a hospital stay, but payments for this purpose were sharply curtailed in the late 1960s when the escalating trend in program costs became obvious. Most public funds for nursing-home care now come from medicaid. Nursing-home care for younger people is also a major drain on medicaid. Altogether, nursing-home care for people of all ages and other outlays for the aged claim about half of the program's resources.

Medicare and medicaid are the most visible components in a long-term trend toward more and more third-party payment for medical services, through health insurance plans in the private sector as well as public programs.[14] Third-party payment has been expanded to insure that cost does not prevent anyone from receiving medical care when it is needed, to remove costs as a consideration when life and health are concerned. The principle is humane and generous—and financially unrealistic. As the nation has poured resources into medical care in its attempt to meet medical need, national health expenditures have risen from 4.5 percent of GNP in 1950, to 6 percent in 1965, and 9 percent in 1979, when they totaled $212 billion.

The 1970s were marked by numerous attempts to control costs without sacrificing the principle of meeting need. The Nixon administration retained price and wage controls governing medical care for some time after controls had been lifted from the rest of the economy. The Ford administration proposed limits on reimbursements under medicare; the Carter administration, on total hospital revenues. Both proposals were rejected by a Congress and a nation not yet ready to concede that rationing, whether through regulation or the marketplace, was inevitable—that benefits had to be weighed against costs in medical care, as in any other use of the nation's limited resources.

But in 1981 the overriding issue is the size of the federal budget, and the Reagan administration has put aside the larger question of the growth in medical care expenditures, promising to return to it in a year or two. At that time they are likely to consider a variation

14. See Louise B. Russell, "Medical Care," in Joseph A. Pechman, ed., *Setting National Priorities: Agenda for the 1980s* (Brookings Institution, 1980), pp. 169–203.

of the "competition" plans introduced by David A. Stockman, director of the Office of Management and Budget, and Richard S. Schweiker, secretary of Health and Human Services, among others, when they were members of Congress. In general, these plans would limit the tax exclusion for employer-provided health insurance and confine federal responsibility for medicare and medicaid to providing fixed voucher payments that beneficiaries could use for the plan of their choice. By these means the plans would encourage people to choose between health maintenance organizations and insurance plans with substantial cost sharing as mechanisms for rationing their use of medical care, with protection against catastrophic expenses in both cases. For now, with the focus on federal rather than on total national expenditures, the administration has proposed cutbacks in a number of federal health programs.

The largest cuts among those proposed are in service programs—the proposals to cap federal grants to the states for medicaid and to combine about forty health and social services programs into four block grants to the states and cut their funding for fiscal 1982 to 75 percent of the fiscal 1981 level. Medicaid funds would be allowed to grow only 5 percent in fiscal 1982—saving almost $1 billion out of the fiscal 1982 outlays estimated in the Carter budget—and by the general rate of inflation thereafter, although per capita medical spending has historically risen much faster than inflation. The cut in funding for the forty health and social services programs is expected to save $1.8 billion from the Carter budget in fiscal 1982.

The health programs, which account for less than half the money involved and range from such venerable institutions as maternal and child health to new programs that are not currently funded, will be consolidated into block grants for services and for prevention. The social service programs will be divided between grants for social services and for hardship assistance. Block grants have been proposed before—President Ford suggested combining sixteen health programs, including medicaid, into a single block grant—and the rationale this time is the same. The Office of Management and Budget argues that redundant bureaucracies can be streamlined and services provided much more efficiently if the states are allowed to set priorities and coordinate efforts through fewer programs. But even if it were somehow possible to eliminate all the federal employees and reporting time associated with these programs, a generous estimate would not put the savings at more than half a billion dollars. The remainder will have to be cut from health services.

The proposed reductions in medicaid are inconsistent with two of the principles the Reagan administration used in choosing programs to cut—maintaining the social safety net and reducing subsidies to middle- and upper-income groups. Focused on the poor, medicaid *is* the social safety net in medical care, and one with quite a few holes in it despite its growth. The Congressional Budget Office estimates that 12 million poor people are not covered by medicaid. Medicare, on the other hand, pays benefits to almost all the aged, most of whom are not poor, and is larger and has grown faster over the last five years than medicaid, so that the potential savings are greater. The only cuts currently proposed for medicare are based on the repeal of new benefits passed last year and not yet in effect.

It would be more in line with the Reagan administration's principles to raise premiums or to cut medicare outlays substantially by introducing more cost sharing. The Ford administration proposed that medicare enrollees should pay 10 percent of the hospital costs they incurred after the deductible was met. This proposal would cut $3 billion from medicare's estimated outlays in fiscal 1982, which would be enough to permit better coverage of very large bills (also proposed by Ford) and some expansion of medicaid to insure that the truly needy do not suffer from the higher levels of cost sharing.

The other cuts proposed by the administration would save less and are often similar to the policies of past administrations. Financing for the education of the health professions has undergone convulsive change in the past decade—first expanding to produce more graduates in order to meet supposed shortages, and then contracting as rising medical care expenditures brought about a consensus that the nation could not afford higher rates of growth in medical personnel. The Carter administration tried unsuccessfully to eliminate general support for institutions engaged in educating health professionals. The Reagan administration is again proposing the elimination of these funds.

The National Institutes of Health have been slated for a smaller increase in funds than the Carter administration proposed, although neither budget gives them enough to keep up with inflation. The Institutes have long been accustomed to steady growth in their collective budget, but that growth slowed in the 1970s, and in each of the past two years outlays lagged behind inflation. The budget proposal would continue that situation for at least the next few years. Many supporters of biomedical research, who argue that research is the nation's best hope for better health and lower costs in the future, will be disturbed by this trend. Others will find it a reasonable policy at a time when the nation is no longer certain it can finance medical care as generously as it has in the past.

Finally, the administration proposes to phase out the health planning system legislated in 1974 and the professional standards review organizations legislated in 1972. Introduced primarily as cost-cutting devices, neither has been able to prove that it can save more money than it costs to run. Federal subsidies for health maintenance organizations would also be phased out, and no money is requested for new national health service corps scholarships, on the ground that the number of students already receiving scholarship funds is more than adequate for the foreseeable future. In addition, in a proposal that is reminiscent of many only partially successful efforts in the past, the administration plans to close the remaining eight hospitals and twenty-nine clinics of the Public Health Service.

Education
Prepared by David W. Breneman

Unlike much of the nondefense budget, federal education programs—with the exception of the guaranteed student loan program—are controllable through annual appropriations. At the elementary and secondary school level, federal grants are allocated to state education agencies and local school districts, usually on a formula basis, to provide additional resources for the education of particular groups of students. The largest program, title I of the Elementary and Secondary Education Act of 1965, provides over $3 billion to 14,000 school districts for compensatory education for over 5 million educationally disadvantaged young people in high poverty areas. Other large programs include education for the handicapped ($1.1 billion in outlays estimated for fiscal 1981), vocational and adult education ($940 million), impact aid ($800 million), and Indian education ($300 million). In all, over seventy categorical grant programs provide federal support for elementary and secondary education, amounting to roughly 9 percent of total school budgets.

Federal support for higher education is provided principally through student aid—grants to low- and middle-income students and loan subsidies and guarantees for all students who borrow. The guaranteed student loan program is the most rapidly growing part of the education budget as a result of the extension of eligibility for interest subsidies to all students in 1978. That change generated an increase in borrowing from $2 billion in fiscal 1978 to an estimated $7.9 billion in fiscal 1982, with the federal subsidy in the latter year estimated at $2.9 billion. Except for the student loan program, however, the growth of federal education outlays is not "out of control."

The Carter budget for fiscal 1982 included two legislative proposals: a youth education and training initiative with annual outlays of $900 million beginning in 1983 and changes in the guaranteed student loan program to reduce federal subsidies. President Reagan dropped the youth initiative, but accepted the revisions in the student loan program. In addition, both the Carter and Reagan budgets include a cut in impact aid from $800 million in fiscal 1981 to $450 million in fiscal 1982 and subsequent years, which reflects the continuing but unsuccessful efforts of every administration since Eisenhower to reduce federal aid to school districts in which federal activities do not place a large burden on the local education system. Perhaps the Reagan administration will succeed where others have failed to end these unjustifiable federal payments.

Budget Issues

Were this not a year when economic and political forces are prompting a search for budget cuts in many areas of the domestic budget, it is unlikely that educational considerations alone would have given rise to proposals for dramatic changes in education programs or funding levels. One exception might have been an effort to consolidate many of the categorical grant programs at the elementary-secondary level into block grants distributed directly to state and local education agencies. Federal policy to date has stressed categorical aid in opposition to general financial support, which is viewed as the responsibility of state and local governments. A reasonable case can be made that the regulations governing these separate programs produce excessive paperwork and, in their cumulative effect on the schools, undesirable overlap and inefficiencies that reduce educational effectiveness. The counterargument is that each federal program attempts to remedy a deficiency that taxpayers and state and local school officials, left to their own devices, might not address. Detailed regulations are considered necessary to ensure that federal dollars provide some additional support, not a substitute for state and local revenues, and that these additional outlays benefit directly the students singled out as exceptionally needy, not the entire school population.

The pros and cons of block grants are conceptually separate from the issue of budget reduction, but the Reagan administration has joined them in a single proposal. Under this plan, forty-four categorical grant programs would be consolidated into two block grants (one for state education agencies, the other for local districts), and outlays would be cut by 25 percent of the total for the separate programs combined. This proposal contains an implicit quid pro quo: increased state and local autonomy in spending federal dollars at a cost of 25 cents on the dollar. State and local education agencies would value increased control, but may judge the price too high. It would be unfortunate if this opportunity to reassess the federal role in education founders on the separate issue of budget cuts.

The block grant approach challenges the existing rationale for federal support of education: concern for the exceptional educational needs of specific groups in the school population. If strings are not attached to the federal money, there is no assurance that these special groups will continue to benefit, nor is it clear on what basis the block grants should be distributed because the eligible populations for each program differ. While some school districts might continue to spend money on special education for disadvantaged and handicapped youth, others would use the federal dollars for general operating purposes. In that case, the original purposes of federal support would be lost, and the only budget question left would be the percentage of total costs to be paid by Washington. The current 9 percent figure at least has a tenuous relation to the educational needs of special populations, but it would have no particular rationale under a system of block grants. Why not 4 percent, or no percent, or even 33 percent, a figure long advocated by the National Education Association?

The Carter administration had started to loosen the strings on federal money in cases in which states and localities could demonstrate that they were adopting federal goals as their own. For example, under the Education for All Handicapped Children Act, if a state can demonstrate that all eligible children are receiving a "free, appropriate public education," federal dollars no longer have to be tracked within that program. This method of reducing federal control seems promising because federal purposes are not lost in the process.

The principal budget issue for higher education is the guaranteed student loan program. Dismay over spiraling subsidy costs of this program prompted the Carter administration to propose a number of major changes, which were largely adopted by the new administration: (1) loans would be limited to a student's remaining financial need after other forms of aid and expected family contribution have been determined; (2) the in-school interest subsidy would be eliminated; and (3) the interest rate on the parents' new loan program would not be subsidized. In addition, the Reagan administration would eliminate borrowing by the Student Loan Marketing Association from the Federal Financing Bank after October 1982, a move that would cut back the secondary market for student loans.

The difficulty posed by this program, which relies on commercial banks as the main source for loans, is that the proposed changes may reduce the willingness of banks to participate. The remarkable growth in loans since the policy changes of 1978 reflects not only the demand for highly subsidized loans, but also the enhanced attractiveness of such loans to the banking community, resulting in an increased supply of credit. Because guaranteed student loans have become a central source of financing for many undergraduate students, particularly in higher-priced colleges, and for many students in graduate and professional schools, it is essential that reforms not jeopardize the supply of bank credit.

Introducing a calculation of remaining financial need into eligibility for loans is an unattractive way to ration access to credit. Borrowing to finance some of the costs of higher education is a perfectly reasonable option for individuals to choose, and ought not to be foreclosed on the basis of a somewhat arbitrary calculation of need. What is objectionable is the large interest subsidy that in essence makes anyone who does not borrow seem foolish, even irrational, at current interest rates. If this subsidy did not exist, no one would be interested in rationing access to credit; market interest rates alone would perform that function by eliminating those borrowers only interested in a source of cheap money. The sensible approach, therefore, clearly involves scaling back—or eliminating entirely—the interest subsidy, requiring accrual of interest while in school and a reasonable repayment schedule that graduates can handle. It may be necessary for the federal government to pay the in-school interest subsidy to reduce administrative costs for the banks, with subsequent reimbursement when loans are in repayment. Whether students from low-income families should continue to have interest subsidized—in effect, reintroducing the income test for subsidy eligibility—depends primarily on the adequacy of federal and state grant programs for such students. With sufficient grant aid available, the rationale for interest subsidy for even low-income students would be largely undermined.

Tuition Tax Credits

The Reagan administration appears determined to force the education community to confront the issue of tuition tax credits once again. Because this ordeal was endured as recently as 1978, no new information or analysis bearing on this proposal will be forthcoming; the issues were discussed at length three years ago.[15] Tuition tax credits commonly proposed for higher education would be regressive, because benefits would flow disproportionately to high-income families; inefficient, because student decisions regarding whether, or where, to enroll would be largely unaffected; and expensive, with a drain on the U.S. Treasury of $1.5 billion or more in the first year and larger amounts in subsequent years, depending upon the configuration of the tax credit. For higher education, therefore, a tuition tax credit simply amounts to a wasteful expenditure (no one would design a grant program with such characteristics), but it would do little damage because behavior would not be affected.

The difficult issues arise when the credit is extended to elementary and secondary school tuition in private schools. In this case, the price differential between tuition-free public schools and tuition-charging private schools would be reduced (unless, of course, private schools raised tuition by the amount of the credit, thereby capturing the subsidy for themselves). Parental choice would be affected to some degree, and the country should be certain that it wants to

15. See David W. Breneman, "Education," in Joseph A. Pechman, ed., *Setting National Priorities: The 1979 Budget* (Brookings Institution, 1978), pp. 117–25.

expand private schooling at the expense of public schooling before embarking on this course. Entanglement of private schools, many of them church-related, with federal tuition subsidies raises constitutional questions and may ultimately threaten the independence of private schools from government control. These concerns, coupled with the drain on federal revenues at a time when emphasis is being placed on the budget deficit, highlight the difficult issues involved in improving the nation's education system.

Housing
Prepared by Katharine L. Bradbury

Three major types of housing programs are supported by the federal government. The first provides direct assistance to low-income households or to operators of housing for low-income households. The second attempts to enhance the operation of the private mortgage market by assuring an adequate supply of mortgage credit nationally and by providing purchase or insurance of mortgages for households or areas not otherwise well served. The third and largest consists of tax expenditures.

The total size of the budget commitment to housing ($33 billion budget authority and $9 billion outlays in fiscal 1980) is a misleading indicator of potential savings from cutbacks in existing programs, at least in the short run, because of the long-term commitments into which the Department of Housing and Urban Development has already entered. The Congressional Budget Office estimates that the $6.6 billion in fiscal 1981 outlays for the assisted housing component would grow to $11 billion by fiscal 1986, even if no additional subsidy commitments were made after 1981.

Housing Assistance

Housing assistance to low-income households has been an important part of federal housing programs for many years, and has grown steadily during the last decade from $733 million in fiscal 1971 to $5.5 billion in fiscal 1980. Currently the major programs subsidize rental housing for low-income households through both direct assistance with rent and subsidies for construction of privately owned low-income units and public housing.

A basic debate regarding federal provision of housing assistance to low-income households centers on the lack of entitlement in housing programs—there are considerably fewer subsidies or subsidized units available than there are eligible and poorly housed households. Still, a large number of households—about 2.6 million in fiscal 1980—are assisted by the two major programs, lower-income housing assistance (section 8) and public housing. The most effective strategy for expanding coverage and limiting annual costs of providing reasonable-quality housing to low-income households is to shift toward greater use of existing housing units, in both the section 8 and public housing programs. Among current housing assistance programs, section 8 for existing housing is the least costly per household aided, section 8 for new construction and substantial rehabilitation is the most expensive, with public housing in between. Although some part of these cost differences is attributable to differences in the quality of housing, they mostly reflect lower rent levels in existing housing. For example, if new section 8 commitments were added at the rate assumed in President Carter's 1982 budget projections, but all were for section 8 existing rather than the assumed 41 percent new and largely rehabilitated units, and if new public housing commitments shifted from virtually all new construction to half new and half purchase of existing units, this might reduce outlays by over $700 million in fiscal 1982, with savings growing by $300 million annually thereafter.[16] The savings could be used to aid additional households or to cut housing expenditures.

In contrast, President Reagan proposed a one-third reduction in 1982 additional subsidized units and a slight shift toward more use of existing units, which saves $19 million in fiscal 1982 outlays and grows to $825 million in fiscal 1986. Whether the objective is to cut the budget or provide better services, a shift to simpler demand-side subsidies for existing housing, which reduces cost per household while maintaining or even allowing expansion of service levels, is a policy change that is preferable to a simple service reduction such as that President Reagan proposes.

16. Outlays begin when the housing project is occupied, so new construction units have a lag between commitment and actual outlays but existing units do not. This means a shift to existing housing would raise outlays initially, but long-run savings would be of the magnitudes cited in the text. This estimate includes direct savings in section 8 and public housing subsidies as well as related savings on "tandem" financing, public housing operating subsidies, and tax-exempt bond sales.

The argument against a shift to existing housing is that it will result in less stimulus to housing construction. However, if existing housing units are available at lower prices than new construction, increases in new construction of low-cost housing are inappropriate on economic grounds.[17] The new administration has indirectly recognized the value of existing housing in proposing a slowing, rather than an elimination, of the public housing modernization program.

Large savings are also possible by increasing the proportion of income that tenants are expected to contribute to rent payments to 30 percent from the current range of 15 to 25 percent, including tenant rents in public housing that are now below section 8 levels.[18] President Reagan has proposed phasing in this increase over the next five years, with savings in outlays of $120 million in fiscal 1982 and $1.1 billion in fiscal 1986.

As part of the decentralization of power sought by the Reagan administration, the transition advisory task force on housing proposes consolidation of the various forms of housing subsidies into a block grant. Housing block grants would theoretically allow local governments more discretion in choosing the mix among subsidy types, although the current section 8 program already attempts to mirror community housing needs as reflected in local housing assistance plans. Because local allotments would be dollars, not numbers of units, one source of the current local bias toward choosing (more expensive) new construction over existing units would be removed. The distribution of funds among localities would probably be similar to the current distribution.

An obvious side effect of block grants is that they would free the federal government from the long-term commitments that currently make the costs of these programs so difficult to control. If annual block grant payments were uncertain, city governments would not be willing to make long-term contracts with landlords or developers and therefore bear the responsibility if costs rose. However, one version of the proposal would, in essence, give budget authority to local governments and enable them to enter into long-term commitments.

17. Most subsidized new construction simply substitutes for unsubsidized construction that would otherwise occur. See Michael P. Murray, "Subsidized and Unsubsidized Housing Starts: 1961–1977," Working Paper, Duke University, Center for the Study of Policy Analysis (June 1980).

18. This has the negative effect of raising the total tax rate on earnings of participant households.

The savings in outlays from a change to block grants depend on funding decisions made annually; proponents argue that budgets could be cut because flexible block-grant dollars would be worth more to localities. The block-grant proposal is not included in President Reagan's first-year changes, but is reportedly under study at the Department of Housing and Urban Development.

Mortgage Credit and Thrift Insurance

Two important elements of the housing credit component of the budget are the mortgage-purchase activities of the Government National Mortgage Association and mortgage insurance provided by the Federal Housing Administration. The former institution guarantees some mortgages insured by the latter and purchases selected mortgages that are below the market interest rate in "tandem" with other programs; these purchases provide a subsidy with net cost equal to the difference between the purchase price (above true value) and sale price. Both outlays and budget authority for these programs are unpredictable and volatile over time because they depend on the timing of asset purchases and sales.

Much of this mortgage-market activity is simply smoothing market operations or providing guarantees or insurance to otherwise ill-served market participants without high budget cost. However, the losses of the Government National Mortgage Association on mortgages with below-market interest rates, tandem costs, interest on Treasury borrowings, and asset sales amounted to over $500 million in fiscal 1980, and were projected to grow to $1.3 billion in President Carter's fiscal 1982 budget. These costs represent subsidies to housing suppliers that enable them to offer units to low-income tenants at lower rents. A shift to increased reliance on existing housing and market responses to subsidized housing needs would automatically reduce these outlays, and thereby make funds available that could be used for additional demand-side subsidies for low-income households. President Reagan proposes discontinuation of the tandem mortgage-purchase program of the Government National Mortgage Association *without* a substantial shift toward existing housing. This is expected to save $4 million in outlays of the Government National Mortgage Association in fiscal 1982, but at the same time it will raise the per unit cost of section 8 housing assistance. The new administration also proposes additional caps on activities of both the Government National Mortgage Association and the Federal Housing Administration, not with the intention of reducing outlays, because most are self-supporting, but to eliminate government interference and "crowding out" in credit and insurance markets.

The Department of Agriculture has a sizable program to improve rural housing, including direct loans and loan guarantees for low- and middle-income families and rental subsidies to low-income households in housing financed by the Farmers Home Administration. Because of the timing of loan purchases and sales, this item also shows considerable volatility. These mortgage loans have effective rates as low as 1 percent, with an estimated average of 3 percent for new loans. The Congressional Budget Office estimates savings of $30 million in fiscal 1982, which would grow to almost ten times that much in fiscal 1986, simply by raising the minimum rate to 5 percent for new borrowers. President Reagan has proposed some cuts in the lending authority of the Farmers Home Administration.

Tax Expenditures

If the federal housing budget must be reduced, some specific cuts in tax expenditures should be considered. These include deduction of interest on home mortgages and of property taxes, deferral of capital gains taxes on sales of owner-occupied homes, exclusion of $100,000 of capital gain on the sale of homes by people over age fifty-five, faster than straight-line depreciation for rental housing, and the tax exemption provided to housing bonds issued by local governments.[19] These provisions, especially the two deductions, offer a fertile field for reducing the federal housing budget because the dollar amounts involved are large—estimated to be almost $40 billion in fiscal 1982. Reductions in tax expenditures for housing would not assist in reducing the size of federal outlays as conventionally measured, but they could be used to alleviate pressure for cuts in direct housing expenditures, thus leaving room for more general reductions in tax rates or reductions in the deficit.

President Reagan has proposed an increase in tax expenditures for rental housing as part of his accelerated cost recovery plan. The proposal reduces the effective life for depreciation purposes from thirty-two years (or twenty years for used structures) to eighteen

---

19. See the tax expenditure sections of this chapter and appendix B.

years and creates a differential for low-income rental housing by reducing its average useful life to fifteen years.

Local Economic Development
Prepared by Katharine L. Bradbury

The federal government provides grants to local and state governments to promote economic development at the local level. The programs of the Department of Housing and Urban Development in this area, including community development block grants and urban development action grants, are focused on cities.[20] The Department of Commerce also provides economic development funds to both urban and rural communities.

Economic Development Programs

The community development block grant program, created in 1974 to consolidate seven categorical grant programs, is by far the largest program in local economic development, with almost $4 billion in fiscal 1981 outlays. These funds are allocated by formula to 521 large cities and 73 urban counties and are awarded on a competitive basis to small cities; the funds are available for a broad range of community development activities with low- and middle-income households as primary beneficiaries. Urban development action grants, begun by the Carter administration in 1978, provide a total of $675 million annually to "severely distressed" cities to promote specific economic development or neighborhood revitalization projects involving financing commitments by local government and the private sector. The Carter administration expected to fund 355 action grant projects in fiscal 1982, which it claimed would attract $5 billion in private money and create or retain 188,000 jobs.

After considerable protests against a plan to eliminate the action grants, the Reagan administration proposed integrating them with the community development grants, incorporating several other programs such as weatherization for low-income families, and allowing local governments more flexibility in the use of the funds. The com-

20. Similar aid is provided to rural areas through the Department of Agriculture's efforts in rural development and business assistance, and to Indians through the U.S. Bureau of Indian Affairs.

bined program would seemingly resemble general revenue sharing in purpose and size, but would retain its focus on considerably fewer communities (revenue sharing distributes $4.6 billion to more than 39,000 local governments). Proposed budget authority for the combined program was reduced by more than the previous administration had scheduled for action grants after fiscal 1983, and the 1981– 86 rate of growth of outlays for the two programs was cut from 5.5 percent annually to virtually zero.

The reasons for enactment of the separate block grant and action grant programs include concern with targeting (what areas receive how much money), the desire to have city government projects address *national* urban goals, and the tension between local political incentives to spend quickly and the long-term nature of significant economic development undertakings. The proposed consolidation is likely to reduce program effectiveness along several of these dimensions, in addition to providing lower total funding for the stated goals. The most important effect of a more flexible grant is that it is likely to reduce city spending on the groups historically ignored by city governments—especially low-income and minority residents. In advocating flexibility, policymakers should weigh the importance of imposing national goals on city government officials, who are apparently often willing to use federal scapegoats to accomplish locally unpopular activities. One of the major criticisms of the block grant program is that uncertain annual funding has curtailed local governments' interest and capacity to deal with the problems of long-term investment in the cities. Yet serious economic development efforts, especially those involving private investment, require coordinated planning and long-term capital commitments. The action grant program has more effectively financed such economic development projects, but whether this can be carried over to a consolidated program depends on program details not yet known.

The Department of Housing and Urban Development also provides subsidized loans to rehabilitate residential and commercial structures (mostly the former) at a cost of $133 million in fiscal 1981, and still spends more than $150 million annually out of its previously unfunded contract authority on the urban renewal program, which was terminated in 1975. Other community development programs of the department—including planning assistance grants, urban homesteading, a new community development corporation, and a neighborhood self-help development program—total about $125 million in estimated fiscal 1981 outlays. Among these programs, the Reagan administration has proposed abolishing planning assistance grants, rehabilitation loans, and the neighborhood self-help program on the grounds that the activities can be financed with community development block grant funds or should be financed locally. The rescission of available budget authority is expected to reduce outlays after fiscal 1982 by over $250 million a year.

The Economic Development Administration since 1965 has provided planning grants, technical assistance grants, public facility construction grants, direct business development loans, and loan guarantees to local governments and private organizations to "reduce substantial and persistent unemployment in economically distressed areas and to react to problems of economic adjustment." The largest items are development grants for community facilities and direct loans (at low interest rates) to retain, construct, or expand industry facilities. The Reagan administration proposed ending the Economic Development Administration, with projected savings of $374 million in fiscal 1982 and $844 million in fiscal 1986.

Overall, federal spending on community development, mostly by the Department of Housing and Urban Development, showed a gradual rising trend from about $2 billion in the early 1970s to $3.6 billion in fiscal 1977–79, with a jump to $4.9 billion in fiscal 1980 and $5.3 billion projected for fiscal 1982 in the Carter budget. Area and regional development outlays by the Departments of Commerce, Agriculture, and Interior showed faster growth during the early part of the 1970s, but then turned down from a high of $4.9 billion in fiscal 1978 to the Carter budget range of $2.8 to $2.9 billion in fiscal years 1981 and 1982, largely as a result of reductions in the local public works program. Thus total economic development activities reached a high of $8.2 billion in fiscal 1978, which would have been reached again in fiscal 1982 under the Carter budget. If the changes proposed by President Reagan are enacted, there will be a reduction in outlays over the next few years, reaching more than $2 billion annually by fiscal 1986. This reduction will affect the budgets of state and local governments that would otherwise have received the funds (see the section later in this chapter on grants to state and local governments), as well as threaten several of the past goals of local economic development programs.

Tax Expenditures

Tax expenditures for local economic development result from the tax-exempt status of local government bonds. General obligation bonds support, among other things, the construction of public infrastructures, such as sewers, that are also eligible for some of the grants and loans outlined above, at an estimated cost of $6.5 billion for fiscal 1982. More controversial are industrial revenue bonds floated by local governments for reduced interest loans for private business development, which are expected to cost $1.6 billion in lost 1982 revenues. The concerns are that these bonds are mostly for subsidizing development that would occur anyway, that they subsidize booming areas as well as distressed places, and that their recent growth has raised the costs of all state and local borrowing.

Urban Enterprise Zones

One of the newest ideas in local economic development is to designate selected distressed areas as "enterprise zones" in which government intervention—taxes, regulation, zoning, social services—is minimized to allow private enterprise to develop or redevelop the area. The Kemp-Garcia bill now being revised in Congress would reduce capital gains and corporate income taxes, speed tax depreciation, subsidize wages (through federal payment of a fraction of the employer share of social security), and reduce local property tax payments for firms locating in designated zones and hiring at least half their work force from among zone residents. The bill would not suspend zoning, other regulations, or the minimum wage, although the wage subsidy would be higher for youth than for those over age twenty-one.

As in all targeted programs, concern has focused on how such areas would be chosen. The bill proposes criteria regarding population characteristics (unemployment rates and poverty incidence) in relatively small neighborhoods, but questions have been raised about whether the poorest residential areas are the best places to expand industry and, if so, whether appropriate local-area data are available. In addition, the usefulness of the plan is seriously undermined (and the cost increased) if too many places are designated.

Because local governments would not be reimbursed for lost property taxes, the primary budget cost of such a plan would be the federal replacement of social security contributions (a transfer from general revenues to the social security trust fund); in addition, business tax revenues would be lost. Although this plan was espoused during the Reagan candidacy, it was not included in the first round of budget changes proposed by the new president.

Energy

Prepared by John E. Jankowski, Jr., of Resources for the Future

Outlays to promote energy production, conservation, and preparedness have been a major source of growth in President Carter's federal nondefense budget. He recommended an increase of 37 percent in energy outlays from $8.7 billion in fiscal 1981 to $12.0 billion in fiscal 1982. President Reagan reduced the 1982 figure to only $8.7 billion. Over one-third of these outlays are for research and development to increase and conserve energy supplies, and two-fifths are for additions to the strategic petroleum reserve. There is also provision in the 1982 Reagan budget for $7.3 billion in energy tax expenditures and $2.0 billion in energy loan guarantees.

The major issues in the energy budget are at what level and in what fashion to support synthetic fuels, how fast the strategic petroleum reserve should be filled, how to promote the development of solar and other renewable energy sources, the degree of federal support to be given to energy conservation, and what the future of the nation's nuclear energy should be.

The Synthetic Fuels Corporation

The Synthetic Fuels Corporation was established by Congress in 1980 as an independent federal entity to provide financial assistance and incentives to the private sector for the development of sources of commercial-scale domestic synthetic fuel. The corporation's goal is a production capacity of 500,000 barrels a day of crude oil equivalent by 1987 and 2 million barrels a day by 1992. The corporation is set up as an off-budget federal entity so that it will be able to operate with autonomy, somewhat like a private financial institution.[21] The activities of the corporation are included in the budget totals

21. Assistance can be provided by the corporation through purchase agreements, price and loan guarantees, direct loans, and joint ventures in small-scale synfuel projects that can expand to full-scale plants. Either house of Congress may disapprove any specific synfuel project proposal. The corporation is scheduled to terminate in 1997.

when funds are transferred from the Treasury, as will obligations through loan and price guarantees if the government must make them good.

The corporation received initial budget authority in fiscal 1980 to assume obligations up to $20 billion. After a period of four years, the corporation must submit to Congress a comprehensive strategy for meeting its synthetic production goals, with details regarding the specific mix of technologies to be supported, the associated environmental effects, and the expected role of the private sector. Congressional approval of the strategy may result in additional budget authority of as much as $68 billion.

The success of the corporation will depend to a large extent on factors that are outside its control, because most of its activities will require the development of new technologies and the construction of large-scale plants, the viability of which will be contingent on future petroleum prices. In the early years, the budget outlays of the corporation will be small, but these outlays could grow substantially in later years if the corporation must fulfill its obligations. If fuel prices rise high enough and the corporation operates mainly through purchase agreements or price guarantees, actual outlays could be small.

President Carter supported the synfuel legislation when it was enacted and proposed no changes in the program in his last budget. President Reagan campaigned on a platform that rejected government financial support for the program. Consequently, while Reagan does not propose changes in the overall funding of the Synthetic Fuels Corporation, he proposes termination of direct funding of coal liquefaction and gasification projects by the Department of Energy, which would reduce the federal outlays for fossil and synthetic fuels by $1.2 billion in fiscal 1982. It is anticipated that the synfuel corporation will consider supporting these projects. President Reagan expects more successful project outcomes because private companies will have more of their own money at risk under the new approaches. However, there remain many economic, technical, environmental, and health uncertainties which, some feel, require direct involvement by the Department of Energy.

The Strategic Petroleum Reserve

The strategic petroleum reserve was established in 1975 to reduce the impact of serious disruptions in world oil markets. The original legislation contemplated a reserve of 1 billion barrels of petroleum, to be filled by the late 1980s. But the early acquisitions were made at a relatively slow rate (partly because of the concern about the possible adverse reaction of Saudi Arabia to a rapid U.S. buildup of its reserve), and purchases actually ceased between March 1979 and December 1980.

The Carter budget assumed that outlays in fiscal 1981 would be used to maintain a fill rate of 200,000 barrels a day, which would result in a total of 171 million barrels in storage at the end of this year. The budget also recommended enough new funding to step up the acquisition rate to 230,000 barrels a day in 1982. At that rate, the facilities would be filled to their current estimated capacity of 252 million barrels at the end of 1982. He also proposed that the storage facilities be expanded to 750 million barrels by the late 1980s. This program would require outlays of $3.4 billion in fiscal 1982 or $2.2 billion more than estimated outlays for fiscal 1981. Although President Reagan made no significant changes in the 1982 budget, he increased fiscal 1981 outlays by $1.3 billion to offset rising acquisition costs resulting from decontrol of domestic oil prices and termination of the crude oil entitlements program.

Consideration is now being given to the use of private financing of the strategic petroleum reserve by selling energy certificates for the petroleum in the reserve, which could then be traded in the commodities markets. By the end of the 1980s, this might cut budget outlays by as much as $17 billion. The Reagan administration has expressed interest in approaches such as this, but has deferred action until after the most urgent budget issues are settled. This procedure would simply substitute another form of borrowing for direct government debt. The apparent budget relief must be carefully weighed against the probability that numerous problems would arise, both in setting up the private financing system and in repurchasing the certificates of oil sold out of the reserve.

Renewable Energy Sources

In mid-1979 President Carter announced a goal of deriving 20 percent of the nation's energy from solar sources by the year 2000—broadly defined—which was to be met through a variety of solar energy programs and solar energy tax credits. The Reagan administration proposes to cut back outlays for stimulating market demand for solar products, including passive solar facilities. The only major long-term solar research and development effort that is currently under way is a program to convert sunlight directly into electricity using photovoltaic devices, for which $1.5 billion was authorized in fiscal 1978 for a ten-year period.

In 1980 Congress created the Solar Energy and Energy Conservation Bank, with expected annual outlays ranging from $130 million to $140 million over the next six years, to promote residential energy conservation and solar technology investments. The Reagan budget does not propose implementation of this subsidy program.

Legislation enacted in 1980 established a goal of 60,000 barrels a day of alcohol fuels production by the end of 1982 and an overall 1990 production goal of at least 10 percent of estimated gasoline consumption. The feasibility of this program has been questioned because it would call for production of between 500,000 and 750,000 barrels a day of alcohol fuels at the end of the 1980s—an objective which, with current technology, would absorb half of the U.S. corn crop. Citing market principles, the Reagan administration has proposed the termination of all federal feasibility studies, co-operative agreements, and loan guarantees for alcohol fuels and biomass energy development.

The fiscal 1982 budget proposed by President Reagan includes outlays of about $210 million for solar energy, which is $380 million less than the amount in the Carter proposal, and more than $200 million of tax expenditures. Both proposals include $200 million for the exemption of gasohol from the 4-cent a gallon federal excise tax, which is worth 40 cents a gallon of ethanol.[22]

Conservation

Before 1975 very little attention was given to energy conservation at the federal level. Government energy policies concentrated on supply rather than on demand. Since then, however, a comprehensive series of measures has been introduced to deal with fuel pricing, tax incentives, information and grant programs, regulatory measures, and research and development to increase efficiency in the use

22. This excise tax exemption is by far the most important subsidy for gasohol. Assuming the targets set in the legislation are achieved, the cost of the exemption will rise to $1.0 billion in fiscal 1986 and $4.0 billion in fiscal 1990.

of energy. The program is a complex set of instruments whose impact on increased efficiency of energy use is difficult to evaluate.

In the belief that existing tax credits and rising energy costs are sufficient incentives to conserve, the Reagan administration proposes to reduce or eliminate a number of federal energy conservation programs. The demise of the Solar Energy and Energy Conservation Bank has already been noted. Other programs whose funding would be terminated include work on energy from urban waste, consumer product design, electric and hybrid vehicles, advanced automotive engine design, and industrial processes. Regulatory programs mandating standards for building and appliance efficiency, which were already under fire within the Carter administration, would also be terminated. In addition, the weatherization assistance program of the Department of Energy would become part of the Department of Housing and Urban Development's community block grant program, but at a reduced level of funding. These actions would reduce conservation outlays by $0.4 billion in fiscal 1982 and by larger amounts in the future.

The major "conservation" program is rising prices, which cause consumers to use energy more efficiently. Regulated energy prices act to insulate energy users from the full effects of rising energy costs which, in turn, affect their energy consumption decisions. Although phased decontrol of domestically produced oil was to have been complete by October 1981, President Reagan ordered immediate decontrol soon after taking office. No changes were made in the schedule established by the 1978 Natural Gas Policy Act, which provides for the gradual decontrol of natural gas over the 1979–87 period, although the Reagan administration intends to propose an accelerated deregulation timetable later in 1981.[23]

The basic issue that has to be decided is the appropriate role of

23. Associated with oil decontrol is the 1980 Crude Oil Windfall Profit Tax Act —actually an excise tax, not a tax on windfall profits—which was imposed to limit the amount of revenues flowing to domestic oil producers from decontrolled oil. During the next decade this tax is expected to raise about $227 billion, the limit on its revenues under the statute. Fifteen percent of the tax proceeds is allocated for energy conservation and transportation programs; 25 percent for helping low-income families pay higher fuel bills; and 60 percent for reducing individual and corporate income taxes. Although the act specifies that tax revenues should be applied toward these three purposes, the allocation is an expression of congressional intent, rather than a budget authorization. Specific programs must first be proposed by the president and approved by Congress.

government in encouraging conservation. On the one hand, past federal regulatory and conservation programs may have been ineffective or even counterproductive, and rising energy costs should by themselves spur future conservation efforts. On the other hand, some argue that there is a role for government to counter factors that inhibit market-based conservation behavior including, but not limited to, imperfect information, institutional barriers, past and present regulations that price some forms of energy below replacement costs, and the need to finance long-run energy conservation research.

Nuclear Energy

Despite the dampening of enthusiasm for nuclear energy following the accident at Three Mile Island in 1979, funding of nuclear energy programs by the federal government continues to be substantial. President Carter placed less emphasis on the development of future fission technologies and reprocessing, and concentrated on such current problems as waste management, fuel storage, and improved fuel-enrichment technologies. On the premise that breeder technology will not be economic until at least the year 2020, funding for breeders was also cut back. In contrast, the nuclear industry and its supporters contend that breeders are a viable option, or even a necessity, for the future and that a major export market will be lost without demonstration of the technology. President Reagan proposes a $0.6 billion reduction in the uranium enrichment and away-from-reactor spent nuclear fuel storage programs, but a $0.2 billion increase for waste management, funding for the Clinch River breeder reactor, and a start on design studies for a large, commercial-size breeder reactor.

Although fusion outlays in fiscal 1980 were only one-third of those for nuclear fission, Congress approved legislation in September 1980 that calls for an operating demonstration fusion-power plant within twenty years and a test facility tackling the most severe engineering problems within a decade. This action was not coupled with any authorization for funding. These congressional deadlines cut in half the number of years the Carter administration recommended for fusion development. The budget proposed by the Carter administration for fiscal 1982 contains outlays of $563 million for the fusion programs, an increase of $120 million over fiscal 1981. The Reagan budget proposes minor changes.

Agriculture
Prepared by Fred H. Sanderson

There are growing indications that the United States may be in the midst of a major readjustment of its agricultural policy. Several factors suggest the need for such a readjustment. The demand for American grains, soybeans, and cotton has exceeded the most optimistic expectations. Instability in world markets has increased, with the burden of adjustment falling almost entirely on the United States because other countries try to insulate themselves from these fluctuations. U.S. agriculture has been transformed into a specialized, heavily capitalized, high-technology industry that no longer needs to be subsidized but continues to be vulnerable to year-to-year fluctuations. Finally, the wage and price structure has become more rigid, and this has made the economy more vulnerable to inflationary shocks emanating from both the food and energy sectors.

Grain Reserves

The need for greater price stability was recognized in 1977 when the Carter administration proposed, and Congress approved, the farmer-owned grain reserve. The reserve could be an effective instrument for bringing greater stability to the grain markets if some of its present defects are corrected. Its principal defect is its inadequate size: a considerably larger reserve is needed to cope with major crop shortfalls in the United States and abroad, such as those that occurred in 1972–75 and again in 1979 and 1980.

A common objection to raising the reserve targets is the budget cost. There are several ways, however, to make the reserve more cost-effective. First, it is not necessary to relieve farmers of all carrying charges while providing them with an excellent chance for a sizable price gain and a guarantee against any loss. One possibility would be to limit the subsidy to storage costs and to charge interest on the loans at a rate reflecting the cost of borrowing by the U.S. Treasury. Another possibility would be to let the market determine what incentive is needed to induce farmers to place grain in the reserve, that is, by requiring them to bid for the storage contracts. Contracts would be awarded to those farmers offering to store grain for three years or until the market price reaches the release level in return for the lowest premiums. Yet another option would be to reintroduce a government-owned reserve, supplementing the farmer-owned reserve and managed according to similar criteria for acquisition and release. A government-owned reserve would cost less than the farmer-owned reserve as it is currently operated because the carrying costs would be largely offset by the gains from price appreciation, which would go to the Treasury rather than to the farmer.

Second, there is no reason why the United States should bear the entire burden of carrying buffer stocks: other countries, both grain exporters and importers, should share this responsibility. A half-hearted attempt was made by the Ford and Carter administrations to negotiate an international system of national wheat reserves. Agreement was within reach among the countries of the Organisation for Economic Co-operation and Development; the negotiations failed in 1979, ostensibly because of differences with the developing countries, but fundamentally because of U.S. ambivalence. The negotiations should be resumed and extended to feed grains.

Third, grain reserves should be managed to serve only one purpose: to keep real grain prices within a predetermined, fairly wide range centered around a price that can be expected to clear the market over a period of years. The objective is to prevent extreme shortages or gluts. A good case can be made for raising the release and call prices for feed grains to the same percentages of the loan rates as already are used for wheat, thus widening the price band. The reserve should not be used for short-term market management. Adhering to stable and rational criteria in managing the reserve will increase its effectiveness and reduce its budget cost. It will also encourage increased stockholding by traders and processors.

Fourth, reserve accumulation would be facilitated, and budget savings could be made at the same time, by scrapping two interrelated policy tools that are no longer necessary or appropriate. Experience in fiscal years 1978 and 1979 has shown how acreage restrictions and deficiency payments can undercut the government's reserve policy. Nine hundred million dollars was spent in these two years to induce corn growers to divert acreage. Target prices for wheat were raised, and $1.6 billion was spent in deficiency payments to persuade wheat growers to cooperate with acreage set-asides. These funds would have been better employed by allowing the extra grain to be produced and placed in the reserve; in this way, the shortage and high grain prices following the 1980 drought could have been avoided.

The Reagan administration has emphasized stabilization, productivity growth, and a reduced government role as its principal agricultural policy objectives. Its proposals to eliminate target prices, deficiency payments, acreage set-asides, national program acreages, and various other techniques of production control and subsidization are consistent with these objectives and with the general trend of farm policy in recent years. The administration can be faulted, however, for not going far enough in correcting past mistakes. Its grain reserve targets are no more adequate than those of the Carter administration. At the same time, it proposes to delete the explicit authority provided in the existing legislation to negotiate an international system of grain reserves that could supplement the U.S. reserve. The administration also wants to retain the option of offering acreage diversion payments for specific crops—a type of program that is no longer appropriate and that has proven to be particularly costly and ineffective. Moreover, it proposes to retain wide discretion to manipulate the terms of the farmer-owned grain reserve, a practice for which the Carter administration had been roundly criticized by grain traders and processors as well as political opponents.

Commodity Programs

Grains have been discussed at length because of their economic importance. In terms of budget costs, however, the dairy program has become more burdensome than all other commodity programs taken together. Now at $1.5 billion, net outlays on this program are projected to rise to $3.2 billion by fiscal 1986 if the minimum support level remains at 80 percent of parity, with semiannual adjustments. The proposal of the Reagan administration to reduce the support level to 70 percent of parity, with annual adjustments, would stabilize program costs at less than $500 million. Further savings could probably be realized by shifting to a more appropriate index for determining milk price supports. The index of prices paid by all agricultural producers that is now used for this purpose does not accurately reflect the specific costs incurred in dairying and also does not take account of productivity growth, which has been exceptionally rapid in the dairy industry. Shifting to a more appropriate index would probably slow the escalation of support prices and federal outlays.

In addition, steps could be taken to increase competition in the dairy industry. One step would be to increase import quotas for cheese and other processed products, which now limit imports to less than 2 percent of domestic consumption, in terms of milk equivalent. Another is to extend the drive for deregulation to the fluid-milk markets that continue to be protected by federal marketing orders. Still another is to open the door to the sale of reconstituted milk as an alternative to fresh milk. More serious efforts also could be made to remove restraints to competition in the bargaining process between producers and processors.

Other commodity programs are less critical because of their limited budget and economic costs. Soybeans and cotton are buoyed by strong and steady foreign demand, making supports largely redundant. Beef import quotas are unnecessary and undesirable. Some programs are not only obsolete but counterproductive. The growing pressure on the cropland base argues for the removal of rigidities such as acreage allotments for tobacco, peanuts, and rice. Scrapping these programs could increase exports.

Sugar policies have saddled U.S. consumers with relatively high domestic prices when world market prices are low, without protecting the consumers from very high prices in periods of worldwide shortage. The exporters' buffer stocks established under the International Sugar Agreement predictably proved to be inadequate. In the long run, the increased competition by corn sweeteners—a product that has already taken one-third of the U.S. sugar and sweetener market—may provide the answer.

Other agricultural programs, such as the new crop insurance program, cost sharing for soil conservation and land development, and lending by the Farmers Home Administration, are subsidized in some degree. A modest level of subsidization can be justified for these purposes. The tax system has also operated to subsidize agriculture. But the present size and distribution of farm subsidies may be questioned for several reasons. They generally go to large farmers who need them least. To the extent that they are retained in the agriculture sector, they tend to be locked into increased land values. This has favored the concentration of land ownership and impeded the acquisition of land by new entrants. To the extent that competition causes the subsidies to be passed on to consumers in the form of lower prices, an increasing share of the benefits goes to importing countries, which often skim them off in the form of import levies.

Total net outlays for the agricultural functions discussed above (plus research and services but excluding international and domestic food assistance) have been about $5 billion. They were expected to be stabilized at slightly above that level by the Carter administration. The Reagan budget proposes savings rising from about $400 million in fiscal 1982 to $1.1 billion in fiscal 1986. These savings would be accomplished by reduced price-support expenditures, especially for dairy products, the elimination of interest rate subsidies, and reduced lending activities.

Gasohol

Even a brief review of U.S. agricultural policies would be incomplete without mentioning the agricultural consequences of the gasohol legislation enacted in 1980. Although billed as an energy measure, this heavily subsidized program owes its existence to farm groups interested in raising grain prices. A previously hesitant Carter administration came out in support of it when it seemed necessary to compensate grain growers for any long-term adverse effects of the Soviet grain embargo.

The program aims at the production of 10 billion gallons of ethanol from biomass by 1990. The principal subsidy is the exemption of gasohol, through 1992, from the federal gasoline tax. This tax exemption alone will have cost the U.S. Treasury $27 billion by the time it expires. The Reagan administration has left this subsidy in place, as well as the special 10 percent investment tax credit, but has terminated the loan and loan guarantee program.

If the gasohol program develops according to schedule, it will raise the real prices of feed grains to twice their 1979–80 levels by the time ethanol production reaches 7 to 8 billion gallons, when it will absorb 70 to 80 million tons of grain. Unless the subsidy is limited or repealed, this is likely to happen sometime during the second half of the 1980s.

The consequences will be far-reaching. A doubling of feed grain prices—and related increases in the prices of other crops competing for the same resources—will increase the consumer's food bill by $30 billion. The total inflationary impact (including multiplier effects) may be estimated at 25 percent on retail food prices and 5 percent on the consumer price index. This would make the gasohol program the most costly price-raising device in the history of U.S. agricultural support programs.

Transportation
Prepared by Theodore E. Keeler

Although the transportation budget is not a large part of total federal outlays ($22.7 billion in fiscal 1980, or 3.4 percent of the total),[24] many who have studied the subject nevertheless believe that it offers significant opportunities for savings. Consistent with this, the Reagan budget proposes cuts (and user-charge increases) of $4.1 billion in transportation in fiscal 1982, and total cuts of $43.2 billion in fiscal years 1982–86, relative to outlays proposed in the Carter budget.

The rationale behind reductions in transportation outlays is straightforward: the transportation budget contains expenditures on projects and facilities that could not pass a benefit-cost test, and are not justifiable either on the basis of providing income to the needy or for enhancement of economic efficiency. Many facilities and services that could pass a benefit-cost test are heavily subsidized, when they could be more efficiently financed through charges on users. These subsidies are spread, albeit unevenly, among all transportation modes.

Air Transportation

The majority of federal air transportation outlays ($3.1 billion out of $3.8 billion in fiscal 1980) is for airports and airways, provided through the Federal Aviation Administration either directly or by grants to local airport authorities. User charges are collected mainly by means of a ticket tax on air passengers, but also by fuel and excise taxes on operators of aircraft. Studies of these charges have indicated that overall commercial airline transportation pays its full share of the costs of this system through user charges, but private and corporate (general aviation) aircraft do not. The Congressional Budget Office estimates, for example, that without addi-

---

24. This includes waterway costs allocable to barge transportation, which are normally in the natural resources component of the budget.

tional user charges, general aviation will fall $800 million short of meeting its costs in fiscal 1982 and $5 billion short in fiscal years 1982–86.

Although the Reagan budget claims to eliminate subsidies for airport and airway users, it does not eliminate the subsidy to general aviation. User charges to general aviation would be raised slightly, but most of the "reduction in subsidy" would in fact come from an increase in the ticket tax for commercial air travel, despite the fact that air travelers already pay their share of the Federal Aviation Administration's costs. Thus general aviation will continue to be subsidized by commercial aviation, which will pay more than 100 percent of the air transportation costs. It is difficult to see what purpose is served, other than a cosmetic one, by replacing a direct subsidy from general revenues with an indirect one from a tax levied on air travelers. Many would argue that making general aviation pay a larger part of the costs it incurs than it currently does would be a step in the right direction.

In addition to proposing more user charges for air transportation, the Reagan administration also proposes cuts in spending. Most of these are accounted for by a $1.5 billion reduction in aid to larger airports for federal airport construction during fiscal years 1982–86, on the ground that airports can finance their own construction. Effectively, however, this would further increase the subsidy from high- to low-density routes; with this change, large airports will increase their passenger user fees, and high-density passengers will continue to pay the increased Reagan ticket tax. The other proposed cut is a $200 million reduction of subsidies for air service to small communities, a cut that would be justifiable on efficiency grounds, but hard to sell politically.

Highway Transportation

Federal highway transportation outlays ($9.5 billion in fiscal 1980) are largely covered by charges on highway users through the highway trust fund. However, present taxes have been forecast to be inadequate to maintain and rebuild the existing system. For this reason, the Carter budget proposed an additional tax on gasoline of 2 cents a gallon, which would be allocated to the highway trust fund. The Reagan administration does not recommend such a tax increase, but instead proposes a reduction in federal highway outlays of $421 million in fiscal 1982 and $7.5 billion in fiscal years 1982–86. However, consideration is being given to an increase in gasoline taxes that would be earmarked for the states for road maintenance. Given the high maintenance needs of the nation's road system and the difficulty that state governments will have raising additional funds, this approach seems to make sense.

Intercity Rail Transportation

As of 1981, Amtrak—which operates the nation's intercity passenger trains—is losing money at a rate of roughly $1 billion a year (including capital outlays), and it is projected to lose over $1.6 billion a year by 1986. A strong economic argument can be made for eliminating Amtrak entirely: many believe (and Amtrak's high deficits support this view) that rail passenger service is neither cost- nor service-competitive with other modes, namely air and automobile. Furthermore, it has been shown that outside the Washington-Boston (northeast) corridor, Amtrak wastes energy, rather than conserves it (and the savings in the northeast corridor are small). Most of Amtrak's deficit could be saved quite quickly if service were terminated. There are some legal and labor-protection costs, but these could be more than paid for by disposing of Amtrak's assets (passenger cars, locomotives, and real estate). Thus the amount of Amtrak's deficit is a conservative estimate of what could be saved by eliminating it.

A less drastic action with regard to Amtrak (but still one affording some savings) would be to limit service to the northeast corridor. Given that short-haul, high-density service of this type is closest to being justifiable on an economic basis, that it does save some energy, and that a significant part of the travel in the corridor is handled by rail, one could justify retaining this service. Such a policy would produce savings of roughly $500 million in fiscal 1982 and $3 billion for fiscal years 1982–86.

One tempting path for extracting savings from Amtrak (proposed by the Reagan administration) is to increase fares, so that more of the costs of the service can be met from fare revenues. This is not a promising solution, because competition from air, automobile, and bus transportation puts tight constraints on what Amtrak can charge without diverting practically all its traffic. In this situation, the Reagan proposal of February 18, 1981, to eliminate services that fail to meet 80 percent of their costs from fares by 1986 is very nearly equivalent to a proposal to eliminate Amtrak by 1986, and should be recognized as such. The Reagan budget of March 9, 1981, seems to recognize this; it states that legislation will be introduced later to cut unspecified Amtrak services and outlays for improvements in its roadbed, with savings of more than $300 million in fiscal 1982. But if Amtrak service is kept in the northeast corridor it should be made more speed-competitive with other modes. Thus the intended cut in the corridor improvement project may be a false economy.

Large savings could be achieved by requiring self-supporting operations by Conrail, which provides freight and commuter service for much of the northeast. The Reagan administration proposes to reduce Conrail's subsidies gradually, making it self-sufficient by 1984, with savings of $1.4 billion relative to current services levels for fiscal years 1982–86. Reductions of almost $400 million are also proposed in rail branch-line subsidies. These cutbacks could be justified on the basis of economic efficiency, but would result in substantial reductions in the number of routes that would be opposed by business and local government groups.

Urban Transportation

Recent research supports the view that, like its intercity counterpart, new urban rail transportation is neither as cost-efficient nor as energy-efficient as competing modes (including, in many cases, the private automobile). To the extent that this is true, a significant savings can be achieved at no cost in economic efficiency to the country by stopping construction of new fixed rail transit. The Reagan budget proposes cutbacks even in funds already committed by the federal government to local governments for rail transit construction, allowing only funding for routes currently under construction and, of those, only to expand routes to "operable transit segments." Funding routes in this way would save $5.6 billion over the fiscal 1982–86 period. This proposal would force local transit authorities to raise fares or subsidies, or reduce service. Such a change would be a move toward economic efficiency, but the affected local governments will doubtless claim that this measure will cause them considerable financial hardship.

In addition to eliminating federal rail transit construction grants, the Reagan budget proposes to phase out federal transit operating subsidies by fiscal 1985, for a total savings of $2.7 billion. The arguments against these subsidies are, first, that some public transit is probably subsidized beyond an efficient level and, second, that to the extent that they are justified, the most efficient decisions on optimal levels of subsidies can be made by state and local governments. There are also arguments in favor of keeping them: first, there is persuasive economic research suggesting the existence of scale economies in bus transit as well as rail, which justify transit subsidies on the basis of economic efficiencies;[25] second, especially in the northeast, where most urban transit service is provided, most state and local governments are not in a good financial position to provide subsidies of this magnitude.

Water Transportation

The U.S. government subsidizes water transportation, both inland and marine, more heavily than any other mode. According to the Congressional Budget Office, without further charges on users, marine transportation will be subsidized in fiscal 1982 by $1.3 billion in outlays for use of harbors and channels, as well as safety services, and inland waterway users will receive subsidies of $1.2 billion. For fiscal 1982–86, the figures are $7.8 billion for marine and $7.7 billion for inland transportation—a total of $15.5 billion for all water transportation. Despite its stated objective of making water transportation self-supporting, the Reagan budget makes relatively modest efforts to eliminate these large subsidies. For inland waterways, great lakes, and ocean transportation, it proposes increases in user charges, with projected additional revenues for user charges for fiscal years 1982–86 of only $3.8 billion, leaving a subsidy of $11.7 billion for 1982–86.

Although there may be some room for disagreement about what part of the ports and waterways system is allocable to commercial traffic, the proposed user charges would not come close to covering the benefits received by commercial users. This relatively favored treatment accorded water transportation by the Reagan administration presumably reflects the political influence of water shipping interests and the persuasiveness of the Corps of Engineers.

25. Herbert Mohring, "Optimization in Urban Bus Transportation," *American Economic Review*, vol. 62 (September 1972), pp. 591–604.

Achieving Economic Efficiency

A strong economic argument can be made for reducing federal expenditures on transportation and for requiring users to pay the costs of the facilities and services they use. The Reagan budget proposals achieve these objectives albeit unevenly among the modes. Thus, it proposes cutting back sharply on urban transit funds and taxing air travelers well beyond the costs they add, while continuing to favor private aviation and shipping by water. Nevertheless, because it brings costs and revenues closer together, the Reagan proposal represents a positive step toward more efficient resource allocation in transportation. As table 3-2 shows, alternative savings of up to $3.5 billion in fiscal 1982 and $22.8 billion in fiscal years 1982–86 could be realized by stricter application of the test of economic efficiency.

In addition to taxation and spending, an important component of the federal government's transportation program is its regulatory policy. The Ford and Carter administrations pressed hard in this area for a reduction of government involvement and further reliance on the free market. In fact, before the Carter administration ended, bills had been passed and signed that considerably loosened federal controls over airlines, railroads, and trucking. The Reagan administration's policies in these areas would appear to reflect a combination

Table 3-2. Some Potential Savings in the Federal Transportation Budget, Fiscal Years 1982–86

Millions of dollars

Category	1982	1982–86
Cutback in Amtrak services, excluding northeast corridor	500	3,000
Elimination of new commitments to fixed rail transit construction	20	1,950
Cost recovery from user charges	3,020	22,840
Inland waterways	1,210	7,720
General aviation	510	2,400
Coast Guard	710	3,970
Deep-draft navigation	590	3,800
Total savings	3,540	22,840

Sources: U.S. Congressional Budget Office, *Reducing the Federal Budget: Strategies and Examples, Fiscal Years 1982–1986* (GPO, 1981), pp. 53–54, 79–97; estimates for Amtrak savings are the author's.

of free-market principles and political expediency. More specifically, given that airlines have shown no opposition to deregulation, the Reagan administration may accelerate the process of dismantling the Civil Aeronautics Board. In the area of freight transportation, while the Reagan administration has given no indications of its intentions for railroads, its policies on trucking are clear. During the 1980 election Reagan stated that he felt that the previous administration had gone too far too fast on truck deregulation and, with the support of the Teamster's Union and the American Trucking Association in mind, promised to appoint commissioners to the Interstate Commerce Commission who are more sympathetic to the needs of the industry. If Reagan delivers on his promises, the commission will continue efforts to restrict entry and keep truck rates above market levels.

Natural Resources and the Environment
Prepared by Paul R. Portney of Resources for the Future

Spending for natural resources and the environment increased significantly during the Carter administration—from $10.9 billion in fiscal 1978 to a proposed level of $14.0 billion in fiscal 1982.[26] The Reagan administration proposes a series of program cuts that would reduce fiscal outlays for natural resources and the environment by $2.0 billion in 1982, $4.0 billion in 1983, $5.7 billion in 1984, and $6.2 billion in 1985. In addition, it proposes increases of $250 to $300 million a year in charges for the use of inland waterways developed and maintained by the U.S. Army Corps of Engineers. Natural resources and the environment, then, is the one area in which the views of the incoming and the outgoing administrations are very different.

The direct federal outlays for environmental protection give a misleading picture of its overall economic significance. Environmental regulation often requires individuals, private firms, and local gov-

---

26. A wide variety of programs makes up the natural resources and environment function of the budget. They include the regulatory activities and sewage treatment grants of the Environmental Protection Agency; the construction, operation, and maintenance of dams, canals, and other inland waterways by the Corps of Engineers; the management of national forests, other public lands, and mineral rights; the conservation of agricultural lands; and the acquisition and operation of national parks and recreation areas, historic sites, wildlife refuges, and wild and scenic rivers.

ernments to purchase and operate pollution control equipment or make other, sometimes expensive, changes in operating practices. It is difficult to estimate the size of these "compliance costs"; they may be twenty or thirty times larger on an annual basis than the $1.2 billion budgeted for the operation of the Environmental Protection Agency in fiscal 1982. These costs must be taken into account along with direct federal expenditures in assessing environmental or other regulatory programs.

Spending for natural resources and environmental protection appears to enjoy continuing popular support. Nonetheless, these programs can hardly be considered untouchable at a time when basic support programs providing shelter, food, and other assistance are being carefully scrutinized. Two principles should motivate any review of the natural resources and environment (or other) programs in the federal budget. First, certain programs have been ineffective or needlessly expensive and should be reviewed with the objective of increasing their efficiency. Second, several spending programs provide benefits to small and easily identifiable groups. In such cases, it seems reasonable to ask the beneficiaries to bear a larger share of the cost of providing these services. In fact, these two principles lay behind several of the proposals made by the Reagan administration.

Water Resource Development

Outlays for water resource development in fiscal 1982 were projected to be $4.6 billion in the Carter budget, or about one-third of total outlays devoted to natural resources and the environment. President Reagan recommends a reduction of $200 million in these outlays that year, to be accomplished by eliminating some projects and delaying the start of several others. In fiscal years 1984 and 1985, outlays for water projects would be reduced by more than $0.5 billion from those proposed in the Carter budget.

Although the new administration has not indicated what projects are to be eliminated or delayed, most observers feel that the water resource projects are a good place to look for reductions in spending. Many of the projects slated for construction or continuation cannot pass a rigorous cost-benefit test. In fact, President Carter tried—with little success—to terminate a number of such projects when he took office. The Reagan administration proposes to eliminate or delay some economically unsound water projects, but resource allocation would be greatly improved if many more were terminated.

In addition, the benefits that do arise from the construction, operation, and maintenance of locks and dams, channels, and reservoirs accrue to relatively few users. For this reason, the Reagan administration proposes a fivefold increase in the fee for the users of inland waterways. Although it will increase the price of goods shipped on those waterways, the increase in user fees is a commendable step that will confront consumers and producers with a greater share of the full social costs of their actions. Congress should look into other ways to offset project costs through fees for users where beneficiaries can be identified.

Construction Grants

The Reagan administration proposes sizable reductions in grants to states and municipalities for construction of sewage treatment plants—by fiscal 1984, outlays are projected to be $2.3 billion below those projected by the Carter administration, a cut of more than 50 percent. Cutbacks in these grants reflect more than partisan differences. For many years the construction grants program has drawn fire from a wide spectrum of critics. It has been alleged by some that improvements in water quality following completion of waste treatment plants have been minor or even nonexistent. This is partly the result of poor operation and maintenance of many plants. In fact, at any given time, one-half to three-fourths of all existing plants are apparently in violation of the terms of their discharge permits; in a recent survey, the General Accounting Office found 87 percent of plants in violation and 31 percent in "serious" violation.[27]

Another criticism of the construction grants program is that the subsidy for municipal waste treatment blunts the incentive that households and businesses would have to eliminate or reduce waste generation if they had to pay the full cost of waste treatment. In addition, the subsidy creates a disparity in the budgetary treatment between municipal polluters (who are heavily subsidized) and in-

---

27. U.S. General Accounting Office, *Costly Wastewater Treatment Plants Fail to Perform as Expected*, Report to the Congress by the Comptroller General of the United States (GAO, 1980), p. 8.

dustrial polluters who receive little or no federal support for compliance with the Clean Water Act. Finally, some evidence suggests that the grants have had little effect on the total number of sewage treatment plants constructed. Rather, municipalities may have deferred projects they might have undertaken on their own in the hope of attracting federal funds.

In proposing to scale back the construction grants program, the Reagan administration cited the small impact some of the projects had on water quality and gave as an example the construction of new interceptor sewers. Although some of these interceptor sewers may be of marginal value, they can play an important role in protecting water quality. This is especially true in areas in which storm water runoff often forces raw sewage to be discharged directly into lakes or rivers. A case-by-case review of interceptor sewers is needed to determine the ones that should be eliminated.

There is another way in which the construction grants could be improved that neither the Carter nor the Reagan administration has addressed. The program currently provides for a subsidy of up to 75 percent of the cost of constructing a new plant, but the funds cannot be used to subsidize the costs of operating and maintaining plants. This led to poor operating performance in many of the plants in the past, as mentioned above, because some communities cannot afford to run the plants properly after they are built. Serious thought should be given to allowing the sewage treatment money to be used for operation and maintenance in places where performance of existing plants could be improved.

Park Acquisition

The Reagan administration proposes eliminating both the land and water conservation fund, which provides federal money for direct park acquisition as well as grants to states to purchase and develop parks, and the urban park grants program, which helps cities rehabilitate park areas. In addition, the administration proposes a reduction of 84 percent in the funds provided for historic preservation. After an allowance is made for additional funds for the improved operation of existing national parks, the reductions amount to about $200 to $500 million a year beginning in fiscal 1982.

Because the benefits generated by state and municipal parks are enjoyed primarily by local residents, one can question the rationale for federal assistance. This is especially true at a time when a number of state governments have budgetary surpluses—it would seem they could afford to purchase park land without federal support. On the other hand, federal assistance may be essential to park development in areas with hard-pressed city governments, where they would benefit large numbers of citizens.

Other Programs

Several other existing natural resource programs might be reviewed with the goal of reducing expenditures or increasing receipts to offset outlays. For example, considerable duplication occurs in the major federal programs directed at soil conservation (which will amount to $565 million in fiscal 1982). Although politically popular, some of these programs pay farmers to take soil conservation measures they would undertake anyway for reasons of private profitability. If farmers took these measures on their own, federal expenditure reductions would satisfy both macroeconomic and microeconomic goals.

Another possible way to help the federal budget would be to increase admission and recreational fees at national parks to cover more or even all of the cost of operation. At certain parks, admission fees of, say, $5 to $10 would provide sufficient revenue to cover costs. This would support the principle that those who benefit from particular programs or facilities should, where feasible, contribute to their support.

Finally, fees charged for irrigation water provided by the government and for grazing rights on public land should be raised to reflect their fair market value. This is especially true of fees for irrigation water. A recent study of federal irrigation projects by the General Accounting Office found that water will be sold for $3 per acre-foot even though it will cost the government more than $130 an acre-foot to provide.[28] At a time when water shortages may limit metropolitan and agricultural growth and new energy development in the western United States, such subsidization of water use is a poor environmental and economic policy.

---

28. Government Accounting Office, *Federal Charges for Irrigation Projects Reviewed Do Not Cover Costs,* Report to the Congress by the Comptroller General of the United States (GAO, 1981), p. 26.

Grants to State and Local Governments
Prepared by Paul R. Dommel

If President Reagan obtains all the cuts he requested, federal grants-in-aid to state and local governments will be about $86.4 billion in fiscal 1982. This is nearly eight times as much as in 1965 when federal aid began to increase rapidly, but it is 13 percent below the amount proposed by President Carter in his final budget and represents a sharp reversal of the steady growth in aid that has occurred since World War II. Moreover, President Reagan's estimates of future spending hold federal aid outlays nearly constant in dollar amounts through fiscal 1984.

Between 1965 and 1970, as the Great Society programs of Lyndon B. Johnson were put into operation, federal aid increased by $13.1 billion, largely in the form of categorical grants with an urban emphasis. Between 1970 and 1976, during the Nixon and Ford administrations, total grants increased by $35.1 billion to finance a new general revenue-sharing program, greatly expanded environmental protection aid, some antirecession programs, and rapidly expanding medicaid. From 1976 to 1979, aid increased another $23.8 billion; during this period, the antirecession programs were significantly expanded by President Carter, with the important effect of raising the amount of direct federal aid to local governments, particularly distressed cities. During 1979–81, few new aid programs were established, and outlays increased at a much slower rate—an average of 7 percent a year in a period when inflation was running at double-digit rates. In real terms, the purchasing power of federal aid declined 2.7 percent in fiscal 1979, 2.9 percent in fiscal 1980, and 8.3 percent in fiscal 1981. If the Reagan budget is enacted, the real decline would be about 20 percent in fiscal 1982.

In recent trends of federal assistance to states and localities there has been a significant difference between payments to individuals and the grants given to carry out the functions of state and local governments. The principal federal grant programs for assistance to individuals that are administered by state and local governments are medicaid, welfare, housing assistance, and nutrition for the elderly and children. In recent years, the growth in outlays for these programs has been significantly greater than the growth in aid to state and local governments for their own use. Overall, payments to individuals increased from 36 percent of total outlays in 1976 to an estimated 43 percent in the Carter budget for fiscal 1982 and 45 percent in the Reagan budget for the same year. Under President Reagan's future spending plans, assistance for individuals would account for 48 percent of federal aid in fiscal 1984; thus these outlays would slowly increase while aid to state and local governments would continue to decline.

The basic factors that account for the slower growth in recent years and now the downward trend in federal aid are the following: (1) the search for items to cut in the federal budget inevitably focuses on grants-in-aid because they multiplied so rapidly in the 1970s; (2) the countercyclical spending that sharply increased federal aid in the latter part of the 1970s is scheduled to end and, given the expected long-term fiscal pressures, a new or revised program of the same proportions is unlikely to be adopted; and (3) the federal government may be better off fiscally than some hard-pressed cities and states, but within the federal system as a whole, it is no longer the strongest.

The federal aid budgets for fiscal 1982 proposed by Presidents Carter and Reagan show sharp contrasts. President Carter's final budget for that year took a "hold the line" approach for federal aid programs. Very few of these programs were significantly cut; most were given small increments; and at least two notable increases were proposed (youth education and employment and expanded medicaid coverage to include about 2 million additional people under age eighteen). President Carter's aid budget of $99.8 billion called for an increase of $5.4 billion over the revised budget for fiscal 1981, two-thirds of which was for programs to assist individuals. As already indicated, this 5.7 percent increase in nominal dollars would mean a sharp reduction in real terms.

By contrast, the Reagan administration has proposed deep cuts in the grant programs. In total, federal aid would be $13.4 billion less than the Carter proposal, $8 billion less than the revised outlays for fiscal 1981, and about $5 billion less than the fiscal 1980 level. Among the major proposed cuts are medicaid, public service employment programs (which would be terminated), health and social services (which would be merged into four block grants), child nutrition, and education. Two education block grants would be established through consolidation of various grants of the Elementary and Secondary Education Act with some other education programs.

The Reagan cuts in grants are the first step of a broader legislative strategy to reduce or eliminate federal government involvement in some policy areas and to obtain better control over the budgets of those programs that will continue to have a large federal commitment. Included in Reagan's fiscal plan is a proposal to consolidate individual grants into block grants in the areas of education, health, and social services, and to expand the existing manpower training block grant by merging the youth programs into it; other block grants are being considered for welfare and housing. The goal is to give states and local governments more discretion in the use of the funds at the same time that total federal grant funds are sharply reduced. Thus grant reform and decentralization are closely connected with the overall budget goals of the new administration.

The Reagan budget revisions also indicate how he will deal with general revenue sharing in the future. Enacted during the Nixon administration, by fiscal 1980 this program was providing states and localities with $6.8 billion a year in grants with virtually no federal restrictions on their use. Congress renewed the legislation in 1980, but provided funds for payments only to local governments in 1981. The legislation authorizes $2.3 billion for the states in 1982 and 1983 if funds are appropriated, but a state will be required to give up an equal amount of categorical grant funds if it wishes to receive general revenue-sharing payments.

The idea behind general revenue sharing was to reduce federal control over state and local grant spending and to provide a measure of fiscal redistribution from the richer to the poorer states. In general, state and local officials support the program, but there is considerable opposition from those who believe that the federal government should exercise control over its own funds to see that national objectives are achieved. The Carter administration agreed with the policy of providing unrestricted grants to local governments but opposed giving any additional grants to the states because they are in a better fiscal position; accordingly, it did not request the $2.3 billion for the state share in the budget. President Reagan is more sympathetic to the general objectives of the program, but his budget does not include the state share in 1982, presumably because of the tight fiscal situation his administration faces. Moreover, Reagan's spending projections for future years do not mention adding an amount equivalent to the state share. Congress could again appropriate money for the states or the local share could be reduced to provide funds for state governments. Such prospects for the states are not bright, however, because Congress also is apparently looking for ways to make major spending reductions.

Interestingly, the Advisory Commission on Intergovernmental Relations, which reflects the viewpoints of state and local officials, has urged not decentralization but federalization of certain functions, including welfare, housing, medical benefits, unemployment, and basic nutrition. Basic redistributive services, they argue, should be accomplished by the broadest based government, while more allocative functions such as law enforcement and highway construction should be accomplished at the state level with minimal locational consequences. The National Governors' Association supported the idea of greater state and local discretion over federal aid at its February 1981 meeting, but backed eventual federalization of welfare and medicaid.

Cutting the cost and decentralization of federal grant programs can be combined in a different way from that proposed by the Reagan administration. In the income security areas President Reagan said he was maintaining the social safety net for the most disadvantaged groups. A similar "fiscal safety net" could be positioned in the neediest places that are likely to suffer adverse consequences from cuts in federal aid. This is particularly true in many fiscally strained cities, where the public service employment program helps provide basic public services. Many of the programs proposed for termination or reduced funding are not ineffective but rather the money is spread too thinly to many locations that do not need it. Directing funds to the neediest places is good fiscal conservatism. It is less expensive than allocating money to places that are well-off and growing. For example, about one-third of the 669 entitlement entities under the community development block grant could meet their development responsibilities from their growing tax bases or by borrowing on their good credit ratings. With several new block grants under discussion, such targeting becomes even more important before the "something for everyone" principle is applied. Selection of fiscally needy communities is politically difficult to achieve, but because so many changes in the rules of the game for federal aid are being proposed, a fiscal safety net approach is worthy of consideration.

Pay and Benefits for Federal Workers
Prepared by Robert W. Hartman

In fiscal 1980 about $61.3 billion, or 10.6 percent, of federal outlays were expended for civilian employment. Three-fourths of the funds, or $46.6 billion, were spent for basic salaries, overtime pay, health and life insurance, and other fringe benefits for 2.2 million government employees. The remainder, about $14.7 billion, was paid in benefits to 1.8 million civilian retirees. (An additional $42.8 billion was spent for active military personnel and retirement pay for the military.) Employment levels are ordinarily determined by particular program decisions, but rules governing salaries, fringe benefits, and retirement benefits are established on a government-wide basis.

Salary Rates

Federal salaries for full-time white-collar jobs are expected to average about $22,000 in fiscal 1981. (Blue-collar jobs are predominantly in the Department of Defense, and issues relating to pay for these workers are beyond the scope of this chapter). The current law states that salary rates at all levels should be adjusted each year in October to correspond to pay rates for comparable jobs in the private sector as determined in a yearly survey taken each March. Pay for high-level executives (both in the career service and in politically appointed jobs) is also supposed to be raised annually by the average of these increases.

Three major problems have arisen with this pay system. First, since 1977 federal pay raises have not been based on the pay comparability standard. President Carter proposed, and the Congress did not change, pay levels each year that were less than those in the private sector. By 1980 the cumulative shortfall in average federal pay was about 4 percent. Second, high-level salaries have been allowed to increase only once since 1977 (by 5.5 percent in 1979). These salaries set a ceiling for all other government workers. As a result of the interaction between the annual raises for most workers and the barely changed ceiling, 33,000 federal employees are earning the same salary. Many of these employees at the top of the salary scale have suffered large losses of real income in the past three years. Third, the pay comparability law itself may be flawed. Differences in fringe benefits between the government and the private sector are ignored in setting pay rates. The government has a single pay scale for the entire country while pay rates vary considerably in different labor markets. The salary survey on which pay comparability is based does not cover state and local government employees, excludes very small enterprises, and samples a limited number of occupations and job levels. Critics contend that, on all or most of these counts, the present system creates an upward bias in the determination of federal pay rates.

Retirement Benefits

Under the civil service retirement system, employees may retire with full annuities at age fifty-five with thirty years service or age sixty with twenty years of service. The annuity is based on the number of years of service and on the highest average salary of three consecutive years. Employees contribute 7 percent of salary to the system. The benefits are fully indexed to the consumer price index and are adjusted twice each year.

The structure of the retirement system gives employees an incentive to retire as soon as they are eligible if pay is frozen or rising slowly. Retirement rates for employees who were eligible to retire and who were at a pay ceiling rose from 18 percent in 1978 to 57 percent in 1980. Retirement rates in early 1981 may have been even higher because a liberalizing provision of the law expired in January. These high retirement rates drive up outlays for the retirement system. In addition, when federal employees retire at an early age, many are employed in jobs in the private sector that are covered under social security. At age sixty-two or sixty-five, the federal retiree is eligible not only for civil service retirement benefits but also for social security benefits (double-dipping). The social security benefit may exceed the ordinary benefit (which is based on career average earnings) because of a special provision providing artificially high minimum benefits (currently $122 a month).

Various commissions have recommended that civil service retirement benefits be made less liberal. The most common proposal is to require new employees to participate in social security and to provide a supplementary retirement program that is more in line with private pension plans. Because the current retirement system is much more costly than such a program, the proposals for universal coverage under social security are the largest budget-saving possibility in the personnel area. But these savings could not be realized quickly, unless the government reneged on its retirement promises to current retirees or current workers.

To achieve more immediate budgetary savings, the Carter administration proposed that the actuarial cost of fringe benefits be combined with salaries in the annual survey to calculate total compensation. Annual salary changes were then to be based on "total compensation comparability." Thus, if government retirement benefits exceeded benefits in the private sector, current increases in federal salaries would be held down by the excess. In its fiscal 1982 budget the Carter administration estimated that pay comparability would require a 13.5 percent increase in salaries in October 1981, while total compensation comparability would reduce that increase to about 8.6 percent. The Carter administration went further and recommended a 5.5 percent pay increase, which would save a total of about $3.8 billion in fiscal year 1982.

President Reagan's Proposals

President Reagan's early proposals include measures that would affect civilian employment and pay as well as benefits. The employment and benefits proposals are minor, while the pay proposals are comprehensive and far-reaching.

EMPLOYMENT CHANGES. Reagan imposed a hiring freeze on all federal agencies upon taking office in January 1981. Because government job turnover is about 11 percent for all grades and is closer to 19 percent for the clerical positions in the lower grades, such a freeze on hiring cannot be maintained for very long before it interferes with productivity. Accordingly, in its March budget revisions, the Reagan administration dropped the hiring freeze and instead specified personnel ceilings for individual agencies. On a full-time equivalent basis, the personnel ceiling for the executive branch for fiscal 1982 would be 1.85 million work-years, which is a reduction of 34,500 jobs, or 1.8 percent, compared to President Carter's estimates for that year. Some agencies, however, would have employment cut much more sharply than the average.

RETIREMENT PROPOSALS. Two relatively minor changes in federal employees' retirement are proposed. The first is an endorsement of a Carter proposal that passed the Senate in 1980 to establish annual rather than biannual inflation adjustment for civil service retirees. This change would reduce outlays by about $0.5 billion permanently ($0.9 billion if military personnel are included). The second change would eliminate the minimum benefit for social security, for both current and future recipients. Social security benefits under this plan would depend solely on the wage history of the retiree. For federal retirees who already receive a full pension this reduction in double-dipped benefits should be significant. (Very low-income recipients of the minimum benefit, according to the administration, would not lose because they would be eligible for supplementary security income or other income-tested welfare programs.) However, because this minimum benefit is currently $1,464 a year, the savings from its elimination cannot compare with the long-run savings possible under more fundamental reforms in federal retirement.

PAY PROPOSALS. In December 1980 the quadrennial Commission on Executive, Legislative, and Judicial Salaries recommended that pay rates for top-level officials be increased by an average of about 40 percent. President Carter, after consultation with the new administration, recommended increases for these positions that averaged about 17 percent. The pay ceiling for the 7,000 top-level career employees in the Senior Executive Service would rise to $61,600 from its current level of $52,750. In addition, President Carter proposed a further increase of 5.5 percent in October 1981, when other employees were to receive a pay raise.

President Reagan's budget revisions withdraw the proposed pay increases for top-level employees "because current economic conditions require that substantial budget reductions be achieved." (The budgetary costs of these adjustments would have been about $180 million.) The new administration, however, has expressed concern about the federal government's ability "to attract and retain high caliber executives" and has promised to work with the Congress "in developing other ways to address this issue" before 1984.

The pay increases that the Reagan administration proposes for civilian white-collar workers continues this austerity theme. It endorses the Carter proposal to base salary changes on the broader total compensation comparability measure (including fringe benefits). However, reasoning that employment by the federal government has many "aspects . . . which make it more attractive" than comparable jobs in the private sector, the Reagan administration proposes that the federal compensation standard be 94 percent of average nonfederal compensation. Application of this standard to the total compensation level in October 1981 (1.086 of 1980 compensation) would have resulted in a 2.1 percent pay increase $(0.94 \times 1.086 = 1.021)$. The administration arbitrarily raised this to 4.8 percent for 1981, but reduced the prospective pay increases in 1982 from 8.9 percent to 7.0 percent and in 1983 from 7.9 percent to 7.0 percent. The end result of this pay curb is that, by 1984, the average federal salary (based on March projections) would be 19 percent below the pay of comparable jobs in the private sector.

In late March 1981, President Reagan submitted his proposal for the Federal Pay Comparability Reform Act. This legislation provides that federal pay plus fringe benefits be comparable to 94 percent of nonfederal pay plus fringe benefits (so adjustments could be made in federal fringe benefits as well as in pay); that the president be given authority to modify sick and annual leave benefits and health and life insurance benefits (subject to certain minimums); that the annual survey of pay and benefits include state and local government workers; and that pay for General Schedule workers be set by locality in keeping with the relation between nonfederal pay in each locality and the national average. In addition, the president's authority is greatly broadened to establish special (higher) rates of pay for occupations or areas in which the government is "experiencing significant difficulty in recruiting or retaining well-qualified individuals." Finally, because of the significance of these changes and the unknown effects of all the new data required under these provisions, the proposed bill specifies that pay rates will be increased 2 percent a year for the first five years, even if the application of the new standard would require a smaller raise than that.

Assuming that these proposals will continue to hold down federal pay, they would have a mixed impact on different groups of federal employees. At lower grades, where federal salaries are currently most comparable to or even above the private sector, and where labor is fairly unskilled, the government will probably suffer somewhat higher turnover rates than previously. In middle-level jobs that are the entry point for professionals, the relatively attractive retirement program is not likely to outweigh the unattractive salaries. Although job slots will not go unfilled, the government's ability to select the best persons from a large pool of applicants is likely to be sharply curtailed. At higher grades, and among experienced workers, the policy of low pay will simply encourage federal employees to retire or to accept offers of employment elsewhere. Recruitment for top-level jobs is bound to suffer under the proposed pay freeze; younger and less-experienced people will be hired for jobs previously filled by experienced hands. Over some period of time, in other words, what the pay proposals foretell is a government work force of less quality and experience than past practice would have allowed.

Regulation
Prepared by J. Elizabeth Callison and Lester B. Lave

Regulation, in its broadest definition, is government intervention in the free market; thus all federal government activities become regulatory and calls for reducing regulation become pleas for less government. A more useful definition of regulation, given by the Domestic Council Review Group on Regulatory Reform, is "federal laws or rules imposing government-established standards and significant economic responsibilities on individuals or organizations outside the federal establishment." The discussion below adopts this interpretation.

Reduction of regulatory costs is a major theme in President Reagan's budget proposals. Yet, total federal spending on regulation amounted to only $7.3 billion, or about 1.4 percent of fiscal 1979 outlays, and were projected in the Carter budget to be $9.6 billion, or 1.3 percent of fiscal 1982 outlays.[29] Reagan proposes to cut these outlays by $0.9 billion to $8.7 billion, more than 40 percent of which would come from reductions in outlays for salaries and operating expenses of the regulatory agencies. But a larger savings in the Reagan budget—$2.1 billion—would come from new or higher

29. These exclude Environmental Protection Agency grants of $3.8 billion in 1979 and $4.2 billion in 1982 under the Carter budget to states and localities for financing construction of facilities to treat waste water. The Reagan budget would cut these outlays by $300 million.

charges and fees for services and products provided directly by the federal government.

Examples abound of services and products supplied by federal agencies to specific beneficiaries who are able to pay for the service. Agencies often make the revealing protest that charging nominal fees that are much less than the full cost of the service would reduce the number of users substantially. The two principal economic reasons for government subsidy are to redistribute income from one group to another (say, from the working population to the aged) and to provide certain "merit" goods or services (for example, providing free schooling to the young so that they can become informed citizens and have more equal economic opportunities). The many programs that fit into neither category should be priced to recover their full costs or turned over to the private sector.

The Commodity Futures Trading Commission, the Federal Maritime Commission, the Securities and Exchange Commission, the Corps of Engineers, the Coast Guard, and many other federal agencies perform services for identifiable individuals and businesses. It is reasonable to require the users who benefit from these services— not the taxpayer—to pay for them. For example, after decades of controversy, inland barge traffic is charged for some of the services provided by the Corps of Engineers. Even when the service benefits the entire population, a user charge is needed to ensure that the service is not overused. The Department of Agriculture spent $834 million for inspections in 1979. If slaughter houses were charged for their share of this service, the cost of of producing meat would rise and there would be some incentive to increase the efficiency of those inspections.

In evaluating the reductions in outlays proposed by President Reagan, agencies that regulate economic behavior should be distinguished from those that regulate health and safety. Given the success in reducing the regulatory authority granted to the Civil Aeronautics Board and the Interstate Commerce Commission, it is evident that society often benefits from less economic regulation;[30] presumably, there can be at least a commensurate reduction in the budgets of

30. See, for example, Roger G. Noll, Merton J. Peck, and John J. McGowan, *Economic Aspects of Television Regulation* (Brookings Institution, 1973), Stephen G. Breyer and Paul W. McAvoy, *Energy Regulation by the Federal Power Commission* (Brookings Institution, 1974), and George W. Douglas and James C. Miller III, *Economic Regulation of Domestic Air Transport: Theory and Policy* (Brookings Institution, 1975).

these agencies. Modest increases in efficiency could probably be realized in the health and safety regulatory agencies by improving management and eliminating duplication of effort. There is no shortage of examples of health and safety regulations that are ineffective or inefficient, but improved regulation is likely to be more appropriate in this area than deregulation.

Spending cuts for the social regulatory agencies can only be achieved by reducing the resources used in formulating and enforcing regulatory standards. It is far from clear that such reductions will lead to more efficient or less intrusive regulation. Unless the goals and responsibilities of the agencies are revised, staff reductions in many agencies would probably be counterproductive. Virtually all regulatory agencies have far too little staff to perform their mandated functions. For example, the Environmental Protection Agency has consistently failed to meet its statutory deadlines under the Toxic Substances Control Act, in part because of insufficient staff. The Occupational Safety and Health Administration has regulated fewer than 20 carcinogens and, because there are only about 500 industrial hygienists to inspect facilities, most workplaces with less than ten employees have never been inspected. Many agencies operate in a frenetic mode; they are unable to fulfill their statutory obligations, are often sued for failing to do so, and are besieged with requests they cannot consider. Cutting staff and budget before redefining goals would make agency actions more arbitrary, would lead to more missed statutory deadlines, and would further undermine public confidence in federal regulatory activities.

Of much greater importance than federal outlays on regulation are the costs imposed on the private sector by the regulations themselves. Many current regulations—from attempts by the Federal Trade Commission to regulate television for children to the standards imposed by the Occupational Health and Safety Administration for the use of benzene—require specific companies to change their customary procedures or to invest in more expensive equipment. Public concern for a clean environment, a safe workplace, and safe products continues, even though the individual regulations are controversial. Cutting the budgets of regulatory agencies is easy; what is difficult is achieving social goals without imposing needless costs on the private sector. This requires improved research and staff work to refine the regulatory instruments used, which in turn may require higher rather than lower agency budgets.

A more promising approach to reducing the costs of health and safety regulation lies in reforming both agency processes and the statutes under which they operate. President Reagan has already begun to make changes in these processes. On the day he was inaugurated, he issued an executive order prohibiting the issuance of new regulations for sixty days. This was followed by another order requiring regulatory agencies to analyze the costs and benefits of alternative regulatory strategies before proposing new regulations. This second order replaces and extends a similar executive order issued by President Carter, but it puts more emphasis on the comparison of costs with benefits of new regulatory rules. Measurement is difficult, and benefit-cost analysis is not a panacea. But such an approach will require major increases in personnel if it is to improve the efficiency and effectiveness of the regulatory process. Because the regulatory agencies imposing the greatest costs on the economy—particularly the Environmental Protection Agency and the Occupational Safety and Health Administration—have a large backlog of regulations in development and many others in the appellate courts, they cannot be expected to comply with such new procedural requirements without more staff, a further falling behind in deadlines, or a changed legislative mandate.

It is clear from even the most casual perusal of health and safety regulation that major cost savings to society can only occur through changes in the fundamental approach to such regulation. These changes have begun at the Environmental Protection Agency but not at other agencies. Simplifying the regulatory approach and relying more on economic incentives (as a substitute for command-control regulation) will be a more effective way of improving health, safety, and the environment. Such changes, however, will probably require revision of the legislative mandates for the individual agencies, a revision that can begin in earnest when Congress considers the Clean Air Act during the 1981 session.

Tax Expenditures
Prepared by Joseph J. Minarik

Eliminating tax expenditure programs might seem to be an inappropriate alternative strategy in the context of President Reagan's proposals to reduce the federal budget because it would increase receipts rather than reduce outlays.[31] However, inefficient tax expenditures are just as wasteful of resources as are inefficient spending programs. At the very least, a tax expenditure that does not efficiently achieve an important national purpose could be replaced by a direct outlay or another more efficient tax expenditure. Alternatively, the funds could be used for reducing tax rates without increasing the deficit.

Tax expenditures in fiscal 1982 will reach an estimated $263.9 billion.[32] This discussion addresses tax expenditures that contribute to reduced saving and investment, the growth in medical care expenditures, and the rising budgetary costs for social security and unemployment compensation. The particular revisions discussed here would increase receipts in fiscal 1982 by almost $19 billion, an amount that would finance a 5.7 percent reduction in income taxes or could be substituted for almost 40 percent of the reductions in outlays proposed by the Reagan administration.

Interest on Consumer Debt and Mortgages

Many observers have faulted the federal income tax for reducing the real net return to savings and thereby penalizing thrift, especially in an inflationary environment; critics of the tax system's rewards for consumption, which have the same effect, have been far fewer. Yet the individual income tax permits the taxpayer to deduct interest paid on consumer loans, which reduces the cost of borrowing and thus encourages consumption. If the deduction for interest on consumer debt were eliminated, tax receipts would be increased by $6.0 billion in fiscal 1982.

Interest on home mortgages is also deductible under the individual income tax. This deduction encourages consumption of housing and diverts investment funds from the stock and bond markets, which provide financing for new industrial capital, to the mortgage market. The income tax subsidy for home mortgages has also contributed to the rapid inflation in the price of owner-occupied hous-

---

31. See appendix B for a definition of the concept and a listing of all tax expenditures in the budget for fiscal 1982.

32. The revenue effects are estimated assuming repeal of each individual tax expenditure with no other change in the tax law. If two or more tax expenditures were terminated, the total revenue gain would differ from the sum of the estimates for the individual tax expenditures.

ing. Elimination of the deduction for interest on mortgages of all existing homes is politically unlikely because it would probably reduce residential property values. However, limiting the amount of deductible mortgage interest to $5,000 or $10,000 would affect only the largest borrowers and would help slow the flow of capital into housing. A ceiling of $5,000 would allow a full deduction on a $41,700 mortgage at 12 percent; a ceiling of $10,000 would allow a full deduction for interest on an $83,300 mortgage at the same rate. Tax revenues in fiscal 1982 would increase by $4.3 billion and $0.8 billion, respectively.

The federal government allows states and localities to issue tax-exempt bonds for financing airport construction and pollution control investments by private firms, other industrial development facilities (for projects of less than $10 million), private hospitals, college student loans, and home mortgages.[33] These bonds reduce investment in productive enterprises by diverting risk or venture capital from the private sector. They also distort the allocation of resources within the private sector and between the public and private sectors. Moreover, the increase in the volume of tax-exempt securities has had the effect of raising interest rates on other tax-exempt financing. If the tax exemption were limited to general purpose debt issued by state and local governments, fiscal 1982 receipts would be increased by $5.6 billion.

Employer Contributions for Medical Insurance

Rising medical care expenditures have been imposing considerable burdens on the public and private sectors, and one of the most important causes of this development is the system of third-party payment. When individuals obtain medical care at no out-of-pocket cost, they ignore the price charged to the third party and request more medical care than they would otherwise receive. As a result, demand for medical care always exceeds supply, and expenditures keep rising at a rapid rate.

The trend toward more comprehensive insurance coverage, and thus more third-party payment responsibility, has been encouraged by the exclusion of employer contributions toward employees' medical insurance premiums from the taxable income of both individuals

33. The exemption for single-family home mortgage bonds has been eliminated beginning in 1984.

and businesses. Because employees do not pay taxes for such contributions, they are encouraged to bargain for more elaborate health insurance coverage than they would choose to buy on their own. One possible way to retard the growth of employer-financed medical care would be to limit the amount of the employer contribution that is excludable from the taxable income of the employee. If the limit for family coverage were set at $120 a month, the differential between insurance contributions and cash compensation would be removed at the margin for about 23 million workers, giving them an incentive to evaluate broader health care coverage more critically. This change would raise federal income tax receipts in fiscal 1982 by $1.9 billion.

Social Security and Unemployment Compensation

During the next few years the social security system will be under serious financial pressure. Although the stress will abate for the remainder of this century and early into the next, the retirement of the post-World War II baby-boom generation is expected to again increase claims on the system beyond payroll tax revenues. With these difficulties in prospect and payroll tax rates already scheduled to rise to unprecedented levels, many experts are seeking solutions other than still higher payroll taxes.

For these reasons, suggestions have been made by expert commissions and task forces that social security benefits should be taxable under the federal income tax. One possibility would be to tax these benefits in exactly the same way as private pensions (that is, allow the tax-free recovery of the previously taxed employee contributions when the benefits begin either until the contributions are recovered or until the end of the taxpayer's expected lifetime). However, this change would impose a considerable burden on the Social Security Administration because workers would not be able to make such calculations on their own. Moreover, employees make contributions not only for retirement insurance, but also for survivors' benefits and for disability insurance. It would not be easy to allocate the contributions among these benefits, except perhaps on an arbitrary basis.

A simpler method would be to tax one-half of all social security benefits (which corresponds to the employer's share of the payroll tax and is therefore not taxed to the employee). This change would affect only a small fraction of the elderly: married couples with social security benefits of less than $14,800 and single persons with benefits of less than $8,600 would not be taxed if they had no other income. A still more generous option would be to use the same method that has been used for taxation of unemployment compensation since 1979. Under this approach, benefits would be taxed only to the extent that total incomes exceed $20,000 for married couples ($15,000 for single persons). At the same time, the treatment of unemployment compensation could be tightened by reducing the current income floors ($25,000 for married couples, $20,000 for single persons) to the same levels as those suggested for social security; this would reduce the budgetary cost of the program and increase the incentive to find work. Tax receipts would increase by $3.5 billion a year for social security, and $1 billion a year for unemployment compensation.

Foreign Economic Assistance
Prepared by William R. Cline

In late January 1981 the press reported a plan by the Office of Management and Budget to cut $2.6 billion from the $9.2 billion budget authority in foreign economic assistance proposed by President Carter for fiscal 1982. The response was immediate and explosive. The State Department insisted on smaller cuts, foreign donor nations protested a breach of U.S. commitments to multilateral lending institutions, and congressional leaders criticized the plan, which the chairman of the House Committee on Foreign Affairs decried as "irresponsible in terms of the U.S. national interest."

The formal budget proposal submitted by President Reagan in February 1981 called for a $1.7 billion cut in budget authority for foreign economic development assistance for fiscal 1982 (excluding security-supporting assistance, which rose slightly), a reduction of 25 percent below the amount recommended by President Carter. Foreign economic assistance is uniquely a budget item with no U.S. constituents as direct beneficiaries, and as a result it is highly vulnerable to budget-cutting pressures. Although during the 1950s and 1960s the United States played by far the dominant leadership role in aiding the economic development of poor countries, today the

United States ranks close to last among industrial nations in the relative amount of aid it provides.

Reasons for Economic Assistance

Maintenance of *long-run national security* is a central reason for providing economic assistance to developing countries. Security-supporting assistance (nearly one-third of the total) goes directly to key allies and strategic nations such as Israel, Turkey, and Egypt. Over the longer term national security is affected by other components of economic assistance that are focused on economic growth and reduction of poverty. In the long run the world is more likely to achieve stable, peaceful conditions if the fruits of economic progress are widely shared than if there are islands of wealth amidst a sea of dire poverty.

Economic self-interest is a second reason for foreign economic assistance. Economic development of the third world means larger future markets for U.S. exports. The United States already exports more to the developing countries than to Europe and Japan combined. The developing countries purchased 38 percent of U.S. exports in 1978. These exports provide jobs. Exports to developing countries account for approximately 6 percent of all production in manufacturing and 15 percent of agricultural output; these exports provide almost 2 million jobs for Americans. If developing economies stagnate, there is a depressing influence on the U.S. economy as exports to these countries stagnate. Similarly, the development of oil and other mineral resources in the third world is crucial to the supply of new raw materials to the United States.

The ultimate reason for foreign economic assistance, however, is the American tradition of *humanitarian* concern. Today an estimated 800 million people live in absolute poverty, primarily in Africa and South Asia, where 62 percent of adults are illiterate, 72 percent of the population has no access to safe water supplies, and life expectancy is only fifty years. In the last decade the United States has concentrated impressively on the needs of the poor at home, but increasingly has turned its back on the poor abroad. In 1966 the United States spent $45 per citizen on social programs at home for every $1 spent on aid to each citizen of poor foreign countries; by the late 1970s the ratio had risen to $360 per U.S. citizen on social programs for every $1 spent per poor person abroad.

There are critics who argue that economic assistance does not work. Foreign aid is beleaguered with charges of wasteful programs, corruption, encouragement of dictators, discouragement of self-help, and so forth. Most criticisms of this nature have been either distorted or refer to atypical instances. Careful studies have shown that economic assistance does make a significant difference to growth, and follow-up evaluations have found good rates of return on World Bank development projects.[34] The cases of Taiwan and Korea are well known. Massive U.S. aid set the stage for economic growth that enabled these countries to develop vigorous economies no longer requiring concessional assistance. Aid from the United States, and later loans from the World Bank, helped propel Brazil to its miraculous economic growth beginning in the 1960s.

Levels and Components of Assistance

The dollar value of foreign economic aid remained practically unchanged over the last two decades, despite inflationary erosion of those dollars, growth in the populations of poor foreign countries, and growth in real U.S. GNP (see table 3-3). When converted to constant dollars at 1980 prices, the figures show a sharp decline in the real level of assistance from the 1960s to the 1970s and a stagnation of aid at a relatively constant level in the past decade. As a percentage of total budget outlays, economic assistance has fallen sharply, from 3 percent in the early 1960s to 1 percent today. The share of GNP given in official development assistance fell from 0.56 percent in the early 1960s, when the United States led the efforts to provide aid, to only 0.20 percent in 1979, when the United States ranked fifteenth among seventeen Western nations on aid-giving as a percent of GNP.

U.S. foreign economic assistance basically takes four forms: multilateral assistance (about 14 percent), bilateral development assistance (33 percent), bilateral "food for peace" (20 percent) and bilateral security-supporting assistance (33 percent). Multilateral aid combines contributions from the United States and other donors through the World Bank, regional banks (Inter-American, African,

---

34. For a discussion of economic assistance and growth see Hollis B. Chenery and Nicholas G. Carter, "Foreign Assistance and Development Performance, 1960–1970," *American Economic Review*, vol. 63 (May 1973, *Papers and Proceedings, 1972*), pp. 459–68.

Table 3-3. Federal Budget Outlays for Foreign Economic and Financial Assistance, Fiscal Years 1961–82

Billions of dollars unless otherwise specified

Fiscal year or period[a]	Outlays		Percent of total federal budget outlays	Percent of gross national product[c]
	Current prices	Constant 1980 dollars[b]		
1961–65	3.6	10.5	3.25	0.56
1966–70	3.9	9.9	2.34	0.38
1971–75	3.0	5.5	1.16	0.27
1976–78	4.0	5.3	0.97	0.26
1979	4.7	5.4	0.96	0.20
1980	5.6	5.6	0.97	n.a.
1981[d]	6.7	6.1	1.01	n.a.
1982[d]				
Carter budget	7.0	5.8	0.95	n.a.
Reagan budget	6.8	5.6	0.98	n.a.

Sources: *The Budget of the United States Government, Fiscal Year 1982*, pp. 600–06; *The Budget of the United States Government, Fiscal Year 1977*, p. 360; *The Budget of the United States Government, Fiscal Year 1975*, pp. 324–28; *The Budget of the United States Government, Fiscal Year 1971*, pp. 587–91; Organisation for Economic Co-operation and Development, *Development Co-operation: Efforts and Policies of the Members of the Development Assistance Committee, 1980 Review* (Paris: OECD, 1980) and previous issues; *International Financial Statistics*, vol. 29 (May 1976), pp. 382–83; *Survey of Current Business*, vol. 60 (December 1980); *Budget Revisions, Fiscal Year 1982*, p. 37; and unpublished data, Office of Management and Budget.

n.a. Not available.

a. The figures for the periods from 1961 to 1978 are annual averages.

b. The OECD deflator is used for U.S. official development assistance, 1967–77; the U.S. wholesale price index is used for other years.

c. Based on the OECD definition of official development assistance.

d. Estimated.

and Asian Development Banks), and programs of the United Nations. "Food for peace" (Public Law 480) provides subsidies and grants for poor countries to buy U.S. farm products. Bilateral development assistance flows mainly through the Agency for International Development for economic development projects. Security-supporting assistance (currently called the economic support fund) provides special assistance to support key allies.

The early proposal by the Office of Management and Budget would have concentrated cutbacks in multilateral assistance; bilateral development assistance and Public Law 480 would also have been greatly cut back, and only security-supporting assistance would have been left relatively intact. The philosophy was to cut back multilateral programs allegedly unresponsive to U.S. interests, and to use aid much more directly as a political tool for short-run rewards to political allies in the third world. The compromise proposed by the

Reagan administration retained its basic objective for foreign aid but nevertheless attempted to honor U.S. commitments to multilateral institutions in view of the sharp response of the allies in industrial countries against any reneging on those obligations.

The World Bank makes loans at market-related interest rates (but for long repayment periods) to middle-income countries. This process is highly efficient, and a small amount of paid-in capital provides the leverage of guarantees for large amounts of lending. Members of the World Bank have recently doubled its capital, and the Reagan administration proposes to go along with this increase. The International Development Association makes concessional (low-interest) loans to poor nations, primarily in Africa and Asia. This agency is the single most important source of concessional assistance for the poor countries. The Reagan budget proposes that the United States meet its international obligation to the new level of funding for the agency of approximately $1.1 billion annually for fiscal years 1981–83 (with a stretch-out and a large final payment in fiscal 1983). For the future, the already small fraction of actual budget outlays on multilateral lending suggests that there may not be much more room for the shift away from multilateral lending that the administration wants without repudiating international obligations and losing influence in these institutions.

The high and rising share of security-supporting assistance reflects the strategy of the new administration to make an even larger portion of assistance overtly political. Public Law 480 assistance has fallen from one-half to the present one-fifth of total aid in the past two decades, a reflection of the transition of American agriculture from a period of excess supply to a new phase of booming commercial exports, relative food scarcity, and concern about inflation of food prices. Congress has led the way in providing bilateral aid with an emphasis on benefits for the poorer classes; if most of these funds were to be redirected toward countries and social groups that might currently be politically more important to the United States, there would be a serious dilemma to resolve between U.S. political and humanitarian objectives.

The Reagan Proposal

For fiscal 1982 the Reagan budget calls for sharp cuts from the Carter projections of foreign economic assistance. The cuts are in multilateral development aid and in the activities of the Agency for International Development, the Peace Corps, and Public Law 480 food aid. The budget authority for security-supporting assistance increased by $150 million (6 percent), however, reflecting the Reagan administration's focus on more direct political objectives. The cuts in development-oriented assistance for fiscal 1982 amounted to $1.7 billion in budget authority; actual budget outlays would be cut from projected levels by only $300 million in fiscal 1982 but by nearly $2 billion by fiscal 1986. (The difference between the cuts in authority and in outlays is caused by the lag of aid disbursements behind commitments.) Essentially the Reagan budget means that the real value of outlays on foreign economic assistance, excluding security-supporting assistance, will be cut by approximately 10 percent between fiscal years 1981 and 1982 and then remain frozen at an unchanging real level for the subsequent five years. (If security-supporting assistance is included, the cut in real assistance is 6 percent from fiscal 1981.) If inflation becomes higher than the administration forecasts, the real value of economic assistance will decline even more.

At a time when national security is receiving renewed emphasis in budgetary decisions, it is worth asking whether the nation's long-run security, economic, and humanitarian interests would be best promoted by a reduction in foreign aid. The shift in emphasis toward bilateral programs with short-run political benefits may also be questioned. Only a large increase in the total foreign assistance budget would seem to allow room for this type of shift. Otherwise, the cuts in multilateral and development-oriented bilateral aid focused on poor countries could mean a breach of international commitments and a blow to the humanitarian goal of U.S. foreign assistance.

Summary

President Reagan has acted decisively on his campaign pledge to reduce the growth of federal spending. Given the constraints he has imposed on the scope of the budget-cutting effort—sparing certain benefits under the social safety net programs while increasing defense outlays sharply—the performance is noteworthy in overall magnitude and in the detail with which it was carried out. Moreover, the president has asked Congress not only to reduce spending but also to decentralize government decisionmaking through the use of block grants, to impose new and higher user charges on the beneficiaries of federal services and facilities, and to accelerate deregulation. These proposals give heavy weight to efficiency considerations; it remains to be seen whether Congress shares the administration's emphasis.

The idea of designating some basic benefits as part of a social safety net is appealing, but it is not clear why particular benefits are included in the net and others are excluded. For example, the Reagan budget does not include any corrections for the overstatement of the inflation adjustments in social security and other federal programs during the last three years, nor does it recommend any changes in the method of adjustment for the future. The medicare program, which pays benefits to the aged regardless of their incomes, is untouched, while medicaid, which assists only those who are poor, would be cut by almost $1 billion in fiscal 1982 and by larger amounts in later years. Similarly, federal outlays are reduced for aid to families with dependent children, despite the fact that this program is included in the safety net and benefits have been declining in real terms for many years. The exemption of the safety net programs requires large cuts in other nondefense programs, which account for less than 40 percent of the budget. Moderate reductions in these programs, such as corrections of retirement and disability benefits for excessive past inflation adjustments and introduction of modest cost sharing in medicare, could have avoided some of the deep cuts in other programs while still meeting the budget targets.

The focus on cutting budget outlays has also diverted attention, at least temporarily, from major structural problems in social insurance and other programs. No provision is made for the possibility that the old age and survivors' insurance trust fund will be exhausted in the next two or three years if taxes and benefits remain unchanged. The complicated and costly welfare program is trimmed down by small economies, but the basic structure of the program remains untouched. Some relatively small reductions in federal health programs are proposed, but the basic problem of sharply rising medical costs in the United States is set aside at least temporarily. The administration is dismantling the employment and training programs for the disadvantaged without proposing any alternative—save for the vigorously expressed faith that a resurgent private sector will provide the necessary jobs it has not generated in the past. It has submitted legislation for comprehensive reform of federal employees' pay and fringe benefits that incorporates a lower standard of compensation than the current law; these changes and the low pay raise proposed for 1981 may impair the government's ability to attract and retain a qualified and experienced work force. Trade-adjustment assistance and extended unemployment benefits are being cut, even though the administration itself expects continued high unemployment for several years. The administration supports the idea of revenue sharing, but it is silent about the denial of grant funds to state governments under present legislation. Consideration of these and other structural issues should not be delayed for long.

To achieve its aims of reducing federal controls over state and local activities, President Reagan intends to eliminate many categorical grant programs and to consolidate them into block grants. Such grants are proposed for education, health and social services, and community development; others are being considered. At the same time, the funds going to the state and local governments through federal grants are slashed by 13 percent, which will mean a cut in real terms of about 20 percent. Unless some safeguards are built into the block grants, the programs for the needy and disadvantaged could be shortchanged, particularly since the cut in federal aid for other programs will place a heavy fiscal burden on the states and local governments. To help resolve the dilemma, assistance under the new block grants could be targeted to fiscally needy communities, but some categorical grants would continue to be needed to target benefits to particular groups (for example, the handicapped, the minorities, the poor, and the medically indigent).

The Reagan administration recommends cuts in several subsidy programs but did not go far enough in a number of instances. While it makes sense for the government to assist research and development, there is little justification for massive subsidies to support commercial production of synthetic fuels. A thorough review of subsidies to agriculture has been long overdue. Costs of some programs (dairy) have escalated; other programs (acreage restrictions) have become obsolete and even counterproductive. Programs that still serve a useful purpose (grain reserves, crop insurance) could be strengthened and, at the same time, made more cost-effective. The external costs associated with soil erosion justify a federal role in its prevention, but it makes little sense to subsidize soil conservation efforts that farmers would undertake on their own. Higher user fees should be collected from users of federally financed parks and inland waterways. The elimination of uneconomical water projects would also serve to improve the allocation of resources and reduce federal outlays.

The new administration is continuing and expanding past efforts to reduce the regulatory burden on the economy and requiring users of federal services and facilities to pay for the cost of the benefits they receive. There are, however, some anomalies and omissions. Staff reductions being proposed for numerous federal regulatory agencies would slow rather than accelerate needed improvements in regulation. The proposed increase in user charges would amount to $2.1 billion in fiscal 1982—only a small fraction of the fees and charges that could be justified on economic and equity grounds. Moreover, large subsidies would remain for general aviation, railroad transportation, the post office, users of the national parks, and beneficiaries of federally supported water projects; competition would continue to be controlled in the trucking industry, and trucking rates would remain above costs; farmers would continue to receive payments for actions they would undertake anyway; and inefficient tax expenditures that cost billions of dollars, misallocate resources, or contribute to inflation would be continued.

The proposed Reagan budget would reduce the real value of foreign assistance for economic development by 10 percent, even though foreign aid in real terms has already fallen 40 percent below levels of the early 1960s and considerations of economic self-interest and humanitarian concern remain. The shift toward political bilateral aid from economic multilateral aid raises questions about U.S. fulfillment of its international obligations and suggests a diminishing concern about the plight of the poorest of the world's poor.

CHAPTER FOUR

The Defense Budget

WILLIAM W. KAUFMANN

EVER SINCE the seizure of the U.S. embassy in Teheran and the Soviet invasion of Afghanistan, an old slogan has acquired an inflationary twist. Americans now favor billions for defense but not one cent for tribute. Exactly how many billions they favor, or even how many billions are needed for defense, is much less clear, especially when the desire for increased defense must compete with the demand for fiscal austerity and balanced federal budgets.

For those who must translate these various signals into programs, a certain caution about defense needs is in order. The military services frequently speak of their requirements as though there were at all times a single set of solutions to the problems of defense. In fact, however, a range of solutions always exists. How much is enough depends on external conditions, conservatism, and cost. What is sufficient for some may seem too little for others who are less optimistic about the future and more prone to minimize risk. It is indeed this kind of choice among risks and alternatives that Congress confronts as it considers the baseline Carter defense budget and five-year defense program, the Reagan amendments, and all the possibilities in between.

This chapter was prepared with the assistance of John C. Baker, Martin Binkin, and Allan V. Burman. Secretarial assistance was provided by Kirk W. Kimmell and Susan L. Woollen.

The Carter Defense Program

On January 15, 1981, President Carter indicated in his fourth and last defense budget that enough would be quite a bit more than he had estimated in the past. For fiscal 1982 he requested $196.4 billion in total obligational authority and proposed $180 billion in outlays. The Carter budget, as can be seen from table 4-1, was supposed to be the first installment on a five-year defense program that would entail an average annual real increase in total obligational authority—with the effects of estimated inflation removed—of about 5 percent between fiscal 1981 (the current fiscal year) and fiscal 1986. Under this plan, outlays would increase on the average by about 4.7 percent each year in real terms. By fiscal 1986, the defense budget, expressed in total obligational authority, would reach $238.7 billion (in fiscal 1982 prices), and $318.3 billion (in fiscal 1986 prices). Cumulative obligational authority for the five years, in real terms, would amount to $1,085.2 billion.

These figures, it should be noted, cover all the military functions of the U.S. Department of Defense, including military retired pay, which will amount to more than $15 billion in 1982. They do not include the so-called civil functions of the department (principally the

Table 4-1. The Carter Five-Year Defense Program, Fiscal Years 1981–86

Billions of dollars unless otherwise specified

Item	1981	1982	1983	1984	1985	1986
Total obligational authority						
Current dollars	171.2	196.4	224.0	253.1	284.3	318.3
Fiscal 1982 dollars	186.5	196.4	206.2	216.5	227.4	238.7
Percent real increase	7.8	5.3	5.0	5.0	5.0	5.0
Outlays						
Current dollars	157.6	180.0	205.3	232.3	261.8	293.3
Fiscal 1982 dollars	172.5	180.0	188.2	197.1	207.0	217.5
Percent real increase	6.1	4.4	4.6	4.7	5.0	5.1
Inflation index						
Total obligational authority	91.8	100.0	108.6	116.9	125.0	133.6
Outlays	91.4	100.0	109.1	117.8	126.5	134.8

Source: *Department of Defense Annual Report Fiscal Year 1982* (Department of Defense, 1981), pp. 10, C-10.

Corps of Engineers); nor do they encompass the costs of nuclear weapons, now estimated at about $5 billion for fiscal 1982 alone, which appear in the budget of the U.S. Department of Energy.

The amounts involved, even without further increases, are huge by any standard. They give the Department of Defense a national income comparable to that of a small industrial nation. The fact remains nonetheless that defense is much less of a burden to Americans than it was only twenty years ago. As shown in table 4-2, only once since World War II have defense outlays taken a smaller percentage of gross national product than has been the case during the last ten years. Despite the increases programmed in the Carter five-year defense program, the share of GNP going to defense outlays would probably not exceed 6 percent by fiscal 1986. Defense outlays as a percent of federal spending, as the table shows, have followed a similar trend. Whereas defense outlays represented 46.3 percent of the federal budget in fiscal 1962, they will constitute about 24.3 percent in fiscal 1982.

It should be stressed that none of these data can be used to demonstrate that the United States is spending too much or too little on national defense. They merely show that as the nation's income has increased, a smaller proportion of it has been dedicated to defense.

Table 4-2. Defense Outlays as a Percent of Gross National Product and Federal Outlays, Selected Fiscal Years, 1944–82

Fiscal year	Gross national product	Federal outlays
1944	35.6	78.7
1950	4.4	27.4
1953	12.1	57.0
1962	9.1	46.3
1964	8.2	41.8
1968	9.3	43.3
1970	8.0	39.2
1972	6.7	32.4
1974	5.6	28.8
1976	5.4	24.0
1978	5.0	22.8
1980	5.1	22.7
1981	5.2	23.2
1982	5.6	24.3

Source: *Department of Defense Annual Report Fiscal Year 1980*, p. 21; *Department of Defense Annual Report Fiscal Year 1981*, p. 18; *Department of Defense Annual Report Fiscal Year 1982*, p. 317; *Budget of the United States Government, Fiscal Year 1982*, p. 611.

They also demonstrate that the United States has not been engaged in an unrestrained arms race or buildup of its defense capabilities.

During most of the four years that Carter was in office, indeed, the administration took the position that relatively modest increases in defense budget authority would be necessary to counter the Soviet military buildup. It was congressional insistence that drove the fiscal 1981 budget to $186.5 billion (in fiscal 1982 dollars)—a jump of nearly 8 percent in obligational authority over fiscal 1980—and increased the procurement account by nearly 17 percent in real terms. In response, the Carter fiscal 1982 budget allows real total obligational authority to grow by only 5.3 percent, and would hold the procurement account to a real increase of only 1.2 percent. By contrast, proposed resources for operation and maintenance rise by 6.5 percent, and for research, development, test, and evaluation by 13.7 percent, both in real terms.

The Reagan Amendments

The Reagan administration clearly believes that defense has been underfunded and that it should take a larger share of both national income and federal spending. In accordance with that belief, President Reagan has submitted amendments to increase the defense budgets for fiscal years 1981 and 1982 and has given the bare outlines of the five-year defense program that he considers appropriate. As can be seen from table 4-3, these amendments would specifically add $32.6 billion in total obligational authority and $5.8 billion in outlays to the Carter budgets for fiscal years 1981 and 1982. Over the period of the five-year program, the Carter estimate of needed total obligational authority would be increased in real terms by about $195 billion. In fiscal 1986, defense would take 7 percent of estimated GNP.

No new administration can be expected in two months to set a definitive course for the next five years. Accordingly, the Reagan projections for fiscal years 1983–86 should be regarded at best as tentative. The large increases projected for those years probably constitute no more than "wedges" reserved by the budget planners for defense in the future. To what extent and how they will actually be used will depend on many factors, not the least of which is the fate of the administration's programs for economic recovery.

Table 4-3. Comparison of the Reagan Amendments and the Carter Five-Year Defense Program, Fiscal Years 1981–86

Billions of dollars unless otherwise specified

Item	1981	1982	1983	1984	1985	1986
Total obligational authority						
Carter defense program	171.2	196.4	224.0	253.1	284.3	318.3
Reagan amendments	178.0	222.2	254.8	289.2	326.5	367.5
Outlays						
Carter defense program	157.6	180.0	205.3	232.3	261.8	293.3
Reagan amendments	158.6	184.8	221.1	249.8	297.3	336.0
Defense outlays as a percent of gross national product						
Carter defense program	5.5	5.6	5.7	5.7	5.8	5.9
Reagan amendments	5.6	5.8	6.1	6.2	6.8	7.0

Source: *Department of Defense Annual Report Fiscal Year 1982*, p. 10; *Budget of the United States Government, Fiscal Year 1982*, p. 611; press release, Office of Assistant Secretary of Defense (Public Affairs), "FY 1981 and FY 1982 Department of Defense Budget Revisions," no. 77-81, March 4, 1981; author's estimates based on Executive Office of the President, Office of Management and Budget, *Fiscal Year 1981 Budget Revisions* (Government Printing Office, 1981), p. 13.

The increases proposed for fiscal years 1981 and 1982, on the other hand, reflect real commitments on the part of the administration. Even so, they are—given the short time in which amendments could be prepared—largely a selection from what the military services already had on their lists of priorities but failed to obtain in the original budgets for fiscal years 1981 and 1982. Thus for all practical purposes (and as should be expected) these amendments can be considered more as full funding of the Carter defense posture than as sharp new departures from it. They propose no radical changes in that posture. They simply request development of a new bomber ($2.4 billion); a few more new ships ($2.7 billion) and the reactivation of three older ones (nearly $1.0 billion); quite a few more aircraft and helicopters ($5.0 billion); additional tanks, wheeled vehicles, and air defense systems ($3.1 billion); increased pay ($2.3 billion); funds to cover cost growth in weapons programs and fuel ($1.8 billion); the nuts and bolts associated with readiness ($10.5 billion); the projection of power to the Persian Gulf ($1 billion); and additional war reserve stocks ($4.0 billion). Major changes in direction or emphasis, if they occur, will probably not come until the administration presents its defense budget for fiscal 1983.

In the circumstances, the opportunity still exists to consider two questions:

1. What are the general directions taken by the Carter defense program as presented in January and augmented in March for fiscal years 1981 and 1982?

2. What might constitute further needs under current defense concepts, or with possible changes in those concepts, considering that not all increases would be of equal priority—with first priority given to urgent programs, second priority to important ones, third to desirable programs; and fourth to programs that are, as the military would say, nice to have?

The U.S. Force Structure

Despite the significant real increase that will take place in the resources allocated to the five-year defense program, assuming that Congress responds favorably to the current requests and projections, the military force structure of the United States is not likely to change appreciably in size during the next five years. Whether the Strategic Arms Limitation Talks treaty (SALT II), signed in June 1979, is ratified or not, U.S. strategic nuclear forces—intercontinental ballistic missiles (ICBMs), submarine-launched ballistic missiles (SLBMs), and long-range bombers—will remain at fewer than 2,100 delivery vehicles.[1] However, the number of warheads loaded into these forces could rise from approximately 9,000 to as many as 14,000, depending on the pace of the Trident nuclear ballistic missile submarine (SSBN) and strategic air-launched cruise missile (ALCM) programs. The so-called theater nuclear forces will also remain relatively stable in size, although if present plans are implemented, approximately 572 longer-range theater nuclear delivery systems will eventually be deployed (originally estimated at 108 Pershing II ballistic missiles and 464 ground-launched cruise missiles, capable of reaching Soviet territory from bases in Western Europe). To counterbalance this deployment, however, about 1,000 nuclear warheads have already been taken out of Europe, and as the Pershing IIs are phased in, an equal number of Pershing IAs will be replaced.

1. For a breakdown of the U.S. strategic forces, see *Department of Defense Annual Report Fiscal Year 1982* (Department of Defense, 1981), p. 53.

U.S. conventional forces will undergo similarly little quantitative change. The active-duty Army and Marine Corps will remain at nineteen divisions and five separate brigades. The Air Force will probably maintain and modernize twenty-six active-duty, fighter-attack wings. The general purpose fleet will grow slightly (largely as a result of past shipbuilding programs) from 526 to about 550 active and reserve carriers, surface combatants, attack submarines, and major auxiliaries. Strategic airlift will continue to be based on about 70 C-5A and 235 C-141 aircraft. Except for mobile logistic ships, sealift, both active and controlled fleet charter, will consist of twenty tankers and thirty-one cargo vessels.

Force Structure and Posture

Substantially increased defense funding combined with a relatively stable force structure does not necessarily mean that the nation will obtain an inadequate return on its defense investment. A defense posture consists of a great deal more than force structure. Divisions, wings, and battle groups must be equipped, manned, trained, maintained, and made deployable and sustainable in combat as well as during peacetime. But the exact degree of modernization, readiness, and sustainability to be sought does not automatically follow from the decision to acquire these units. The range of possibilities is large. At one end, the force structure can be fully equipped and manned, highly modern and trained, and well maintained. A more or less significant percentage of it can be stationed in overseas theaters and can be rapidly reinforced from the continental United States. It can be sustained in combat with men, matériel, and supplies for an indefinite period of time. At the other end of the scale, it can be precisely the same force structure, but a hollow shell that is undermanned, under-equipped, poorly maintained, and without mobility or sustainability.

Posture Choices

Exactly where the U.S. defense posture should be along this range of possibilities is to a large extent a matter of tradition and judgment. Because readiness, deployability, and sustainability are costly, mundane, and supposedly recoverable on relatively short notice, U.S. policymakers for most years since World War II have engaged in a compromise about the kind of posture they should support. With a few recent exceptions, they have tended to keep the strategic nuclear forces both modern and highly alert, with demanding standards of training and maintenance. They have followed a much more traditional practice with respect to the larger, more costly, and more controversial tactical or general purpose forces.

These forces have been subjected more nearly to the old "feast or famine" policies that characterized what passed for U.S. defense planning before World War II. It was assumed then that, before the United States became engaged in major combat overseas, it would have ample time to mobilize, equip, train and deploy its expeditionary forces. Therefore, during peacetime it could afford to restrain the cost of readiness, mobility, and sustainability—especially when resources were scarce. It made more sense to invest those scarce resources in the maintenance of the cadres and the prototype equipment needed for mobilization when the famine ended and the feast began.

Admittedly, the periods of famine have become shorter and less severe since the Korean War, but the fluctuations in spending for combat-ready general purpose forces have continued. Whether the Carter five-year defense program and the Reagan amendments—prepared, it should be remembered, at a time when the United States is at peace—will mark the end of this tradition, and whether the country is ready to adopt more stable peacetime funding for its general purpose forces, remains to be seen.

The Basis for Readiness

Certainly the case for departing from a mobilization strategy and posture should be well known by now. In the period since World War II, the United States has developed worldwide economic, political, and strategic interests. Moreover, these interests are likely to expand rather than contract in the future as national economies become more interdependent, other nations gain a comparative advantage over the United States in the production of certain goods and services, and U.S. self-sufficiency in raw materials declines.

INTERNATIONAL DANGERS. That these interests could be threatened by military means is now taken for granted. Not only does the United States have adversary relationships with the Soviet Union, North Korea, Vietnam, and Cuba; the dangers from them appear to have grown with the Soviet support of radical regimes in Africa and the Middle East, Soviet invasion of Afghanistan, and the threat to Poland; with the Vietnamese takeover of Cambodia and incursions into Thailand; with the increasing turbulence in Central America and the Caribbean; and with the heightened instability of the Middle East, marked most recently by the revolution in Iran, the continuing war between Iraq and Iran, the conflict between Libya and Chad, and the turmoil in Lebanon.

This kind of turmoil and the possibility of great power confrontations show no signs of abating in the foreseeable future. Local and regional animosities in Africa, the Middle East, and Asia have not been removed. Discontent with existing regimes continues to smolder and flare in Latin America, some of it stimulated and exacerbated from the outside, and in Eastern Europe. Disputes over energy supplies, raw materials, and economic practices have already begun and are likely to grow.

ALLIES. The United States can count far less now than in the past on friends (now allies) to deal with these dangers. While all of them have more than recovered from the ravages of World War II, they are no longer willing, or able individually, to play the forward defense roles that formerly permitted the United States to decide where, when, and how to become involved in major international disputes. Like it or not, times have changed; now it is the United States that mans the first line of defense in Europe, the Middle East, and Asia. Even if the allies in these theaters should substantially increase their defense efforts, the odds are not great that the United States could extricate itself from these forward positions in the foreseeable future. Such a withdrawal would not, in any event, make the continental United States any less vulnerable to direct attack from the combined power of nuclear weapons and long-range delivery systems.

THE SOVIET UNION. Worst of all, the Soviet Union, despite impending changes in its leadership, economic problems, and potential demographic and ethnic difficulties, gives every indication of continuing its military buildup. Because of the secrecy surrounding most Soviet activities, controversy attends the methods used to analyze the buildup and the scale and purposes of the effort. Attempts to specify the resources devoted to the Soviet defense establishment and to compare them with the U.S. allocation to defense have been criticized on a number of grounds, not the least of which is that they overestimate or underestimate the magnitude of the Soviet commitment to defense. That issue aside, problems arise in trying to determine how efficiently the USSR converts these resource inputs to outputs. Still further hazards are involved in attempting to assess the effectiveness of their military products. Nevertheless, the evidence of the buildup itself remains striking, and no one can seriously question the growth in sophistication of Soviet weapons and equipment during the past twenty years.

A few examples will illustrate both the nature of the evidence and the difficulty of determining its significance. To the best of American knowledge, since about 1964 the Soviet Union has enlarged its ground forces from about 145 divisions of varying size and readiness to more than 170 divisions of equal diversity. Current divisions, while smaller than their American counterparts, are supposed to be larger than their Soviet predecessors. The forward deployed divisions are substantially better equipped, with sizable inventories of modern tanks, armored fighting vehicles, self-propelled artillery, and organic air defenses. It is also the case that the increase in the total number of divisions coincides with the increase in the number of divisions deployed to the border of China. What is more, many Soviet divisions —whether in the East or in the West—are no better equipped and no more ready for combat than U.S. National Guard and Reserve divisions, and it seems to take the Red Army about three months to set up a major attack force—whether against Czechoslovakia in 1968, Afghanistan in 1979, or Poland in 1981.

More spectacularly, the Soviet Union has increased its strategic ballistic missile force (ICBMs and SLBMs) from about 220 in 1964 to approximately 2,350 in early 1981. All of the current missiles have better accuracy than their relatively primitive ancestors of twenty years ago, and as many as 900 of them are now armed with multiple independently targetable reentry vehicles (MIRVs). At least hypothetically, the Soviet Union will soon be capable, with about a third of its ICBM force, of destroying a large majority of the U.S. Minuteman and Titan ICBM silos, all nonalert bombers, and any SSBNs that might be in port. Although this represents a dramatic change in capability from the early 1960s and belies the notion that the Soviet Union only reacts to advances in the U.S. posture (which lacks a comparable capability), it is also the case that the Soviet strategic forces maintain a lower day-to-day alert than do the U.S. strategic forces (a state of affairs subject to conflicting interpretations), and that Soviet SSBNs are noisier and more prone to breakdowns.

Thus, while there is a continuing trend of expansion in some categories of Soviet forces, and across-the-board modernization, the purposes of these increases and changes remain uncertain. As usual, U.S. policymakers know less about Soviet problems and intentions than they do about their own.

Dealing with Uncertainty

Because of this asymmetry in information and knowledge, the U.S. military is frequently charged with using "worst cases" in its force planning. A more precise description of its practice would be that, given a range of uncertainty about adversary intentions and capabilities—and to a lesser extent about its own—the U.S. military tends to analyze future contingencies at the less favorable end of the range. However, even if the military picked more favorable cases or examined all the major possibilities along the range of uncertainty, policymakers would still have to decide how much to hedge, and at what cost, against the less favorable or less plausible cases. As the more abstractly inclined might put it, there is no single-point solution to the problem of U.S. security. What is usually at issue, given the uncertainties, is the level of confidence the United States should have in its ability to fulfill its responsibilities—through deterrence if possible, through combat if necessary—knowing that high confidence in defending against a modest and moderately competent foe could turn out to be very low confidence against a malign and highly competent enemy.

Is the world a relatively benign place, or is it a tinderbox about to burst into flames? Does the United States face at one extreme a long-range Soviet planner armed with a superbly equipped and trained force, which he is itching to use, or at the other a bumbling and defensive peasant who cannot quite come to grips with modern warfare and technology? Or do the realities fall somewhere in between?

The Approach of the Carter Five-Year Defense Program

The Carter defense program takes what might be characterized as a moderately optimistic attitude toward these uncertainties and the amount of insuring that should be done against the possibility of proving wrong. The world is seen as a more dangerous place than in the past, but not as in any way analogous to the situation in the years immediately preceding World War I or II. Leonid I. Brezhnev, indeed, is probably considered to be something of a force for restraint in a system of jealous and selfish bureaucracies—each intent on maximizing its income and power—and concerned for his part largely with the preservation of the Soviet empire. Nonetheless, the alleged ability of the Soviet marshals to unleash powerful forces with little or no warning, regionally as well as intercontinentally, has been given increased emphasis. The Soviet invasion of Afghanistan combined with the volatility of the Middle East has underscored the renewed importance of what are perhaps mistakenly described as minor contingencies, after three years of almost exclusive focus on the problems of defending Europe. Caution but not alarm might be said to be the operative watchword of the last Carter five-year defense program.

The Reagan administration currently sees the Soviet Union in a less favorable light. There is no evidence so far, however, that the president and his senior advisers rate the international climate as any more volatile than the Carter administration did in its last year. The new administration has been more willing to call a spade a spade (and even a bloody shovel); it has not been more willing to argue that the United States faces a worldwide emergency.

Strategic Nuclear Problems and Programs

This attitude of restraint no doubt derives in part from the official assessment of the current and future military balance. The five-year defense plan, with the Reagan amendments, avoids proposing any crash programs. In effect, it considers the nuclear deterrent to a direct attack on the United States as holding firm. For force planning purposes, it acknowledges that the ICBM leg of the Triad is becoming increasingly vulnerable (as shown in figure 4-1). At the same time, it accepts the probability that even after this and other possible losses (in nonalert bombers and SLBMs in port) the second-strike forces of the United States would be able to cover a majority of the targets that are incorporated into current and projected war plans. This expectation is shown in figure 4-2. The implication is that, depending on the nature of the hypothetical Soviet attack and the response option chosen by the National Command Authorities, as many as 3,000 or 4,000 warheads could be launched against the USSR.

Figure 4-1. U.S. ICBM Silo Survivability, 1979–85[a]

Expected percent surviving missiles

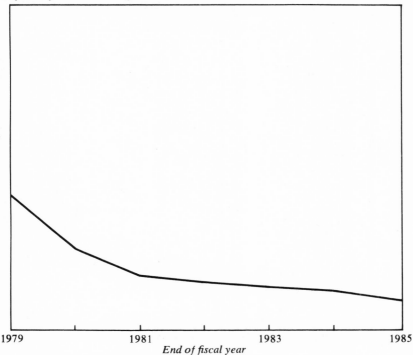

End of fiscal year

Source: *Department of Defense Annual Report Fiscal Year 1981*, p. 128.
a. This figure was designed to show the slope of the curve only. The data for the expected percent surviving missiles are classified.

Despite this retaliatory capability, the Carter defense program addresses what are seen as four problems of the U.S. strategic nuclear forces:

1. The bombers and SLBM platforms are growing old and need replacement.

2. The probability is declining that manned bombers, as currently configured, will be able to penetrate modernizing Soviet air defenses.

3. The potential loss of the ICBM leg of the Triad means that there would be fewer reliable warheads on which to count for second-strike targeting, and that the other two legs of the Triad could be eroded, because the Soviet Union would no longer have to invest

Figure 4-2. U.S. Surviving Warheads after Soviet First Strike, 1979–89[a]

Number of warheads

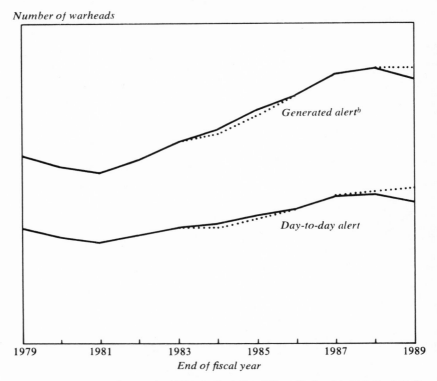

End of fiscal year

Source: *Department of Defense Annual Report Fiscal Year 1981*, p. 87. See also *Department of Defense Annual Report Fiscal Year 1982*, p. 57.
  a. This figure was designed to show the slopes of the curves only. The data for warheads are classified.
  b. The dotted lines indicate uncertainty about whether the Soviet Union will deploy a single reentry vehicle (RV) or a payload of ten RVs equipped with MIRVs on the new ICBM allowable under SALT II.

heavily in countersilo capabilities and could switch resources to anti-submarine warfare or air defenses.

4. The United States lacks a major, hypersonic, hard-target kill capability in its strategic nuclear forces. Such a capability is seen as needed to increase U.S. flexibility in the event of a Soviet attack confined initially (and perhaps solely) to strategic nuclear targets, to limit damage to the United States from follow-on strikes by Soviet ICBMs (which would otherwise enjoy a sanctuary for as many as eight hours), and to oblige the Soviet Union to commit further resources to reducing the impending vulnerability in its own ICBM

forces. Under these conditions, essential equivalence (an ill-defined concept) would be restored.

To resolve these problems, the Carter defense plan continues three major strategic acquisition programs and expands research and development in several related areas. Despite the continuing delays and difficulties in the production of the Trident submarine, a total of fifteen boats will be funded by fiscal 1986, of which six are included in the Carter plan. Backfitting of the Trident I missile into the twelve newest Poseidon boats is on schedule and will be completed by the end of fiscal 1982.

These programs are intended to ensure the survivability and safety of the SSBN force and to keep the number of warheads based on submarines at roughly current levels. Eight of the ten Polaris boats (each with sixteen launch-tubes) are scheduled for conversion to attack submarines (and possibly to platforms for cruise missiles). Warheads in the remaining Poseidon missiles (about 304, all of which are equipped with MIRVs) will be increased on the average from 10 to 14—an increase permitted under the terms of SALT II.

The Carter plan initially did not contain any acquisition program for the replacement of the B-52 and FB-111 bomber fleet. Instead, it continued programs to convert 151 B-52Gs to platforms for launching cruise missiles (20 for each bomber eventually), and to upgrade the 96 B-52Hs in their role as the main penetrating bombers of the 1980s. As Soviet look-down and shoot-down defense capabilities improve and expand, the intention was to rely increasingly on cruise missiles to penetrate these defenses, and on a possible revival of a modified, subsonic B-1 aircraft as the platform from which to launch them. However, pressure from Congress (and no doubt the Air Force), questions about the effectiveness of cruise missiles under certain conditions, and the desire to lock Soviet resources into air defense modernization programs caused research and development funds to be considerably expanded for a new bomber based on the so-called stealth technology. The Reagan administration now proposes to go a step further in this process and fund the development (at $2.4 billion) of an interim long-range combat aircraft, which could be either the subsonic B-1 or a lengthened version of the FB-111.

The most ambitious of the strategic programs, of course, deals with Missile-X. Actually, the Carter plan continues and expands two programs: one for the new missile (MX) and the other for a complex basing mode which, with the movement of 200 missiles among hardened "garages" built along specially constructed roads in the Great Basin of Nevada and Utah, would attempt to ensure the survival of at least half the missiles, even in the event of a heavy Soviet attack. The missile itself will be 92 inches in diameter—too large to fit into the Trident SSBN launch-tubes—and will weigh about 192,000 pounds. It will presumably carry 10 MIRVs, each with a yield of about 335 kilotons. Its hard-target kill capability should be much greater than that of the Minuteman III with the MK-12A nose cone. Using the cold launch technique, it could be backfitted into existing Minuteman silos without any violation of the SALT treaties.

Under the currently approved MX basing mode, which the Reagan administration has questioned, each missile would be moved on a transporter-erector-launcher among a series of twenty-three hardened "garages" branching off a straight road. If 200 missiles are deployed (with fewer than the number of warheads actually needed to cover all Soviet silos and other hard targets with two warheads), they will require 8,000 miles of roads and 4,600 garages, all of which the USSR would presumably have to hit in order to destroy the force. The destruction of this target system might require about 9,200 warheads of the appropriate yield and accuracy. The Soviet Union, in principle, could acquire such a capability by the late 1980s, especially if SALT II constraints on ICBMs armed with MIRVs were not imposed and then extended beyond 1985. As a response to this threat, the first step probably would be to lengthen the roads and add more garages for the missiles, on the assumption (which has been challenged) that it would be less costly for the United States to add roads and shelters than for the Soviet Union to add warheads, missiles, and silos. However, if the competition continued, the roads grew too long, and the United States ran out of appropriate real estate, it could, as a second step, install a ballistic missile defense of the area. Such a step would require modification or abrogation of the antiballistic missile treaty between the United States and the Soviet Union that was signed and ratified in 1972.

At present there are three major competitors to the proposed MX system. The first, intended as an interim measure, would redesign several hundred Minuteman IIIs (with the MK-12A nose cone) to make them portable and add additional silos at existing Minuteman sites to expand the number of targets for the Soviet ICBMs. At a later date the MX missile could replace the Minuteman III as the movable missile; and as a third phase the silos could be defended by a ballistic missile defense system. To relocate 200 missiles in a silo-based system would take about forty-eight hours, compared with the twelve hours to relocate the same number of missiles in a garage-based system.

The second competitor would simply deploy the MX missile to the current Minuteman silos and defend the silos with a hard-point ballistic missile defense system that is currently under development. The third competitor would be the Trident II missile, which could be backfitted into the Trident SSBNs, possibly beginning in the late 1980s. This missile could presumably have an accuracy comparable to that of the MX, but without the ability to deliver as many warheads of comparable yield. Although there is no agreement about how much each of the candidates would cost for an equivalent second-strike capability, the differences among them are unlikely to be large, especially because each incorporates a comparably expensive basing mode and method of protection.

The budget for the strategic nuclear forces could easily grow to $25 billion (in fiscal 1982 dollars) by the end of the Carter five-year plan. Despite this growth, it is doubtful that all these forces will require much more than about 10 percent of the total resources allocated to defense, including pay for retired military personnel.

Theater Nuclear Problems and Programs

Essential equivalence is said to exist between the strategic forces of the United States and the Soviet Union. It is said to be absent from the long-range theater nuclear balance in Europe and in Southwest and Northeast Asia. This is not a new situation. For more than twenty years, the Soviet Union has deployed a large force of medium-range nuclear delivery vehicles—bombers and missiles—oriented toward Western Europe and other regions on the periphery of the Soviet Union. For some years now, the USSR has been replacing this aging force with more capable Backfire bombers and mobile SS-20 ballistic missiles equipped with MIRVs.[2]

2. See Raymond L. Garthoff, "Brezhnev's Opening: The TNF Tangle," *Foreign Policy*, no. 41 (Winter 1980–81), pp. 82–94.

The nations on the periphery of the USSR do not appear any better or worse off than they were in an era of alleged American nuclear superiority as a consequence of essential equivalence at the strategic level or the lack of it in various theaters. In the past, to the extent possible, the United States has targeted the Soviet medium-range delivery vehicles with its strategic forces; no doubt it will continue to do so in the future. In the circumstances, it is doubtful that either side has, or thinks it has, an exploitable nuclear advantage in one or more of these theaters. It is equally doubtful that the United States would be any more willing to fire at targets in the USSR from platforms in Europe than from ICBM silos in America or from submarines in the Atlantic.

Be that as it may, the publicity surrounding SALT, essential equivalence, and the newer Soviet peripheral attack systems, the recent rediscovery of the long-standing strategic nuclear stalemate, especially in Europe, and the academic theories about the nature of theater nuclear conflicts and the importance of what is called escalation dominance have led some Europeans to the conclusion that the Soviet peripheral attack systems must now be directly countered. The Carter administration, for its part, was eager to demonstrate not only its willingness to deploy new nuclear systems to Europe, but also its consistency and tenacity in such a policy. Its determination was reinforced by the argument that, because the allies consider the nuclear balance in Europe to have changed, the United States must respond to this perception. The outcome has been twofold: a program to begin deploying approximately 108 Pershing II ballistic missiles and 464 ground-launched cruise missiles (GLCMs) to Western Europe by 1983 and the initiation of negotiations with the USSR to limit the deployment of long-range theater nuclear forces.

The Pershing and GLCM deployment program will entail a cost to the United States of about $5 billion over the period of the five-year defense program. The arms control negotiations will almost certainly last well beyond the program. The costs of these negotiations in terms of further U.S. deployments (to achieve essential equivalence, or some other standard) are not yet known.

Nonnuclear Problems and Programs

A basic theme of the five-year program has been that the problems of U.S. and allied conventional forces are much more serious than those of the nuclear forces and are more costly to overcome. Except for the Navy, which continued to shrink during the Carter presidency (because of small shipbuilding programs in the Nixon and Ford years), the conventional forces themselves are not yet seen as requiring any major growth, especially given the real difficulty of manning existing capabilities. The rationale behind the five-year plan has been that these forces are large enough to deal with any two nonnuclear contingencies that might arise, including even a large-scale attack by the Warsaw Pact on Central Europe. Whether the conventional forces could respond to the contingencies in a timely fashion, fight with full effectiveness, and sustain themselves in combat at least as long as potential enemies has been, however, considered much less certain, particularly when the Soviet Union, despite its record, is credited with being able to attack areas contiguous to it on very short notice.

The problems of effectiveness are judged to have arisen primarily from the shortage of funds for the spare parts, major overhauls, and experienced military personnel required to help keep operational equipment in good working order. Because operation and maintenance activities are alleged to have been shortchanged in the past and because military pay has been eroded by inflation, key enlisted personnel have been leaving the services for more lucrative civilian work, and substantial percentages of U.S. ships, aircraft, and tracked vehicles have not been considered capable of performing their assigned missions. Flying hours and steaming days have fallen, not only because of maintenance and overhaul problems, but also because of the rising cost of petroleum products. Combat effectiveness allegedly has fallen commensurately.

From the standpoint of the five-year defense program, at least in its current form, the quickest and cheapest way to restore combat effectiveness is not to add more maintenance-prone force structure but to repair and exploit fully the capability of those forces already in existence. In line with this philosophy, military pay in general was increased by 11.7 percent in fiscal 1981, and the Reagan administration plans to raise the total by $420 million in 1981 and by nearly $1.9 billion in 1982. In addition, special efforts are being made to retain military personnel critical to matériel readiness. Operation and maintenance accounts are being funded at levels that will reduce overhaul backlogs to appropriate peacetime levels (usually considered to be 10 to 15 percent of the equipment), restore inventories of spare parts to the point at which deliveries are prompt and cannibalization of other systems is abandoned, and increase operating rates for ships, aircraft, and ground combat vehicles. As a consequence, operation and maintenance has grown from $46.6 billion in fiscal 1980 to $64.1 billion in fiscal 1982. The real increase over the two-year period amounts to more than 15 percent. This "full funding" of the accounts will presumably be maintained over the period of the five-year defense program.

What constitutes responsiveness to a contingency depends on the nature of the threat and the theater being threatened. For three years the Carter administration, in focusing almost exclusively on the European theater, postulated a threat to Germany from the Warsaw Pact that would be nearly ninety divisions in size and would materialize in several weeks. Since the European allies were not expected to furnish more than a few major reinforcements to the units already on the line, this meant that the United States would have to bear the main burden of stabilizing the central front. Yet U.S. reinforcements, with the airlift then on hand or likely to become available in the foreseeable future, would not arrive early enough to prevent a large, fast-moving Warsaw Pact attack from rupturing the allied line.

To extract additional contributions from the European members of NATO and to lay the groundwork for a much speedier deployment of American reinforcements, the United States once again (as it had several times before) launched an elaborate long-term defense plan for the Alliance. At its center has been a U.S. program to store full sets of army division equipment (known as POMCUS) and large war reserve stocks in Germany. These would permit troops to be flown rapidly to Germany, where they would draw the stored equipment and move to the front before an attack.

Whether such a scheme could be made to work on a large scale, or could even be fully tested, has been questioned. Nonetheless, four division sets have already been pre-positioned in Germany, and the Carter program calls for adding two more. At the same time, preparations are being made to deploy as many as forty-two squadrons of fighter-attack aircraft to Europe within ten days. Although the movement of so many ground and air units would put a heavy strain on the KC-135 tanker force—and do so at a time when the Strategic Air Command would need heavy tanker support also—the Carter 1982 budget does not call for the acquisition of any new KC-10 tanker aircraft beyond the twelve already funded through the fiscal 1981 budget. Now, however, the Reagan administration requests $500 million for eight additional KC-10s and about $220 million to begin replacing the engines in the old KC-135 tanker fleet. The newer tankers would be available to support deployments to another theater, as well as Europe, provided that such deployment occurred well before or after the European contingency.

Potential trouble in the area of the Persian Gulf became a source of major concern to the Department of Defense even before the oil embargo of 1973. However, the threat remained difficult to define for planning purposes, and did not begin to attract funding and forces until after the seizure of the American hostages in Iran and the Soviet invasion of Afghanistan. The headquarters for a Rapid Deployment Force was put together in the wake of these events, with a deployment to the Persian Gulf as its first mission. Soon thereafter, two attack carrier battle groups drawn from the Sixth Fleet (in the Mediterranean) and the Seventh Fleet (in the Western Pacific) went on patrol in the Arabian Sea. Since then, the carrier battle groups have become a more or less permanent fixture in the area, and a reinforced Marine Corps battalion aboard amphibious ships has also been deployed to the Arabian Sea.

Despite these changes, the Carter administration took the position that the capabilities already incorporated in the force structure for a minor contingency (say three or four divisions and five or six fighter wings) were sufficient to cope with an emergency in the gulf. The problems raised by this particular set of dangers were seen to be of a different order than would be solved by additional combat force structure. These problems arose from such difficulties as the increased probability of short-warning attacks by Soviet land forces in the vicinity of the theater; the distance from the United States to the Persian Gulf, computed for airlift at about 9,500 nautical miles; the lack of any en route or forward bases under U.S. control nearer than Diego Garcia in the Indian Ocean, or of war reserve stocks and communications close by; and finally, the difficulties of terrain and climate and the acute shortage of potable water in key parts of the theater—so different from the problems of Europe and Northeast Asia.

Not only did the Carter administration direct its main programs for the Persian Gulf both in fiscal 1981 and in the current five-year defense program toward the solution of these problems; the Reagan administration seems to have accepted these solutions also. The new naval and Marine Corps forward deployments in the vicinity of the gulf have apparently been considered sufficient for presence and to guard against surprise attacks from the north. Hence the key short-term measures have emphasized the acquisition of base rights (however tenuous) in Kenya, Somalia, Egypt, and Oman, and the improvement of ports and bases in these countries and expansion of the base at Diego Garcia in the Indian Ocean; the earmarking, training, and equipment of general purpose forces for operations in the theater; and the improvement of the U.S. capability for rapidly reinforcing the deployed forces. Particularly noteworthy has been the acquisition of seven commercial cargo ships that are now stationed in the Indian Ocean with the equipment and initial supplies for a full Marine Corps brigade force of 12,000 men. In the event of a crisis and warning of an impending attack, they will permit the troops of the brigade to be flown to the theater in a few days and to join the equipment. In the short run, perhaps an additional light brigade with its equipment could be airlifted to the area within a week, and as much as a division could be brought in by fast sealift ships within thirty to forty days.

For the longer term, the Carter defense program, as it now stands, stresses the acquisition of 12 specially designed maritime pre-positioning ships for the forward deployment of additional equipment and supplies, up to 130 new CX long-range airlift aircraft to supplement the current fleet of C-5s and lengthened C-141s, and the buildup of stocks of war reserve matériel and combat consumables. In addition, the Army is beginning to experiment (presently at modest cost) with the concept of a new light infantry division that would be much more easily airlifted than current units—which are not tailored to existing aircraft—but would have the firepower and mobility to deal with even the heaviest of the Soviet tank divisions.

All these preparations, both short term and longer run, as shown in table 4-4, will presumably make the Rapid Deployment Force an all-purpose, minor-contingency force, just as the preparations for Europe are alleged to provide the United States with a flexible major-contingency capability—able to go anywhere anytime. The greater likelihood, however, is that the country will end up with forces

Table 4-4. Estimated Ten-Year Costs of Rapid Deployment Force Programs in the Carter Defense Program

Program	Billions of 1982 dollars
130 outsize airlift aircraft (CX)	17.2
12 maritime pre-positioning ships and equipment	7.3
8 SL-7 fast sealift ships	0.9
12 additional KC-10 long-range tanker aircraft	1.0
Improvement of facilities at Diego Garcia and other bases	2.0
Pre-positioned war reserve stocks	1.0
Naval presence in the Indian Ocean and Rapid Deployment Force exercises	3.5
Total	32.9

Source: *Washington Post*, August 10, 1980; author's estimates, which include the costs of minor and major procurement.

trained for and able to deploy to Europe and the Persian Gulf but not particularly adaptable to or available for deployment and combat in other parts of the world.

It was the hope in the early 1960s that a strategic economy of force could be achieved by minimizing overseas deployments and concentrating most U.S. ground and tactical air forces in the continental United States. With the support of selected stocks pre-positioned overseas, fast deployment logistic ships, and airlift, these forces would then be able to move from this central location and respond to contingencies wherever they might occur.

Whether this degree of flexibility has ever been realistically attainable during the past twenty years is open to question. But successive administrations have, for all practical purposes, endorsed the concept at the same time that they have withheld from the forces (particularly the ground forces) the wherewithal to implement the strategy. What were considered the necessary amount and balance of overseas pre-positioning, logistic ships, and airlift have not been acquired. Deployed units (if not numbers of people) have been increased rather than decreased in Europe, and the attempt to withdraw forces from Korea has been abandoned. The renewed alarm about a surprise conventional attack in Europe has had the effect of orienting the majority of the general purpose forces to the central region of NATO. Perhaps most important of all, the task of training and orienting large and complex organizations for a particular contingency—whether in Europe, Korea, or the Persian Gulf—appears to be so great that it precludes the kind of flexibility and all-purpose conventional capability that was envisaged in the strategic concept of the early 1960s. If indeed that is the case, it suggests that the basis for planning U.S. force size and composition will have to change in the future.

The one branch of the U.S. military that can be said to have preserved a large measure of flexibility is the Navy. As it demonstrated by its deployments in the Indian Ocean, it can with a small number of key overseas bases shift its capital ships from one ocean to another without elaborate changes in training, equipment, and logistics. It is evident, however, that the shift did not occur without a certain amount of pain. The Navy, like the other services, lacks the personnel to man and maintain fully the equipment it already has. What is more, the total operating force of general purpose ships (active, reserve, and auxiliary) will consist of only 526 ships in fiscal 1982, whereas the Carter administration had foreseen the need by 1990 for about 550 ships to execute its strategy of long-range blockade, convoy, and power projection. This led to a fourth Carter five-year shipbuilding program of 80 new ships over the period of the five-year program. Such a program, together with the 79 ships previously authorized but not yet delivered, was expected to enable the Navy to reach the goal of 550 ships and even stabilize the force at close to that level through the 1980s, provided that older ships were not phased out more rapidly than is now planned.

The Reagan amendments add to this program in several ways. First, they increase the fiscal 1982 shipbuilding program from fourteen to eighteen ships (about the same as planned by the Carter administration a year ago in a previous five-year shipbuilding program) by adding an AEGIS-equipped air defense cruiser (CG-47), two frigates (FFG-7s), and one nuclear attack submarine (SSN-688) at a cost of over $2 billion. Second, they reactivate two battleships, the *New Jersey* and the *Iowa,* and one aircraft carrier, the *Oriskany,* at a cost of more than $1 billion by fiscal 1983. Third, they request long-lead items for a new amphibious ship (LSD-41) and a new nuclear attack carrier (CVN-72) at a cost of about $700 million. Full funding for these two ships will be requested in fiscal 1983. Presumably the older and less capable ships being reactivated not only will respond "perceptually" to the appearance of the new Soviet *Kirov*-class strike cruisers; they will also provide the nucleus for fifteen battle groups until such time as the Navy again can reach its traditional peacetime goal of fifteen modern, large-deck carriers. Achieving that goal will take quite a few years and many people and dollars.

In the Carter fiscal 1982 budget, funding for the general purpose forces would amount to $74.4 billion (compared to $14.5 billion for the strategic forces). This total does not include more than $3.4 billion for airlift and sealift or $10.3 billion for the National Guard and Reserve forces, even though both programs contain what are primarily general purpose forces. At least 75 percent of the defense budget now goes to these forces and their support. The Reagan amendments actually increase this percentage by adding more than $17 billion to the three programs, with $15.1 billion for the general purpose forces alone.

Assessing the Future Military Balance

The Carter defense plan had five major objectives for its programs: modernization of all three legs of the strategic nuclear Triad; strengthening of the theater nuclear deterrent in Europe with the deployment of intermediate-range ballistic and cruise missiles; improvements in the rapid deployment capabilities of the general purpose forces, with emphasis on the European and Southwest Asian theaters; increased readiness for these forces; and gradual modernization of the nonnuclear ground, naval, and air capabilities, with a growing emphasis on all-weather, precision delivery systems. The Reagan amendments essentially accelerate somewhat the process of reaching these goals.

Are they the appropriate goals for the United States? Should the nation accept the direction and pace of the Carter program? Should it do so but move at the more rapid rate inherent in the Reagan amendments? Or does the future suggest that still other goals and programs should be considered?

One way to answer these questions is to assess what U.S. military capabilities can actually accomplish. Inevitably, judgments on this score are bound to vary, especially when the popular but questionable comparisons of equipment and other inputs are abandoned. Nonetheless, what might be considered a median assessment—using less than the most pessimistic assumptions about American, allied, and enemy performance under hypothetical combat conditions—would yield conclusions of the following order about the so-called military balance in the years ahead.

The Strategic Balance

U.S. strategic nuclear forces on a second strike should have a high probability of covering a fairly comprehensive target system in the Soviet Union, of withholding attacks against parts of that system as directed by the National Command Authorities, and of maintaining a postexchange reserve of perhaps one hundred or more deliverable warheads. But the programmed forces would still lack a high-confidence ability to destroy hard targets during the first hour or so of a nuclear exchange. Furthermore, if the later-arriving cruise missiles and gravity bombs were dedicated to hard-target destruction, other important parts of the target system could be left uncovered. There is also at least a small probability that penetrating bombers—whether lengthened FB-111s, modernized B-52Hs, or B-1 aircraft—would suffer higher attrition than estimated because of improved Soviet air defenses.

It is now rather widely accepted that neither the United States nor the Soviet Union is capable of a full disarming first strike against the other's strategic forces. It is increasingly recognized that strategic target systems can, and probably should, comprise more than urban areas and population, and that it might be desirable to withhold attacks on some of these targets. Less fully understood is the fact that strategic forces, while they now have a limited retargeting capability, are relatively inflexible instruments of war, and that parts of the total (even if they survive) have limited endurance. In the circumstances, it is conceivable that after an initial exchange one side could cover more types of targets, and a greater number of targets, than the other. How significant these asymmetries would prove in the chaos and disaster of nuclear war is open to debate. It remains difficult at present to explain the process by which a Soviet-American exchange, however initiated, could result in such large, meaningful, and exploitable asymmetries as to tempt either side to launch an attack and thus make mutual deterrence unstable. Because of this stability, it is equally difficult to understand why policymakers would be intimidated in a crisis by the prospect of these asymmetries. But it is undoubtedly the case that, with increased funding, the U.S. deterrent could be given a higher probability of covering its designated target system on a second strike. It is unlikely that extended deterrence of nonnuclear attacks by means of the strategic forces—if that deterrence ever existed—could be restored by increased funding of these forces.

The Theater Nuclear Balance

For what it may be worth, U.S. theater nuclear forces, at least those based on land, will probably continue to be vulnerable to a Soviet surprise attack, especially if such an attack preceded any conflict at all. The deployment of Pershing II ballistic missiles and GLCMs will not appreciably alter the situation. It is not clear, however, that this vulnerability has the same implications as would a comparable weakness at the strategic level. As the Soviet Union has acknowledged, limiting the use of nuclear weapons to a battlefield or even a theater would probably prove difficult. The presence or absence of these forces has not been demonstrated to be of critical importance to the outcome of a full-scale nuclear exchange. Still, the case can be made that even the very low probability of controlling escalation should be exploited. Rather than more delivery systems, however, steps in this direction would mean greater peacetime mobility for delivery systems, more survivable command-control-communications in the theater, and better data on both sides about the origin and destination of aircraft and missiles.

The Conventional Land Balance

Any assessment of the conventional military balance must consider both the specific theaters of potential conflict and the possibility that two or more of these theaters might become active simultaneously or in close sequence. Estimates of the situation in Europe usually assume that the Soviet Union will continue its military modernization at about current rates, and that the other Warsaw Pact nations would join in a full-scale assault on Western Europe. Under these conditions, NATO has sufficient forces to give it a fair chance of withstanding the early phases of such an attack. Although this assessment will seem excessively optimistic to some, it could be asserted with even fewer qualifications if it were not for three continuing risks. The first is that the Alliance would not respond promptly to the warning of the Warsaw Pact buildup. The second is that the Soviet Union would draw on its forces in the Far East and Central Asia to launch a second attack on the western front before NATO could recuperate from the first attack and deploy further reinforcements. The third risk is that the European allies would deplete war reserve stocks earlier than would the Warsaw Pact.

Despite the well-advertised buildup of North Korean ground forces in the 1970s, there is still no persuasive evidence that these forces would have a high probability of outflanking or breaking through the heavy fortifications south of the demilitarized zone and defeating South Korean forces before U.S. ground and tactical air capabilities on the scene, and other units in Okinawa, could intervene. Indeed, if all the U.S. ground and air forces in the theater deployed before the attack, the odds would strongly favor a bloody repulse of the North Korean assault.

Assessment of the situation in the Persian Gulf is complicated by major uncertainties about future U.S. deployments near the theater, and how a major military challenge might arise. For planning purposes, a Soviet invasion of Iran has been considered the relevant contingency, but the Iraqis have also been characterized as the Prussians of the Gulf. If the Soviet Union continues to follow past practice and takes several months to make ready an attack force based on the ground and air units it stations in the Trans-Caucasus Military District, and if the United States uses this time to increase its tactical air forces in the theater, the chances are better than even that the Soviet Union, under attack from the air, could not move (much less support) a large ground capability south of the Zagros Mountains. Only relatively modest U.S. ground forces might then be necessary to hold a beachhead along the upper reaches of the Persian Gulf—if that were the initial objective. However, if U.S. policymakers did not exploit this warning time and neither significant U.S. tactical air nor ground forces were within striking distance, the Soviet Union would have a high probability of advancing through the difficult terrain of Kurdistan. The probability that the United States could then establish a major beachhead in southwestern Iran would be correspondingly low.

The five-year defense program will admittedly fund a considerable amount of additional airlift to facilitate the rapid deployment of tactical air and ground forces. But whether the necessary land bases would be available to receive such a deployment is not at all certain.

Thus, without somewhat larger forces stationed in the theater, it is conceivable that even a quite modest defense objective in or near Iran could not be achieved.

The Maritime Balance

At sea, there is good reason to believe that the programmed naval forces would have a high probability of preventing the main Soviet surface fleets from operating outside their home waters in the Barents Sea and the Sea of Japan. Soviet submarines and long-range naval aircraft would thus become the main threat to the Navy's ability to control those sea-lanes needed to reinforce and supply U.S. and allied forward deployments and to conduct power projection operations with carrier and amphibious forces against moderately defended areas.

In the face of the submarine and aircraft threat, the standard expectation is that naval antisubmarine warfare and antiair warfare forces, especially with the addition of the AEGIS air defense system, would have a high probability of destroying Soviet submarines, aircraft, and cruise missiles through a process of long-range blockade and attrition. U.S. losses of capital ships and merchant vessels would probably be substantial but acceptable during a campaign estimated to last about three months. However, the programmed forces would not be able to perform these missions and at the same time take aggressive action against Soviet home naval bases, if that should be thought desirable. Command of the seas in the Nelson or Mahan tradition of defeating the enemy fleet in a naval battle thus would almost certainly prove beyond the Navy's reach. This, it should be added, would probably be the case whether the Navy had twelve, fifteen, or eighteen battle groups.

Multiple Contingencies

Whatever the probability that the United States and its allies can handle any single contingency, that probability changes for the worse if more than one contingency develops in a short period. The five-year defense program supposedly provides the capability to deal more or less simultaneously with one major and one lesser contingency. Should these two contingencies arise in Europe and Korea, the force structure would not necessarily be strained beyond its capacity, although strategic mobility forces and logistic systems might well snap under the combined pressure. The Navy might also find that it lacked sufficient antisubmarine and antiair warfare capability and particularly surface combatants to protect fully the sea-lanes in the Atlantic, the Mediterranean, and the Pacific, although the European allies could contribute in this regard. Should the two contingencies occur in the Persian Gulf and Europe, the difficulties could prove still greater. How much greater would depend in part on the size and readiness of U.S. and allied deployments in the gulf. But still another problem could arise in that a military emergency in Europe or the gulf would probably set off the alarm bells in other parts of the world, and particularly in Northeast Asia. If U.S. forces there became tied down, policymakers would find a force structure deficit on their hands. Somehow they would have to allocate that deficit—as many as four divisions—between Europe and the gulf. Obviously if military crises occurred more or less simultaneously in Europe, the gulf, Korea, and the Caribbean, the deficit would prove even larger and more dangerous.

Net Assessment

It is relatively easy, in sum, to visualize conditions under which the Carter defense program forces would fail to achieve such relatively straightforward objectives as fully covering a comprehensive nuclear target system in the USSR, surviving a surprise nuclear attack in Europe, and establishing firm forward defenses with conventional capabilities under the pressure of attacks in two or more theaters. Thus the issue for the future becomes: how seriously should these more testing conditions be taken, and how far beyond the Carter defense program, as it now stands, might it be desirable to go in order to hedge against what could be a more threatening future?

The Range of Uncertainty

No doubt there are some who see the current international situation as reminiscent of 1938 and assume that the Soviet gerontocracy is like a dog straining on the weakening leash of deterrence. But even such pessimists do not propose programs commensurate with the purported peril. Nowhere is there a demand for prompt national mobilization, the freezing of weapons designs, the accelerated production of as many equipped and trained combat units as time permits. The implicit assumption, even among those most concerned about U.S. military vulnerabilities, seems to be that deterrence is decaying but has not yet collapsed. Obviously if their proposals to reduce Minuteman vulnerability and increase high-energy laser and particle-beam research are any indication of what they have in mind, they must postulate that a span of some years is available in which to begin the process of halting the alleged decay in the U.S. deterrent, becoming competitive with the Soviet Union, and restoring American military preeminence.

This assumption could prove optimistic. The Munich analogy may be a weak one. Still, it is not difficult in 1981 to imagine a rapid deterioration in international stability brought on by events outside the immediate control of either the United States or the Soviet Union. This is not to suggest that greater stability is out of the question, but only that it tends to be less expected. As usual, the crystal ball is clouded. Uncertainties abound about the future weight of the many factors that must be taken into account in U.S. defense planning.

Allied Contributions

Certainly a matter for argument is whether the allies, more than the United States, can be held to an elaborate, long-term defense plan or to a fixed annual real increase in their defense budgets. Such an expectation is even less likely to be realized when arms control and cooperation with the Soviet Union have been given so much play, and when so little is done to dissuade the allies from their long-standing belief that the nuclear deterrent and the threat of a U.S. first-use of nuclear weapons relieve them from the need to make a costly conventional defense effort. Indeed, to the extent that the United States might hope that Europe would assume an increased responsibility for its own nonnuclear defense, and thereby release U.S. resources for the protection of the Persian Gulf, that hope seems likely to be dashed. Without a full-scale review of and new consensus about the problem of collective defense in this quasi-nuclear age, the European and Japanese allies of the United States, despite all their collective wealth, will probably continue to act as poor relations in the realm of international security.

SALT Constraints

It seems equally evident that such constraints as SALT has imposed on the strategic nuclear competition are likely to weaken with time unless the Reagan administration suddenly reverses itself and supports the ratification of SALT II. Until now, both the United States and the Soviet Union have abided by the terms of SALT I, even though its terms expired in 1977. The provisions of SALT II may be similarly honored, and the United States at least may continue to insist that any of its new strategic systems be manageable within the SALT framework and permit adequate verification of their numbers and characteristics. The higher probability, however, is that pressures will grow to make verification secondary to the survivability of the systems, and that hard-point ballistic missile defense will return to favor as a way of solving the problem of ICBM vulnerability, even if it should entail a modification or abrogation of the 1972 antiballistic missile treaty that is to be reviewed in 1982.

Soviet Nuclear Planning

Exactly how the USSR might attack their strategic nuclear planning problem under these fluid conditions is bound to be a major uncertainty. The Carter administration consistently asserted that, without the constraints of SALT II, the Soviet Union would exploit its "hot" production lines to add to its already large total of ICBMs and SLBMs, and would fractionate still further the nuclear payloads of these missiles, thus ending up with far more strategic nuclear delivery vehicles and warheads than the United States could possibly deploy in the same time. But whether the USSR would actually embark on such a costly program—and at the same time refurbish its air defenses, begin its own ballistic missile defense deployments, produce a new long-range bomber, and continue or expand its current civil defense efforts—is quite uncertain. The constraints of SALT II will permit the Soviet Union to deploy at least 12,000 warheads on its ICBMs, SLBMs, and bombers. Such an inventory will enable it, even on a second strike, to cover an enormous target system in the United States—military, economic, political, and urban. Additional warheads would appear to be superfluous, and a further fractionation of missile payloads would only serve to complicate the USSR's targeting and control problem, if it has any serious interest in selective targeting, options, and control. The history of Soviet endeavors nonetheless shows a fascination with sheer numbers, and the Soviet leadership may feel somehow more secure or more threatening with a quantitative advantage over the United States in strategic nuclear delivery vehicles and warheads. A continued Soviet nuclear buildup cannot therefore be precluded if SALT II remains in limbo or becomes the subject of lengthy renegotiation.

The Role of Strategic Asymmetries

How much difference such a buildup would make is another matter, given the number of targets the USSR will be able to cover within the constraints of SALT. Much of the debate about the nuclear balance is conducted in traditional terms, and ratios—especially those favoring the USSR—are often used to project the outcome of a strategic nuclear exchange. But it is by no means clear that beyond a certain point these force or warhead or throw-weight or megatonnage ratios have much meaning. When nuclear weapons are used they destroy targets and contaminate the atmosphere; they do not seize, hold, or occupy territory. There are, moreover, only so many targets of value to a society, and there is only so much atmosphere to contaminate.

To develop strategic nuclear options, to have the choice of hitting or not hitting a range of military, economic, political, and urban targets—while desirable—is a costly business. Weaknesses in surveillance and command-control are not easy to overcome; strategic forces cannot be fully retargeted at great speed; information for retargeting may be difficult to acquire during a nuclear exchange. Under the circumstances, flexibility can best be achieved by deploying sufficient nuclear delivery vehicles and warheads to cover the entire target list designated by the National Command Authorities and by slicing up the list into option packages that can be covered by specified forces. Thus the entire force could be released in an all-out attack on the enemy target list, or portions of it could be withheld, depending on the objectives of the enemy and the National Command Authorities. The rigidity of these capabilities, in other words, complicates the achievement of any economy of force; more targets mean more forces. Still, there is a point beyond which adding more targets to the list and more weapons to cover them makes little if any sense, regardless of what an opponent might be doing.

This is not to say that the United States has already reached such a point. However, U.S. forces, even without ICBMs, will continue to have the capability to cover a long list of soft targets on a second strike; under the programs in the Carter defense plan hard targets will be reliably covered, as will an increased number of soft targets. Adding to the Carter plan—as the Reagan administration proposes to do with $2.4 billion allocated in fiscal 1982 for the development of a long-range combat aircraft—may still be worthwhile, both to assure a higher probability that aerodynamic vehicles can penetrate Soviet defenses in the late 1980s and to add the appearance of equality to the long-standing reality of nuclear stalemate and stability. But it is hard to argue convincingly that the uncertainties in this area have grown to such magnitude as to warrant crash programs in the near-term or high priority in the longer run. Perhaps such a case can be made; it has not yet been persuasively argued.

The Role of Theater Nuclear Asymmetries

Much the same conclusion seems warranted where the long-range theater nuclear forces are concerned. It is bound to be troublesome politically that the Soviet Union, while professing a desire for restraint in the nuclear competition, should have taken the initiative in modernizing its long-range theater nuclear forces. It is even conceivable that there are those in the USSR who believe it possible to gain an advantage at the nonnuclear level or at the level of battlefield nuclear exchanges, and at the same time, through escalation dominance—that is, great enough power to discourage the United States or NATO from escalating to longer-range nuclear exchanges —to keep any campaign controlled in a way that would ensure the achievement of Soviet military and political objectives.

There could possibly be circumstances in which it would be desirable to remove any serious prospect of such escalation dominance and go beyond the program of the Carter defense plan. But one would have to be hard pressed to argue that escalation dominance for NATO (and perhaps all other U.S. allies) or its denial to the USSR should be a matter of urgent concern or high priority. Politics may have required the Pershing and GLCM programs: prudence dictates caution in pursuing these expensive developments beyond existing commitments.

This is not to say that the systems already deployed or programmed for Europe should be left as vulnerable as they now are. Nor is it to argue against the deployment of enhanced radiation weapons ("neutron" bombs) and other more modern, economical, and controllable short-range nuclear capabilities, however much their benefits and dangers may have been exaggerated. But whether more needs to be done in shoring up the tactical nuclear deterrent, or done more urgently than in the five-year defense program, is highly debatable. The United States is no more willing than it has been for thirty-five years to initiate the use of nuclear weapons, and there is no strong evidence to suggest that the Soviet Union favors nuclear adventure either. As used to be said, but has since been forgotten, any use of nuclear weapons is a leap into the unknown. Certainly American political leaders have avoided such leaps, especially upon discovering that no one could describe operationally how to exploit a nuclear advantage, how to bring an end to the "war," or how to avoid catastrophic damage.

Soviet Nonnuclear Planning

While it is difficult to say that the United States will behave any differently than it did when it allegedly enjoyed meaningful nuclear superiority, the argument has been made that the Soviet Union with nuclear superiority (assuming it can be defined) will behave more bellicosely and aggressively than it has in the past—when it seized Eastern Europe, blockaded Berlin, supplied the North Koreans and the North Vietnamese, and deployed nuclear missiles to Cuba. Certainly the possibility cannot be precluded, although the current evidence for it is mixed. On the one hand, there is the case of Afghanistan (even though it may represent no greater departure from a harsh tradition than the suppression of Czechoslovakia in 1968) and the disruptive support for South Yemen, Syria, Angola, Ethiopia, and Libya. On the other hand, there is the relative restraint shown toward China, over which the Soviet Union surely commands an impressive nuclear superiority. Indeed, the general impression of the USSR is that it remains as defensively paranoid as ever, however superficially glittering its nuclear prospects may appear to be.

Any optimism on this score, however, must be tempered by the caution that in the "thee or me" world apparently inhabited by the Soviet leaders, the absence of control over neighboring and even more distant nations is considered potentially threatening; therefore, opportunities must be seized to cause difficulties for and weaken those potential enemies—whether in Europe, Africa, the Middle East, or Latin America. In addition, of course, if the Soviet empire itself shows signs of crumbling, as well it may under the shocks of revived regionalism, ethnic rivalries, energy shortages, and economic dislocations, the danger that a decaying but militarily still powerful Soviet Union could lash out against imagined foreign foes cannot be entirely discounted. Indeed, the distinction between the defensive and the all-conquering USSR, while important for many purposes, may not be all that significant from the standpoint of U.S. and allied defense planning.

How much lashing out the Soviet Union is capable of doing, particularly with its nonnuclear capabilities, is one of the largest uncertainties confronting the U.S. planners. Generally speaking, Soviet forces are more mobile than in the past now that, in addition to large quantities of tanks, they have acquired modern armored fighting vehicles, self-propelled artillery, organic air defenses on tracked vehicles, helicopter gunships, and relatively long-range, sophisticated fighter-attack aircraft. The USSR has shown, moreover, that it can sustain modest military operations in Afghanistan, hold its other forward deployments more or less in place, and still put together a threat of major proportions to Poland.

But despite the increased firepower and mobility, despite the growing possibility that the Soviet Union can create military threats in several theaters more or less simultaneously and that states such as North Korea, Vietnam, and Cuba might be tempted or encouraged to exploit such a tense international situation, some of the old problems remain with the Soviet conventional forces. Only about a third of the ground forces would qualify as approximately combat-ready by U.S. standards. Many of the divisions in this category lack the maintenance and support units necessary to sustain them in combat. For these reasons, whether it was Czechoslovakia in 1968, Afghanistan in 1979, or Poland in 1980–81, the Soviet Union took several months to set up its deployments and ready its forces for action. This mobilization time may decline in the years ahead. But the probability should remain low that the USSR could or would launch surprise nonnuclear attacks out of the blue, without the warning that would come from an international crisis, the call-up of ill-trained reservists, and the movement of troops.

Even so, the United States already faces, and will face increasingly in the years ahead, serious problems of its own. One set has to do with the most effective way of dealing with warning. A second set centers on how to cope with the possibility of several more or less simultaneous military crises.

Warning and Its Use

Warning can be exploited through some mix of forward deployed forces, airlift, sealift, and pre-positioned equipment and supplies. If warning of an attack comes early, is reliable, and is acted upon promptly, forward deployments can be minimized and relatively cheap sealift can be used to move forces and equipment into position. If warning comes late, is more unreliable, or exploited belatedly, forward deployments had better be increased and greater emphasis placed on airlift and the pre-positioning of equipment.

The United States continues to try to minimize forward deployments while emphasizing pre-positioned matériel and airlift. It assumes, in effect, that warning will come quite early but may be ambiguous and acted on only after some delay. Thus nearly six division-equivalents and twenty-seven fighter squadrons are regularly stationed in Europe to help guard against surprises from the Soviet forces in Eastern Europe, with the expectation, in the event of a Soviet buildup, that as many as nine more divisions and forty-two more fighter squadrons would be moved in on short notice by means of pre-positioning and airlift. Much lighter forward deployments characterize the situation in Korea and the Persian Gulf.

Force Flexibility

Despite the increased specialization of forces to these three theaters, as perhaps has been inevitable, the assumption remains that U.S. forces are "fungible." There is an increasing probability, however, that the assumption is becoming more fiction than fact, and that in any event conditions could arise in which the need to reinforce more or less simultaneously in such disparate and distant areas as Europe, the Persian Gulf, and Korea would appear urgent. Under these conditions, the active-duty forces would be too few in number to cover all three theaters; reserves would not be sufficiently ready to make up the deficits; and airlift would fall far short of the demand.

Strategic Concepts

The Carter defense program contains a number of efforts to reduce the strain on the airlift: more pre-positioning of equipment in

Europe, maritime pre-positioning ships for the Persian Gulf and other theaters, and increased airlift. However, the forces are still planned on the basis of having to deal simultaneously with no more than one major and one lesser contingency, all forces supposedly being flexible enough to adapt rapidly to any theater regardless of current equipment and previous training.

Whether this is any longer a realistic basis for planning even for the immediate future is open to question. The uncertainty is particularly great given what might happen in the gulf, where the stakes are high, U.S. deployments are modest, and worldwide repercussions would follow from a further disruption of oil supplies to the industrialized nations. If more is to be done in shoring up U.S. military capabilities, there is a strong case for giving the highest priority, both now and in the longer run, to strengthening the U.S. forces oriented toward the Persian Gulf, Europe, and Korea, and in that order. Next in importance, especially given the amount of U.S. equipment and supplies being committed to Europe through the POMCUS program, is the buildup of war reserves for the other two theaters.

Constraints

If these considerations and the uncertainties surrounding them argue for increases in the original fiscal 1982 budget and Carter defense program, certain other factors dictate that additional resources be applied with considerable selectivity. Despite the flexibility and power of the U.S. economy, a large and relatively youthful population, and an abundance still of many of the raw materials needed for military purposes, there are several constraints on the ability of the country to change its military posture with great speed.

MILITARY PERSONNEL. Perhaps the most troublesome of these constraints relates to the acquisition and retention of military personnel. With the roughly two million active-duty and more than 850,000 reserve personnel now in the armed forces, the military services seem to be able (with some difficulty) to man the currently authorized force structure according to the standards prescribed by Congress. With the new pay scales that have now gone into effect and the further increases proposed by the Reagan administration, whether the right mix of recruits and career specialists can be maintained still remains to be tested. What has already become evident, however, is that significant additions to the forces will prove expensive (even if their cost can be kept from cascading through the rest of the forces) and that the draft—or more accurately, selective service—will remain a politically difficult step to take, short of a generally recognized national emergency. Proposals for additions to the five-year defense program will have to take these difficulties into account and develop realistic measures to deal with them.

THE WAR PRODUCTION BASE. At the same time, recognition will have to be given to the shrinkage in the U.S. war production base that took place in the 1970s as the United States withdrew from Vietnam and reduced the force structure and posture below its prewar size and composition. The production base obviously can be expanded again, but the expansion will not be immediate and will compete with other programs for resources. Even with such an expansion, moreover, modern weapons—if they remain as complex as they are now—will take a considerable amount of time to produce in quantity. If the United States were to decide immediately to produce four new nuclear-powered attack carriers, and Newport News Shipbuilding were to open a second graving dock (as would be feasible), it would probably take eight years to deliver the first two carriers and another six years to deliver the next two. In some instances, increased production could also place a strain on existing supplies of domestic and imported raw materials and might require the development of more available substitutes.

To the extent that new orders through the regular defense acquisition process could remove these constraints, the problem would obviously disappear. It is conceivable, however, that increased demand would simply result in large backlogs for the contractors and that, in any event, it will prove desirable to expand parts of the production base before deciding on a larger force structure. Without such planning and insuring, the production throttle might be moved forward briskly, but to no discernible effect.

Hedges against Uncertainty

Several conclusions suggest themselves from any examination of the uncertainties and constraints that face the nation in providing for military security during the coming decade. The first is that while the Carter defense program and the Reagan amendments appear to make good progress toward meeting what might be termed the standard or median dangers, they do relatively little to insure against a more testing yet not implausible set of dangers—dangers, it should be added, that are more likely to be nonnuclear than nuclear in character. The second conclusion is that not all the risks are of equal priority. Some, indeed, can be considered sufficiently low in probability so that they warrant long-term and carefully paced programs at best, and even then programs that would fall at the end of the queue as far as the allocation of additional resources is concerned. Other threats might justify hedges against their occurrence, but only provided that resources were not in urgent demand from the nondefense sectors of the society. The highest priority would necessarily go to measures designed to exploit more fully the combat potential of the existing force structure, and at the same time to minimize costly and difficult personnel increases.

First Priority

A generally accepted proposition in defense planning is that it makes little sense to add forces to the posture unless they can be deployed forward in threatened areas during peacetime or rapidly deployed to those areas in an emergency. At present, the United States has too large a force structure by this definition because there is not enough airlift to move many of the more or less ready ground units in what is considered to be a timely fashion—defined as between ten days and several months. To increase peacetime deployments overseas in most land areas would be costly and politically troublesome; in addition, it would probably aggravate the problem of retaining experienced enlisted specialists. However, there is no reason why as much as a brigade of Marines with its amphibious lift could not be concentrated in the Arabian Sea. Roughly a brigade has for some time been kept on station but has been scattered in the Atlantic and Caribbean, the Mediterranean, and the Western Pacific. Bringing these battalions together near the Persian Gulf might increase the risk elsewhere. But it could be minimized by giving Army units in Italy and the southern United States some of the responsibilities previously held by the Marine Corps battalions afloat. The added strength in the Arabian Sea, sufficient to establish and defend a small beachhead, seems somewhat more commensurate with what is at stake in the area. The costs of the redeployment should be minimal.

To minimize early dependence on politically unreliable land bases, at least seven cargo ships could be put on station to provide the brigade with combat consumables for at least forty-five days. The ten-year investment and operating costs for such a program would be modest.

The Carter five-year defense program continues the buildup of airlift, with all the complications it entails in the acquisition of further land bases, the storage and maintenance of vulnerable additional matériel overseas, and the marrying of men and equipment in large quantities. An alternative would be to cancel the expensive CX airlift aircraft program, halt the pre-positioning of division sets in Europe, and acquire forty-eight additional fast sealift ships. The penalty for this trade-off is that sealift would deliver all its tonnage at about the time that the airlift would have completed a comparable deployment. In principle, this is not an unacceptable penalty because sealift tends to be easier to organize than airlift, and warning should be more than sufficient—whether in the Persian Gulf or in Europe—to permit the delivery of the programmed forces before an attack could be launched (D-day).

There remains the problem that the warning might not be exploited fully, and that sealift, accordingly, might prove too slow. However, overseas deployments already provide one hedge against this risk; existing airlift and POMCUS pre-positioned in Europe and the Persian Gulf furnish another. Instead of betting so much on the relatively untested and difficult process of airlift and pre-positioning—adopted to a considerable degree because of exaggerated estimates of the Soviet ability to launch surprise attacks with conventional forces—cheaper, more reliable sealift should be given greater consideration for most of the U.S. reinforcement capability. If the allies are concerned about the time it takes to deliver these reinforcements, they can always provide more of the high-readiness, early-deploying forces themselves. Furthermore, they and the United States have the option of introducing major field fortifications along parts of the German frontier, as has been done in Korea. Such fortifications are by no means impregnable, but they can buy the time to bring reserve units on line. Surely they are worth the relatively modest incremental cost entailed.

The deployment problem can undoubtedly be solved more rapidly by the acquisition of fast sealift than by developing the next generation of wide-bodied cargo airlift or by reopening the C-5 production line. Furthermore, with an early improvement in sealift, it makes sense to remove the force structure deficits that would arise in the event of multiple contingencies. It is now time, surely, to incorporate the National Guard and Reserve fully into U.S. contingency plans. Admittedly this was attempted in the early 1960s when eight Army divisions and one Marine Corps division in the Guard and Reserve were assigned an early role in dealing with two major contingencies and a lesser one. But for a variety of reasons the attempt proved premature. Circumstances have now changed, however. Air Force squadrons in the Guard and Reserve have been and remain of superior quality. What they need above all is modern equipment rather than hand-me-downs, and equipment they can keep regardless of any sudden need to resupply an ally. Ground force units are of less certain quality, and the Army has had little incentive to improve their proficiency. Local politics and demands also have been a problem. However, once the Army fully understands that owing to the high cost of incremental manpower for the active-duty forces, with or without the draft, it will not be able to acquire more regular units (except in the event of a grave national emergency, by which time it may be too late), it may prove more willing than it has in the past to cooperate in bringing selected Guard and Reserve units to a high state of readiness. To do so will require more, and more serious, training and full sets of modern equipment that the units can be assured of keeping.

About thirty-six Army maneuver battalions from the reserve component are already associated with regular Army divisions for the purpose of rounding out and augmenting those divisions in the event of their deployment. An additional four divisions from the reserve component—three Army and one Marine Corps—could be fully equipped with funds now programmed in the five-year defense program for more POMCUS and made ready for mobilization within four weeks. These divisions would remove the deficit in ground forces that could occur in the event of multiple contingencies.

Along with these divisions, the reserve Marine Corps air wing and fifteen Air Force reserve fighter squadrons could be modernized with A-10 attack and F-5G fighter aircraft and given a similar mobilization schedule. At the same time, inventories of modern ground and air munitions would be filled to forty-five days of combat for 23 divisions, 35 land-based air wings, and 180 ships (with 9 Navy air wings).

These programs, once completed, would permit the following

more or less simultaneous combat deployments within forty days of an order to mobilize (M + 40):

Table 4-5. Potential U.S. Combat Deployments at M+40

	Forces				
Location	Army divisions	Marine divisions	Marine air wings	Air Force fighter wings	Navy attack carriers
North Atlantic	...	...	...	...	2
Central Europe	15	...	...	23	...
Norway	...	1	1	...	1
Mediterranean	...	...	...	...	2
Persian Gulf	2	2	2	4	2
Korea	2	1	1	4	...
Pacific	...	...	...	...	2
Total	19	4	4	31	9[a]

Source: Author's estimates.
a. The three remaining carriers are assumed to be undergoing overhaul.

All this additional capability could be acquired without exceeding the levels of active-duty and reserve military personnel currently assumed in the five-year defense program. Moreover, the program would give the United States the military resources, in conjunction with allies, to deal more confidently than now with the most serious nonnuclear threats to those areas of the world in which it has the greatest stake.

The readiness of this capability will depend in no small way on the number and quality of the people in the armed forces. Whether pay rates and bonuses already in effect are enough to fill the force structure, active and reserve, with enough qualified volunteers remains to be seen. There are good reasons, however, to doubt that current levels of compensation will suffice to stem the exodus of skilled noncommissioned officers, fill the reserve ranks, and alter the socioeconomic makeup of the ground forces (if that should be desired).

Recruitment shortfalls could develop as early as 1982. If they do, the nation will face the choice of relaxing standards, reinstituting conscription, reducing the size of the armed forces, or increasing the military payroll. If the last course is chosen, its budgetary impact will depend on the specific measures taken. Across-the-board pay increases of the kind recommended by the Reagan administration will cost much more than targeted increases; deferred education benefits will cost more than cash payments. But whatever the detailed programs, real pay increases over the decade could reach 10 percent. This means that annual military payroll costs should probably be increased by $3 billion. The programs in this first-priority group and their ten-year costs (estimated in 1982 dollars) are listed in table 4-6.

Second Priority

There are a number of ways in which the U.S. defense of the three main theaters could be strengthened and steps taken to deter further contingencies. The addition of the amphibious airlift ships for three more Marine Corps brigades would permit the stationing of a second brigade in the Arabian Sea or the restoration of current peacetime deployments of reinforced battalion landing teams in the Caribbean, Mediterranean, and Western Pacific to respond to minor contingencies in those areas. If another amphibious brigade were stationed in

Table 4-6. Estimated Ten-Year Costs of First-Priority Increments to the Carter Defense Program

Program	Billions of fiscal 1982 dollars
Programs proposed for addition	**61.2**
Persian Gulf	
1 marine brigade on station	. . .
7 cargo ships on station with combat consumables	1.9
Central Europe	
3 Army Reserve component division-equivalents fully equipped	3.0
1 Marine Corps reserve division fully equipped (Norway)	1.0
1 Marine Corps reserve air wing fully equipped[a]	2.1
15 Air Force reserve fighter-attack squadrons fully equipped[a]	5.3
Fortifications for the U.S. sectors of the central front	1.0
48 fast sealift ships	5.9
Worldwide application	
Modern munitions for forty-five days of combat[b]	11.0
General pay increases and special incentive bonuses and pay	30.0
Programs proposed for cancellation	**19.2**
130 outsize airlift aircraft (CX)	17.2
2 division sets of European POMCUS army division equipment	2.0
Net ten-year costs	**42.0**

Source: Author's estimates, which include some operating costs as well as major and minor procurement.
a. A mix of A-10 and F-5G aircraft.
b. For 23 divisions, 35 air wings, 180 ships (including 9 carriers). For further data see Melvin R. Laird with Lawrence J. Korb, *The Problem of Military Readiness*, Special Analyses (Washington, D.C.: American Enterprise Institute, 1980), p. 14.

the vicinity of the Persian Gulf, it should be accompanied by seven more cargo ships stocked with forty-five days of combat consumables—for a total of two brigades and fourteen support ships in the Arabian Sea.

Under most conditions, the Navy could draw on its existing force of surface combatants to give close-in protection to these two brigades and fourteen cargo ships. In a worldwide emergency, it might need as many as thirty more frigates for that purpose. An additional thirty frigates (for a total increment of sixty) would make possible more assured close-in convoy protection in the Western Pacific and Indian Ocean.

A worldwide emergency would obviously place a heavy strain on the twenty-six active-duty Air Force wings and the twelve carrier wings of the Navy. Both forces have been losing aircraft through attrition and retirement more rapidly than replacements are being acquired. The Reagan administration proposes to begin correcting this situation in its amendments to the budgets for fiscal years 1981 and 1982, which request roughly $4 billion for new tactical aircraft. Even so, the Navy and the Air Force will each continue to need on the order of one hundred more front-line aircraft a year to keep existing units at authorized levels of strength. The cost of these increments will be large, but such a maintenance of strength should not require any increases in military manpower.

It is open to question whether the Soviet Union could or would bring an additional thirty or so divisions into an assault on Central Europe during the first three months of a buildup, or (as would be more likely) after a phase of initial offensive operations. Nonetheless, it might be worth taking a hedge against such a possibility by fully modernizing nine more Army Guard and Reserve division-equivalents and twenty-seven Air Force reserve fighter squadrons, and making them ready for deployment within forty-five days of the order to mobilize (M + 45). Such a step would mean that about twenty-four divisions and thirty-two fighter wings from the United States alone, would be available for Central Europe. The total force deployable to the three main theaters would consist of approximately thirty-two division-equivalents (plus independent brigades), forty-four land-based air wings, and nine carrier-based air wings (assuming that 75 percent of the carrier force would be put on station in a worldwide emergency)—not an unimposing capability.

The incremental ten-year costs (in 1982 dollars) of reaching this level of capability are shown in table 4-7.

Third Priority

As should have been expected, the Soviet Union has come a long way with its land and tactical air forces from the days of towed artillery and short-range interceptor aircraft. Still, standard analyses indicate that when the United States and its allies are able to deploy their forces fully before an attack—whether in Europe or in Southwest Asia—they have the firepower and tactical mobility to withstand what might be characterized as the expected threat. That is why warning and its efficient utilization have become so crucial to the success of modern collective security.

There are a number of ways to exploit warning and gain valuable time without forcing political leaders into difficult, overt mobilization and deployment decisions. These measures could be more desirable than last-minute, large-scale, and untested deployments by air to vulnerable stocks of weapons overseas. Be that as it may, one way to insure against a failure to obtain or exploit warning would be to restore the program for a substantial increase in U.S. outsized airlift

Table 4-7. Estimated Ten-Year Costs of Second-Priority Increments to the Carter Defense Program

Programs proposed for addition	Billions of fiscal 1982 dollars
Persian Gulf	
Amphibious lift for 1 Marine division	30.4
7 cargo ships on station with combat consumables	1.9
60 frigates to protect stationed forces and convoys	25.4
Central Europe	
9 fully equipped Army Reserve division-equivalents	14.0
27 fully equipped Air Force reserve squadrons[a]	9.5
Worldwide application	
100 additional Naval fighter-attack aircraft annually	33.0
100 additional Air Force fighter aircraft annually	22.4
Modern munitions for forty-five days of combat[b]	4.0
Total ten-year cost	140.6

Source: Author's estimates, which include some operating costs as well as major and minor procurement.
a. A mix of A-10 and F-5G aircraft.
b. For 9 divisions and 9 wings.

capability and for the eventual pre-positioning of five more division sets in Europe. Another and perhaps more desirable hedge would entail the acquisition of seven more Air Force active-duty wings of A-10 aircraft. These wings could be deployed rapidly to Europe, provided tanker support and base facilities were available, and would constitute a powerful, mobile reserve of firepower behind a forward screen of ground forces, as was demonstrated in Vietnam. They might, indeed, substitute for as many as five more divisions in the short run if they could generate four sorties per aircraft a day.

As indicated previously, the Navy's twelve deployable carriers are sufficient to provide air support with up to two battle groups in the Arabian Sea, air defense barriers in the North Atlantic and Western Pacific—with two battle groups in each ocean cooperating with land-based air—air support with two battle groups for indigenous ground forces in the eastern Mediterranean, and initial air cover with one battle group for a Marine division in Norway. It has been argued, however, that the United States should have a total of eighteen deployable carriers to maintain six on station in peacetime (in the Mediterranean, Indian Ocean, and Western Pacific) for whatever value in presence and demonstration these deployments might have. It has also been suggested that a force of eighteen carriers would permit the Navy not only to perform defensive sea-control functions, but also to gain immediate command of the seas by attacking either the Kola Peninsula and Murmansk or Vladivostok and Petropavlovsk. Whether four battle groups could survive for long in these high-threat waters or, if they could, whether these attacks would contribute significantly to the campaign for sea control is uncertain. A great deal more certain is the acquisition cost of six new and heavily armored nuclear-powered carriers along with their deckloads of aircraft, escorts, and underway replenishment ships: about $72 billion in fiscal 1982 dollars.

This large investment (with its uncertain return) is not included in the ten-year costs (in fiscal 1982 dollars) for the third-priority forces. These costs are shown in table 4-8.

Fourth Priority

Although improvements in the nuclear forces are given the highest priority in most proposals for augmenting the defense budget, in this

Table 4-8. Estimated Ten-Year Costs of Third-Priority Increments to the Carter Defense Program

Programs proposed for addition	Billions of fiscal 1982 dollars
130 outsize airlift aircraft (CX)	17.2
5 division sets of POMCUS army division equipment	7.5
21 active-duty Air Force squadrons with A-10 aircraft	16.2
Modern munitions for forty-five days of combat	1.0
Total ten-year cost	41.9

Source: Author's estimates, which include some operating costs as well as major and minor procurement.

chapter they receive the lowest. This ranking is assigned for two reasons. First, with the forces already programmed in the Carter five-year defense program, the United States will continue to have a powerful second-strike capability through the 1980s, despite the hypothetical vulnerability of the ICBM force and some question about the ability of current manned bombers to penetrate Soviet air defenses in the late 1980s. Second, the probability of any use of nuclear weapons should remain low. Nevertheless, it could increase during the decade if U.S. and NATO general purpose forces gain in effectiveness, and if the Soviet political leaders are faced with the onus of a nuclear decision. Thus, as a complement to improvements in the general purpose forces, it could make sense—depending on the nature of any future SALT constraints—to provide higher confidence in the performance of the U.S. nuclear second-strike forces.

The five-year defense program already includes measures to increase the survivability of the strategic command-control-communications system. In the short run, with an augmentation of flight and maintenance crews and spare parts, further strategic aircraft (82) and weapons (656 or more) could be added to the second-strike forces simply by increasing the bomber alert from 30 to 50 percent of the B-52s and FB-111s. To improve the second-strike capability of the long-range theater nuclear forces, eight of the older Polaris boats could be converted from SSBNs to platforms for submarine-launched cruise missiles (SLCMs). About half the boats (with alternating blue and gold crews) could be maintained on station at any time. As a replacement for the penetrating component of the B-52 and F-111 force, simply proceeding with the development of the

Stealth bomber would probably make more sense than to buy an expensive interim bomber such as the B-1. Because the five-year defense program already allows for that option, it would not require the new resources programmed by the Reagan administration for the long-range combat aircraft. However, as insurance against cancellation of the currently planned MX basing mode, additional funds could be allocated to research and development on hard-point ballistic missile defense to permit deployment of such a system in the late 1980s for defending the existing complex of ICBM silos.

To minimize the fallout effects of a nuclear attack on U.S. military installations (usually considered the most plausible opening move in an implausible contingency) a civil defense program could be funded to protect 40 million people in the general vicinity of these installations. This would substitute for the unworkable plans to evacuate the major cities that would be least likely to come under attack during a nuclear exchange.

Table 4-9 shows the incremental ten-year costs of these programs. All programs would improve the second-strike performance of the nuclear forces. However, as already noted, one of them, hard-point defense, would contravene an existing arms control agreement. Another, SLCMs, would seriously complicate the problem of verifying compliance with any future agreement. A third, civil defense, would no doubt generate vocal domestic opposition as making nuclear war more likely, despite the existence of a great many "provocative" shelters in the Soviet Union.

Table 4-9. Estimated Ten-Year Costs of Fourth-Priority Increments to the Carter Defense Program

Programs proposed for addition	Billions of fiscal 1982 dollars
Nuclear forces, offense	
Increased bomber alert rate (from 30 to 50 percent)	6.0
8 Polaris submarines converted to SLCM launchers	3.5
Nuclear forces, defense	
Increased research and development for ballistic missile defense	2.0
Fallout shelters for 40 million people near military installations	10.0
Total ten-year cost	21.5

Source: Author's estimates, which include some operating as well as procurement costs; see also Congressional Budget Office, *Resources for Defense: A Review of Key Issues for Fiscal Years 1982–1986*, p. 19.

Summary

To give a sense of the major increases that might be made in the Carter defense plan, table 4-10 shows the ten-year costs of the four priority programs in aggregate form and how they relate to major defense functions. Table 4-11 indicates how these programs would progressively increase the totals of the Carter plan. Both the original plan and the highest priority increment to it could be implemented without major increases in the currently authorized level of active-duty and reserve military personnel. However, the other three increments would require a significant growth in the war production base if larger capabilities are actually to be forthcoming during the decade of the 1980s, and more people would obviously be needed to man, maintain, and support the expanded capabilities. It remains to be seen whether the nation and Congress are yet persuaded that an uncertain future requires either this many large and costly hedges or the more mechanical and equally costly increases already proposed and foreshadowed by the Reagan administration.

Sir John Slessor once wrote, to the subsequent applause of many, "It is customary in the democratic countries to deplore expenditures on armaments as conflicting with the requirements of the social services. There is a tendency to forget that the most important social

Table 4-10. Summary of Estimated Ten-Year Costs of Priority Increments to the Carter Defense Program

Billions of fiscal 1982 dollars

| Program priority | Allocation of increments | | | | |
	Persian Gulf	Europe	Worldwide	Strategic forces	Total
Urgent	1.9	16.3	23.8	...	42.0
Important	57.7	23.5	59.4	...	140.6
Desirable	...	41.9	...	...	41.9
Low-priority	...	...	...	21.5	21.5
Subtotal	59.6	81.7	83.2	21.5	246.0
Capital fund[a]	37.5	49.4	48.8	7.3	142.7
Total costs	96.8	131.1	132.0	28.8	388.7

Source: Author's estimates based on tables 4-6, 4-7, 4-8, and 4-9.

a. This fund reflects the depreciation of the equipment being acquired and the resources required to replace it systematically with the next generation of equipment.

Table 4-11. Estimated Five-Year Cost Impact of the Priority Increments on the Carter Defense Program

Billions of fiscal 1982 dollars

Program	Carter defense program (five-year costs)	Capital fund[a]	Augmented defense program	Percent increase
Carter defense program	1,085.2	...	1,085.2	...
Proposed programs				
Urgent	21.0	7.6	28.6	
Subtotal	1,106.2	7.6	1,113.8	2.6
Important	70.3	40.5	110.8	
Subtotal	1,176.5	48.1	1,224.6	12.8
Desirable	21.0	10.3	31.3	
Subtotal	1,197.5	58.4	1,255.9	15.7
Low-priority	10.8	3.2	14.0	
Total costs	1,208.3	61.6	1,269.9	17.0

Source: Author's estimates, based on table 4-10.

a. This fund reflects the depreciation of the equipment being acquired and the resources required to replace it systematically with the next generation of equipment.

service a government can do for its people is to keep them alive and free."

In the abstract, it is difficult to quarrel with Sir John's sentiment. As a practical matter, the national income is not infinite and defense can never have it all. Calculated underfunding of U.S. military programs in the past is no excuse for overfunding them in the future. A five-year defense plan based on automatic percentage increases, a fixed share of gross national product, a mirror-image of alleged Soviet spending, or round numbers such as 600 ships are poor substitutes for analysis, whether proposed by the Department of Defense or permitted by the Office of Management and Budget. Both the executive branch and Congress have a duty to search more systematically for the defense policy and programs that are appropriate for the country in these ambiguous times. As Sir Winston Churchill might have put it, even this pudding should have a theme.

CHAPTER FIVE

The Budget Outlook

ROBERT W. HARTMAN

PRESIDENT REAGAN's budget proposals for fiscal year 1981 especially, and even for 1982, were constrained to some extent by past budgets. Only by looking at the future year implications of what his administration proposes can the full plan be understood. In this chapter the history of federal budget activity is discussed to provide a backdrop for President Reagan's proposals. This is followed by a discussion of the implications of his proposals through fiscal year 1984. Because of the controversy surrounding both the economic assumptions on which the budget is based and the magnitude of the tax and spending policy changes that are advanced, the chapter concludes with an assessment of what might happen if some things do not work out as assumed.

Budget History, 1960–80

A conventional accounting of the last twenty years of federal budget activity indicates the source of much of the current frustration over federal finances. Outlays grew from 18.5 percent of gross national product in 1960 to 20.3 percent in 1970, 22.0 percent in 1975, and 22.5 percent in 1980 (see table 5-1). Government receipts roughly kept pace with expenditures in the 1960s (the average

I am grateful to Henry Aaron, Thomas J. Cuny, Darwin G. Johnson, John L. Palmer, and Charles L. Schultze for their comments and for providing data; to Michael K. Kuehlwein for research assistance; and to Vickie L. Corey for secretarial assistance.

Table 5-1. Federal Budget Outlays, Receipts, and Surplus or Deficit as a Percentage
of Gross National Product, Selected Fiscal Years, 1960–80

Item	1960	1965	1970	1975	1980
Outlays	18.5	17.9	20.3	22.0	22.5
Receipts	18.5	17.7	20.0	19.0	20.3
Surplus or deficit	0.1	−0.2	−0.3	−3.0	−2.3

Source: Office of Management and Budget, Fiscal Analysis Branch, Budget Review Division, "Total Government Finances," January 1981 edition, tables 1, 3, and 6.

deficit was less than 1 percent of GNP), but in the 1970s the gap between expenditures and receipts widened (the average deficit in the 1970–80 period was 2 percent of GNP).

In the 1970s a growing concern over federal fiscal activities became evident, symbolized by the movement to enact a balanced budget amendment to the Constitution.[1] The nature of this concern, however, is highly varied and complex. Attempts to boil it down to "the deficit" obscure legitimate issues, such as the size of government, the burden of taxation, the burden of the public debt, and the crowding out of private business investment. Each of these needs to be put in context so that the relevant government budgetary action can be highlighted. Accordingly, the following discussion of the budget in the 1970s is organized around these themes, and appropriate budget concepts are applied to each.

The Major Components of the Budget

Outlays in the unified budget can be disaggregated into three major components that differ in their impact on the economy and in the degree of control Congress can exercise.

Program outlays either directly purchase goods and services for the government's use (such as national defense or employees' pay) or provide income for people (social security benefits), governments (educational grants), or businesses (agricultural subsidies). These are the elements of the budget that economists emphasize when they analyze the effect of federal spending on total demand and the gross

1. For a discussion of the balanced budget amendment, see Bruce K. MacLaury, "Proposals to Limit Federal Spending and Balance the Budget," app. A, in Joseph A. Pechman, ed., *Setting National Priorities: The 1980 Budget* (Brookings Institution, 1979).

national product. For the most part, these outlays are under congressional control either through appropriations laws that limit spending or through substantive laws governing eligibility for receiving transfer payments or grants.

Direct loans are advanced by government agencies for a variety of purposes ranging from rural sewers to inner-city small businesses. The unified budget includes the value of loans advanced in a year net of repayments of past loans and net of sales of loans by on-budget agencies. Most of the loan sales are made to the Federal Financing Bank, an off-budget entity (see appendix A). While off-budget outlays are not included in the unified budget, they give rise to Treasury borrowing in the same way as the budget deficit. Economists studying aggregate demand generally exclude loans or repayments of loans because they do not affect anyone's income—they are an exchange of assets between the government and the private sector. The budgetary process until recently had inadequate procedures for congressional oversight in limiting the current lending activities of either on-budget or off-budget agencies.

Net interest outlays in the budget represent the difference between total interest on the public debt and interest earned by federal accounts (primarily trust funds) on U.S. securities they own. (In addition, interest paid by the Federal Financing Bank to the U.S. Treasury is an offset to interest on the public debt.) Thus these are interest payments on the debt held outside federal agencies. In any given year these outlays are beyond governmental control because they depend on the inherited public debt and on interest rates set in the market.

Table 5-2 shows federal spending rearranged into these categories for selected years from 1970 to 1980. Several important relationships are important to note. First, while total outlays grew faster than GNP throughout the 1970s, the gap was much larger in the first part than in 1976–80. Second, program outlays of the government increased significantly faster than GNP from 1970 to 1976 but grew more slowly than the economy from 1976 to 1980. The financial activities of the government—loans and net interest—were far and away the fastest growing elements of the budget throughout the 1970s. Their rapid growth more than accounts for the increase in the ratio of federal outlays to GNP in the last half of the decade.

Table 5-2. Federal Budget Outlays by Major Category, Selected Fiscal Years, 1970–80
Billions of dollars unless otherwise specified

Category	1970	1976	1979	1980	Annual rate of change (percent) 1970 –76	1976 –80ᵃ
Program outlaysᵇ	179.2	335.5	445.0	517.6	11.0	10.7
Direct loan outlays	3.0	10.9	19.6	24.2	24.0	20.6
On-budget	3.0	4.2	6.0	9.5	5.8	21.2
Off-budget	0.0	6.7	13.6	14.7	. . .	20.3
Net interest outlays	14.4	26.7	42.6	52.5	10.8	17.2
Unified budget outlays						
Excluding off-budget	196.6	366.4	493.6	579.6	10.9	11.4
Including off-budget	196.6	373.1	507.2	594.3	11.3	11.6
Addendum						
GNP	968.9	1,642.7	2,357.8	2,567.5	9.2	11.1
GNP price deflatorᶜ	91.0	131.7	162.9	176.8	6.3	7.2

Sources: *The Budget of the United States Government, Fiscal Year 1982*, pp. 611–12; Office of Management and Budget, Fiscal Analysis Branch, "Federal Credit Programs: Historical Data, 1950–1980" (October 7, 1980), p. 6; *Special Analyses, Budget of the United States Government, Fiscal Year 1982*, p. 150; and unpublished data from the Office of Management and Budget.
a. The period 1976–80 contains 4.25 years.
b. Unified budget outlays minus net interest and on-budget direct loan outlays.
c. Fiscal year 1972 = 100.

The Size of Government

Aside from the allegedly heavy hand of federal regulation, what most people mean when they say that the government is too large or is growing too rapidly is that spending for programs is commanding too large a share of the nation's output or that too many services are being provided. Tables 5-3 and 5-4 summarize program outlays in the federal budget from these perspectives.

The essential story of the growth of federal program spending in the 1970s is that it expanded rapidly in the first part of the decade (a continuation of the late 1960s expansion) but slowed in the last half of the decade. The second fact is that total spending masks disparate trends in the defense and nondefense sectors.

If Jimmy Carter's first term had ended with fiscal 1979, he could have much more easily defended budget performance during his administration. He inherited programs that had risen from 18.5 percent of GNP in 1970 to 20.4 of GNP in 1976; by 1979 these outlays rep-

Table 5-3. Program Outlays as a Percentage of Gross National Product, Fiscal Years 1970–80

Category	Average, 1970–74	Average, 1975–76	Average, 1977–78	1979	1980
National defense	6.7	5.6	5.1	5.0	5.3
Nondefense					
Payments for individuals	7.8	10.5	10.1	9.6	10.6
Retirement and disability insurance	3.8	4.7	4.7	4.6	4.8
Health	1.5	2.0	2.1	2.1	2.3
Unemployment compensation	0.5	1.0	0.7	0.5	0.7
Other grants	1.8	2.3	2.5	2.3	2.2
Other operations	2.1	1.9	2.0	1.9	2.1
Total program outlays	18.5	20.2	19.7	18.9	20.2

Sources: Office of Management and Budget, "Federal Government Finances," March 1981 edition, pp. 44–45, 74–75, and 81; *The Budget of the United States Government, Fiscal Year 1982*, pp. 252, 603–04, and 611–12; unpublished data from the Office of Management and Budget; and table 5-2.

resented only 18.9 percent of GNP, a reasonable achievement (although most of the reduced ratio was attributable to cyclical factors and to a continuing erosion of the national defense share; see table 5-3). In 1980, however, program outlays grew sharply, by 4 percent after correction for inflation, and the ratio to GNP was back to its 1976 level. The reasons for the 1980 jump in spending are discussed in chapter 2 of this volume; I note here only that both defense and nondefense spending accelerated significantly.

In the 1970s federal spending on programs in constant dollars rose at 3 percent a year, about the same rate as real GNP rose over the decade.[2] Constant dollar expenditures for national defense, however,

2. The constant dollar expenditures reported in table 5-4 and discussed in the text are the official OMB series (see *The Budget of the United States Government, Fiscal Year 1982*, p. 612). Defense expenditures are deflated by a special deflator that is essentially a compensation index for personnel costs in the defense budget and a purchase index for other items. Grants to state and local governments and "other operations" are similarly deflated. Payments for individuals are deflated by the consumer price index, not by price indexes suited to each type of transfer payment. The implicit assumption of no productivity gain for government employees, the failure to recognize that the consumer price index has typically overstated inflation, and the decision not to deflate such programs as medicare by a health cost index all impart some biases to the resulting measures. In any event, the fact is that the implicit price deflator for these outlays rose faster in the 1970s than the GNP deflator. This explains why, although program outlays rose faster than GNP in current dollars, they increased at about the same rate as GNP when measured in constant dollars.

Table 5-4. Program Outlays in Constant 1972 Dollars, Fiscal Years 1970–80

Billions of dollars unless otherwise specified

Category	Average, 1970–74	Average, 1975–76	Average, 1977–78	1979	1980	Annual rate of change (percent)		
						1970–76	1976–80	1970–80
National defense	77.3	67.7	67.4	70.1	72.5	−4.9	1.9	−2.1
Nondefense								
Payments for individuals	88.6	125.3	132.9	132.8	139.4	11.3	1.5	7.1
Other grants	21.1	26.7	31.5	31.5	30.8	8.4	2.4	5.9
Other operations	23.9	22.9	25.9	27.4	29.6	−2.0	6.0	1.3
Total program outlays	210.8	242.4	257.7	261.7	272.2	3.5	2.1	2.9
Addendum								
Payments for individuals excluding unemployment compensation	83.1	112.7	123.8	126.5	130.1	10.2	2.6	7.0

Sources: Same as table 5-3.

declined steeply in the first part of the period and recovered at a moderate real rate after 1976. Payments for individuals rose at a 7.1 percent real rate for the decade (table 5-4). This is more than double the rate of growth of real personal consumption over the decade. The largest increases, however, came in 1970–76, when the annual real rate of growth of these transfer payments reached double-digit levels.

There are four major reasons for the explosion of transfers in 1970–76. First, the period ends with the aftermath of a sharp recession, and unemployment compensation was thus unusually high in 1976. Second, in 1970–72 three increases in social security benefits, whose cumulative effect was to raise payments by over 50 percent, were put into effect. (This was before indexing of social security, which did not start until 1975.) Third, increased use of the services provided by medicare and medicaid (plus a differential medical care cost increase) drove up health care costs in the budget. Finally, participation in new programs such as food stamps and supplemental security income grew significantly.

The boom in payments for individuals fell off sharply after 1976. In constant dollars these expenditures (excluding unemployment compensation) slowed to an annual growth rate of 2.6 percent, less than the estimated trend rate of growth of real GNP. The real growth in these programs in recent years was the result of a growing number and rising wage base of recipients of social security, the continuing rise in costs and utilization of health care programs, and the increased eligibility for a number of assistance programs (trade-adjustment assistance, food stamps, and low-income energy assistance are examples).

Aside from national defense and transfer payments, the aggregate of the rest of the program activities of the government rose in constant dollars at about the same rate as real GNP. In the first half of the seventies, grant programs (excluding those that provide payments for individuals) rose relative to GNP, but these programs leveled out after 1977 (see chapter 2). The other activities of the government—largely overhead costs, research support, and the costs of operating bureaus such as the National Park Service and the Federal Aviation Administration—held at a 2 percent share of GNP throughout the decade.

The point of this discussion is that when people complain about the size of the federal government, and aside from irritation over federal regulations, the numbers indicate that they must be expressing frustration at the increased amount of aid going to individuals as transfer payments. With the widespread (and incorrect) belief that living standards fell during the 1970s,[3] it is not surprising that many people resented the growing amount of publicly supported consumption. And the fact that many of the benefit programs are indexed automatically while most wage earners view themselves as having to struggle to stay even with inflation adds to the frustration. It is unlikely that Congress would have enacted the myriad of transfer payment liberalizations if it had foreseen the apparent resentment of nonbeneficiaries.

Some people are concerned about the size (or growth) of government because they associate it with inflation. But there is no substantial body of economic theory or obvious statistical evidence that supports this association. Table 5-5 shows recent inflation trends of industrial countries in relation to the size and growth rate of government. One highlight is that Germany and Italy had nearly identical measures of size and growth of government and yet experienced the lowest and highest inflation of the ten countries listed.[4]

The outlook for the size of government as the nation enters the 1980s can be summarized as follows. By 1980 federal program outlays consisted of national defense outlays (representing roughly 25 percent of outlays), social security (also 25 percent), other transfers (about 30 percent), and other programs (20 percent). If national defense expenditures move to the real growth path charted by President Carter (of roughly 5 percent annual real growth) in the early 1980s, if social security and other transfer programs are held to the 2.5 percent annual real rate they attained in the late 1970s, and if other programs grow at a 3 percent real rate as they did throughout the 1970s, the real growth in the program budget will be about 3.2

---

3. Real consumption exclusive of transfer payments per capita rose by about 1.9 percent a year between 1970 and 1980. A slowing of the rise in real wage rates was offset by a growing number of earners—mainly women—to support this higher living standard. Between 1978 and 1980 increases in real consumption exclusive of transfer payments per capita did in fact come to a halt, as inflation and recession offset wage and employment developments.

4. Table 5-5 lists total government *at all levels*. This is the main reason the U.S. ratio (for federal, state, and local governments) to national output is so much higher than previous ratios discussed in this chapter.

Table 5-5. Size and Growth of the Public Sector and Rates of Inflation in Ten Industrial Countries, 1970–78

Country	Government expenditures, 1978		Growth of government expenditures as percent of gross domestic product, 1970–78		Inflation, 1970–78	
	Percent of gross domestic product	Rank	Percentage point increase	Rank	GDP deflator (percent)	Rank
Australia	29.9[a]	9	8.0[b]	7	11.7[b]	3
Canada	37.8	7	5.6	9	8.3	7
France	43.5	3	5.6	6	9.0	5
Germany	41.3	5	9.7	4	5.5	10
Italy	42.5[a]	4	10.4[b]	3	13.7[b]	1
Japan	23.0	10	9.0	5	7.9	8
Netherlands	53.1	2	13.4	2	8.4	6
Sweden	57.1	1	20.0	1	9.5	4
United Kingdom	40.5	6	7.3	8	12.9	2
United States	32.1	8	1.8	10	6.5	9

Source: United Nations Statistical Office, *Yearbook of National Accounts Statistics, 1979*, vol. 1: *Individual Country Data* (New York: UN, 1980). Government expenditures based on data for current disbursements.
a. For 1977.
b. For the period 1970–77.

percent.[5] With the outlook for real growth in GNP over the next few years at about the same rate or lower, the prospects for reducing the size of the budget in relation to the economy are slim, unless a deliberate program to reduce some of these historical patterns of growth is implemented.[6]

Taxes and Tax Burdens

Many people have no strong philosophical view about how much the government should spend; almost everyone would like to pay less tax. It is clear that a large part of the growing public antipathy toward federal spending stems from the pain of federal taxes. At the same time there is a commonly held view that unless the government

5. Defense contributes 1.25 percentage points of real growth (0.25 × 0.05), social security and other transfers 1.4 points, and all others 0.6 point.
6. Moreover, to hold program outlays to a given fraction of nominal GNP, further reductions will be necessary if the prices of government purchases and services continue to grow faster than the overall price level.

Table 5-6. Federal and State and Local Receipts, Fiscal Years 1970–80

Item	Average, 1970–74	Average, 1975–76	Average, 1977–78	1979	1980
Federal receipts as percent of					
Program outlays	102.5	92.0	97.7	104.7	100.5
Program outlays plus net interest	95.0	85.3	90.2	95.5	91.2
GNP	18.9	18.6	19.2	19.8	20.3
State and local receipts as percent of GNP	10.5	10.7	10.7	9.9	9.9
Federal, state, and local receipts as percent of GNP	29.4	29.3	29.9	29.7	30.2
Distribution of federal receipts (percent)					
Individual income taxes	45.4	43.8	44.6	46.8	46.9
Social insurance taxes	26.6	30.8	30.6	30.4	30.9
Corporate income taxes	15.3	14.2	15.1	14.1	12.4
All other	12.8	11.3	9.8	8.7	9.7
Individual income tax as percent of personal income	10.7	10.1	10.7	11.5	11.6
Individual income tax plus employee social security tax as percent of personal income	13.1	12.9	13.6	14.6	14.7
Addendum					
Federal receipts (billions of dollars)	217.6	290.5	379.9	465.9	520.0

Sources: Office of Management and Budget, "Total Government Finances," January 1981 edition, table 1; OMB, "Federal Government Finances," March 1981 edition, p. 8; *The Budget of the United States Government, Fiscal Year 1982*, pp. 552 and 613; Department of the Treasury, Office of Tax Analysis, "Individual Income Tax Liability and Employee Social Security Contributions as a Percent of Income," revised, March 30, 1981; and Bureau of Economic Analysis, National Income and Product Accounts. Figures are rounded.

raises enough receipts through taxation to cover expenditures, federal borrowing to cover the deficit will fuel inflation and crowd out private borrowers.

Table 5-6 assembles some of the pertinent facts about taxation over the decade of the 1970s. The first thing to note is that throughout the decade, except for the recession-influenced years of 1975–76, federal receipts were just about sufficient to cover program outlays.[7]

7. The Federal Reserve System is defined as part of the public for purposes of budget accounting. Interest payments to the Federal Reserve are counted in net interest outlays. But federal receipts include the remittance of interest earnings by the Federal Reserve System to the Treasury. The deposits of earnings by the Federal Reserve were $11.8 billion in 1980; if these are excluded from receipts, the resulting ratio of taxes to program outlays would fall to 98 percent in 1980. In 1970–74 the ratio was 100 percent.

Borrowing, in other words, was mainly to finance loan outlays and net interest payments. The desirability of borrowing for those purposes is discussed in the next sections.

By 1980 federal receipts had risen to 20.3 percent of GNP, a ratio exceeded in the last forty years only in 1944–45 and in 1969, both years in which special taxes to pay for a war were in force. Thus the rising tax burden reflects not so much that a tighter tax policy in relation to program outlays was adopted, but rather that inflation-boosted revenues were used to finance the relative growth in the size of government.[8]

The rising federal tax burden has been significantly offset by a decline in state and local taxes relative to GNP, especially since 1977. With the "tax revolt" that resulted in the passage of tax limitations in many states, state and local taxes (from their own sources, excluding federal grants) were a lower fraction of GNP in 1979 and 1980 than in any other year of the decade.

Examination of the composition of federal taxes allows one to zero in on the source of current pressure to lower taxes. Individual income taxes accounted for about 45 percent of federal receipts both in the early 1970s and in 1977–78 (table 5-6). Since that time, the fraction has risen to around 47 percent. The difference is that, from 1970 to 1977, a number of revisions of the individual income tax code offset the built-in tendency of a progressive tax system to take a larger fraction of income as it rises. No such offsets have been legislated in the last few years, and individual income taxes rose in relation to personal income, from 10.7 percent in 1977 to 11.6 percent in 1980. The employee share of social security taxes (part of social insurance taxes) has risen even faster than income taxes, as legislation has raised the payroll tax rates and the base to which they are applied. The upshot is that individual income taxes plus the employee share of social security taxes in 1980 represented 14.7 percent of personal income, although they were only 13.1 percent in the early 1970s. Whether this rise in the federal direct tax burden alone would be a major political concern is arguable; in combination with a slow-

---

8. The reader will note that the ratio of receipts to GNP is equal to the product of the ratios of receipts to program outlays and program outlays to GNP. The first ratio is a measure of the tightness of tax policy and the second of the size of government. The former ratio barely changed from 1970 to 1980 (table 5-6) while the latter grew by 9 percent (table 5-3).

Table 5-7. Estimated Marginal Tax Rates under 1980 Tax Law and under 1970 and 1975 Laws Indexed for Inflation, by Selected Income Class, 1981

Selected adjusted gross income class, 1981 (dollars)	Marginal tax rate			Change, 1970–80	
	Indexed 1970 tax law	Indexed 1975 tax law	1980 tax law	Percentage points	Percent
5,000–10,000	14.6	14.5	15.7	1.1	7.5
10,000–15,000	16.7	19.1	20.2	3.5	21.0
20,000–25,000	20.7	21.6	25.6	4.9	23.7
50,000–100,000	32.5	37.4	46.8	14.3	44.0
100,000–200,000	48.9	53.1	58.6	9.7	19.8
All classes	18.2	18.0	21.6	3.4	18.7

Source: Joseph A. Pechman, "Anatomy of the U.S. Individual Income Tax" (working paper, Brookings Institution, 1981).

down in the growth of real wages and the continued growth of indexed transfer programs, the public political awareness of taxes was evident by 1980.

The frequent income tax cuts in the 1970s were not concentrated on reducing marginal tax rates (the tax rate in the bracket where the last dollar is earned) but rather on raising personal exemptions and the standard deduction and widening the range of tax brackets. At the same time, Congress passed up virtually every opportunity to subject more forms of income to taxation, which would have provided room for tax rate cuts (see appendix B). As a result, an increasing portion of the population found itself in higher marginal tax brackets.

The effect of inflation on marginal tax rates at various levels of 1981 real income under the tax laws of 1970, 1975, and 1980 is given in table 5-7.[9] For the average of all tax classes the marginal tax rate rose from 18.2 percent in 1970 to 21.6 percent in 1980, an increase of 3.4 percentage points, or 18.7 percent. The increase was greatest for those with 1981 incomes of $50,000–$100,000 and smallest in the lowest and highest income classes.

9. The table shows the marginal tax on an additional $1 of ordinary income in various adjusted income classes under the 1980 tax law. For earlier years the marginal tax on the same level of income is computed on the assumption that these earlier tax laws had been indexed—that is, their rate brackets, exemptions, and standard deductions were adjusted for the change in the GNP deflator to 1981. The entries therefore show the marginal tax rates in each year for a taxpayer whose income rose at the rate of inflation.

As the taxpayer's bracket goes up, the incentive to seek tax shelters (legal) and to earn money in unreportable forms (illegal) increases and the incentive to save and expend work effort may be eroded. These economic effects are discussed in chapter 2; whatever their magnitude, the historic highs reached by income and payroll taxes are a cause for concern.

If tax laws are not revised in the early 1980s, the trend of rising direct tax burdens will continue and even accelerate. Payroll and income taxes would rise from 14.7 percent of personal income in 1980 to 17.7 percent by 1984. Total federal receipts would rise from 20.3 percent of GNP to about 23 percent of GNP. In no peacetime four-year period in modern American history have tax burdens risen at such a fast pace.

Federal Lending and the Quality of Investment

The federal government has become a major lender, either directly or indirectly. Appendix A discusses the growth of federally assisted lending in some detail, and notes that, of all credit advanced in the United States, loans made under federal auspices accounted for 23 percent of the total in 1980, up from about 14 percent in the early 1970s. Many of these loans would have been made without federal assistance, and it is doubtful that federal lending expands the total volume of credit. What then is their significance?

One answer is that this credit assistance alters investment decisions. It may help to think of a lineup of potential borrowers, standing before the door of a superbank, ranked according to the rate of return that each borrower expects to earn on the investment to be made with the loan. The government lending official then appears and discovers near the end of the line a college student borrower. He is moved up to the front of the line. A prospective rural housing borrower is moved up as well. A potential importer of U.S. airplanes is the next to move to the front. The small businesses are moved up. And so on. After all this rearranging the superbank opens its door and makes the same dollar volume of loans that would have been made without government intervention. The level of income, output, and investment in the economy is little different from what it would have been without all the government lending activity; what is different is the nature of the investments that are financed. If the government is systematically giving an advantage to housing, students, and small businesses, then some nonhousing, nonstudent borrowers that would have received credit will be left out (through higher interest rates or failure to qualify for credit) when all the credit is allocated. Thus federal lending activity may lower the average market productivity of new investments as the price of achieving nonmarket, social objectives.

In some cases the government may reason that the market, left to its own devices, would have made the wrong choice; for example, a synfuel producer developing a new and untried process may be placed at the end of the line by wary lenders uncertain about a risky project. Here the government's intercession may move an investment with a high economic rate of return to a favorable position. Indeed, some have argued that to revitalize American industry the government should become a more active lender by creating, in effect, a superbank to sort out industries that are potential "winners" and encouraging their expansion.

Assuming that some loans under government sponsorship should be made, how should they be controlled and what are their implications for taxing and borrowing? Current federal budget practice is as follows. When an agency makes a direct loan, the full value of the loan is counted as an outlay of the agency. If the agency receives repayments of principal on past loans, these are counted as negative outlays, reducing the agency's outlay total. If the agency sells its loan asset to the Federal Financing Bank, that transaction is a negative outlay in the unified budget but is an outlay of off-budget federal entities. These off-budget outlays are financed by the issuance of federal debt in the same way that an ordinary budget deficit is financed. Aside from repayments, agencies ordinarily obtain money for lending by borrowing from the Treasury (or the Federal Financing Bank). They normally pay the current government borrowing rate on the loan. If the loans made by the agency bear interest rates below the Treasury rate—as they usually do—the agency each year shows a loss: its interest received is less than the interest it pays to the Treasury, and this interest subsidy shows up as an outlay of the subsidizing agency. Guaranteed loans that are not subsequently purchased by the Federal Financing Bank do not show up in the budget (or require any federal financing) at all unless they default.

These accounting conventions can be illustrated for 1980 as follows (see table 5-8). In that year government agencies made on-

Table 5-8. Federal Lending Activity, Fiscal Years 1978–80
Billions of dollars unless otherwise specified

Item	1978	1979	1980
Funds advanced under federal auspices[a]	58.9	73.8	80.8
On-budget lending			
Direct loans made	32.2	31.9	37.8
Less: Repayments and adjustments	12.3	14.0	15.8
Sales to Federal Financing Bank and other	11.3	11.9	12.5
Equals: Direct loan outlays	8.6	6.0	9.5
Off-budget lending	50.3	67.8	71.2
Direct loans	11.2	13.6	14.7
Guaranteed loans	13.9	26.1	32.4
Government-sponsored enterprise loans	25.2	28.1	24.1
Direct loans outstanding[b]	120.5	140.5	163.9
Addendum			
Funds advanced under federal auspices as percent of total credit advanced in U.S. markets	15.3	17.8	23.2

Sources: Office of Management and Budget, "Federal Credit Programs: Historical Data, 1950–1980," table 2; *Special Analyses, Budget of the United States Government, Fiscal Year 1982*, pp. 144 and 150–51; *Special Analyses, Budget of the United States Government, Fiscal Year 1980*, pp. 142 and 148; and *Special Analyses, Budget of the United States Government, Fiscal Year 1981*, pp. 150 and 157. Figures are rounded.
a. Direct loan outlays plus off-budget lending.
b. On-budget agencies and off-budget entities only.

budget direct loan obligations (essentially promises to lend) of $39.6 billion (not shown in the table). They actually lent $37.8 billion. But since repayments totaled $15.8 billion and the agencies sold loan assets of $12.5 billion, net on-budget lending was only $9.5 billion. This is the amount shown in table 5-2 (as on-budget direct loan outlays) and in appendix A. Also, agencies were paying out more in interest than they received, but these interest subsidies cannot readily be identified in the budget totals.

It is clear that direct lending cannot be controlled by just controlling net loan outlays. For this reason, the "credit budget" that now accompanies the unified budget bases its restraints on the level of obligations to lend that an agency may undertake in any year. The credit budget deals with guaranteed as well as direct loans. Control over interest subsidies per dollar of lending is another matter. Generally the low interest rates or favorable terms of direct federal loans are embedded in the underlying legislation that created the program, and the subsidy generally grows as interest rates rise. To control interest subsidies usually involves dealing with substantive law, not just taking budgetary actions; unchanged laws in times of rising inflation imply growing subsidies.

Assuming that a loan is to be made and that any interest subsidies should be included in the budget,[10] how should the government finance the capital for the loan? Specifically, since the principal on the loan is presumed to be repaid in later years, does it make sense to raise taxes in the year the loan is issued and to reduce taxes in all subsequent years? Most economists would answer that tax finance for loans makes no sense; it is permissible in a sound financial plan, in other words, for the government to borrow to finance loans. This practice of treating the capital value of direct loans as if they did not have to compete with other government operations would essentially equalize the treatment of direct and guaranteed loans in the federal decisionmaking process, a long-time objective of budget reformers.[11] The reader will now understand why, in the previous discussion, federal taxes were matched up with program outlays or net interest but not with loan extensions.

Federal Borrowing and Crowding Out

One of the reasons people are concerned about the size of the federal government's deficits is that the government's borrowing may "crowd out" someone from capital markets. In the 1970s particular attention was paid to private nonfinancial business being squeezed, to the detriment of long-run productivity and economic growth.

The government did in fact account for about 15 percent of all borrowing in the 1970s, and nonfinancial businesses, which commanded over 45 percent of funds raised in the early 1970s, drew only about one-third of borrowing in the last three years of the decade (table 5-9). But federal borrowing was concentrated in the re-

---

10. Current budgetary practice counts the subsidy only as it accrues as a cost each year. The preferable treatment would be to count the present value of all future subsidies that would derive from a loan at the time the loan was made. This would discourage politicians with short time horizons from converting grant programs into long-term, highly subsidized loans that appear to be saving the government's money in the first few years.

11. See Robert W. Hartman, *Credit for College: Public Policy for Student Loans,* Report for the Carnegie Commission on Higher Education (McGraw-Hill, 1971), chap. 3.

Table 5-9. Share of Funds Raised in Nonfinancial Credit Markets by Borrowing Sector, Fiscal Years 1970–80

Percent

Sector	1970–74[a]	1975–76[a]	1977–78[a]	1979	1980	1970–80[a]
Nonfinancial business	46.6	31.2	31.7	38.0	36.3	39.4
U.S. government	8.5	30.5	16.2	8.1	20.5	14.9
Home mortgages	19.6	18.8	27.4	26.7	24.1	21.9
Consumer credit	9.2	5.0	12.2	11.7	1.6	8.5
State and local government	9.4	6.8	6.0	3.9	5.5	7.4
All other	6.8	7.7	6.6	11.6	12.0	7.8
Total	100.0	100.0	100.0	100.0	100.0	100.0

Source: Board of Governors of the Federal Reserve System, Flow of Funds Accounts. Figures are rounded.

a. Average of yearly shares.

cession years 1975–76 and 1980 (as a result of automatic stabilizers in the budget); in the recovery years 1977–79 federal borrowing in relation to the total market for credit came down, making room for other claimants. The jump in federal borrowing in 1980, however, causes some concern.

The major culprit—if there is one—in squeezing out nonfinancial business was household borrowing, especially for mortgages. From 1972 to 1979 (both prosperous years) mortgage lending grew at an annual rate of 16.9 percent and consumer credit at an annual rate of 14.9 percent. These rates are much in excess of the growth of nominal GNP (10.7 percent) or of residential construction (10.4 percent) over the same period. It is a fair guess that some of the mortgage borrowing financed consumption expenditures or nonresidential investments during the 1970s.

The reason for the boom in mortgage lending that resulted in enormous increases in the selling price of existing homes is by now common knowledge. For a long time the government maintained regulatory control over the passbook interest rate that banks and savings associations could pay; the rate was kept low and mortgage money was cheap. When savers got wise and turned to other forms of holding wealth, the government stepped back in and authorized lending institutions to offer certificates at more competitive interest rates; this kept the flow coming in. If the flow ebbed, an assortment of government agencies were ready to buy up existing mortgages to reliquefy the market. At the same time people were realizing that federal taxes gave differential advantages to homeownership over almost any other form of investment.[12] The income (rental value) of the home is not taxed, and some of the expenses (interest and property taxes) are deductible from income. Capital gains on homes are deferrable if you buy another one. In the mid-1970s a one-time exclusion from any tax of the first $100,000 of capital gains on owner-occupied homes sold by people over fifty-five years old further increased the attractiveness of housing as a tax shelter.

To a lesser extent, consumer borrowing was fostered by similar government regulatory and tax policies. There are actually people alive today who saved money in order to buy an automobile. The 1970s made that only a memory. Since interest rates on consumer loans are tax deductible, a great many people found that the after-tax cost of borrowing was less than the rate of inflation in car prices. This provided an incentive to borrow and buy rather than save and wait. No one knows how many consumers used similar logic to justify borrowing to purchase antiques, coins, and other items.

State and local government borrowing was fairly limited in the 1970s. But even the small share of such borrowing did take funds away from other borrowers. These governments, moreover, are able to borrow at better terms than business because interest on the bonds they issue is not taxed by the federal government. To the extent that governments were raising funds for housing, student loans, industrial development, and the like because their interest costs are so low, it is not unlikely that some alternative business investment project was crowded out.

In sum, government is to blame for some of the high interest costs or lack of funds that crowded out some business borrowing. But federal borrowing as such played a small part in the years of high economic activity when it really mattered. More important were government regulations and tax expenditures that channeled borrowing and lending toward house equity, unproductive investments, and consumption.

Government borrowing is often said to contribute to inflation because of an alleged tendency of the Federal Reserve to expand its holdings of government securities (and thus expand the monetary

12. See Anthony Downs, "Too Much Capital for Housing?" *Brookings Bulletin,* vol. 17 (Summer 1980), pp. 1–5.

base) when government is borrowing at a fast pace. This would be the case, for example, if the Federal Reserve attempted to hold down interest rates. (In that event high government borrowing would not crowd out anyone since the volume of total credit would be expanded by the Federal Reserve's purchases. But the expanded money base might be inconsistent with long-run inflation control.) This is not the place for an evaluation of Federal Reserve policy in the 1970s, but by the end of the decade the central bank had made it clear that it is primarily concerned with the management of monetary aggregates—not interest rates—and that it has no intention of allowing its policies to be affected by ups and downs in government borrowing.

Will the next decade be different? Suppose federal borrowing is held in check and incentives for investment by nonfinancial business are increased. Will the loanable funds actually get to the business sector? Since the tax incentives discussed above are among the most sacrosanct in the tax code, the possibility certainly exists that in the next decade many people will continue to want to "invest" in housing. The principal change from the 1970s, however, will be a transformation in the financing mechanism for housing. Passbook interest rates have been deregulated and will gradually rise. Moreover, lending institutions have realized that making long-term fixed-interest mortgages in an era of rising inflation is not a wise policy. As a consequence, the 1980s will almost certainly see fewer lenders willing to lend at a fixed rate; instead they will offer renegotiable-rate mortgages in various forms. This development will shift some of the risk of rising inflation and interest from the lender to the borrower-investor and may lessen the attractiveness of housing investment. If the government is serious about opening an adequate window for the financing of corporate investment in the 1980s, it must keep an eye on such parts of its house as fiscal and monetary policies, financial regulation, and tax benefits that skew investment decisions.

The Federal Reserve's announced policy of lowering the growth of monetary aggregates could pose problems in the 1980s. If there is a spurt in demand for credit arising from the government, households, or business and if the Federal Reserve sticks to its policy of moderate money growth, interest rates could soar and somebody will be crowded out. Obviously, the likelihood of a stop-and-go economy of this sort is minimized if the federal government's own borrowing path is consistent with the Federal Reserve's planned expansion of the monetary base.

Net Interest

Interest payments on the public debt cause many problems of analysis, especially when inflation rates are changing. This is because what is ordinarily termed interest really consists of two components: "true interest" and "repayment of capital." An example should help here. Suppose that a government in a noninflationary world maintained a ten-man army at annual wages of $5 each and in addition had outstanding $100 worth of public debt on which it paid $3 in interest. The budget outlays of this country would be $53, $50 for defense and $3 for interest. Now suppose that inflation at the rate of 10 percent suddenly and permanently invaded the nation. Defense expenditures would go up by 10 percent, to $55, as the all-volunteer army demanded a 10 percent pay boost. But interest expenditures would rise to $13.30, a more than fourfold increase. The bondholders would demand that their true interest be adjusted for inflation (from $3 to $3.30) and that they be compensated for the fact that when the $100 is returned it will be worth only $90. Thus the "interest rate" of 13.3 percent has a true interest component of 3.3 percent and a "repayment of capital" component of 10 percent; the latter presumably would be reinvested so that in future years the value of the bondholder's principal would not be eroded. The only "income" payment made by the government is $3.30 (up 10 percent from the previous year); the rest simply restores the owner's capital.

The first thing to note is that when interest rates rise government expenditures for interest rise disproportionately.[13] This is exactly what happened to federal expenditures for interest in the 1970s. In 1970 the average interest rate paid on outstanding debt was 5.5 percent; in 1980 it was 8.8 percent. Thus interest payments on the debt would have risen by 60 percent even if the federal government had

---

13. It is the *increase* in interest rates that drives up the government's interest outlays, not the *level* of interest. In the example in the text, defense expenditures would continue to rise at a 10 percent rate while interest outlays remained constant (if the government financed the initial increase in interest by taxes) or increased at a 10 percent rate (if the government borrowed to finance the initial increase). Thus the bulge in interest outlays is greatest when interest rates rise. In the real world of federal debt, the adjustment takes place more slowly because part of the debt outstanding is in the form of long-maturity Treasury bonds.

borrowed nothing during the decade. The same thing is true in reverse: if a budget plan is put forth in which interest rates are assumed to decline, there will be a disproportionate decline in outlays for interest, even if the debt itself rises somewhat. Thus whenever a policymaker wishes to show a balanced budget in any given future year, the task is considerably eased if he can forecast inflation in that year low enough to push down interest outlays.

If the government's interest outlays are partly a repayment of capital, the ordinary reasons for wanting to cover such outlays by taxation may not hold. A true interest payment would be treated as income by the recipient and be indistinguishable from a social security benefit payment or a salary paid to a military official. But a payment that is viewed as the return of an asset by the recipient is not likely to be put back into demand for goods and services and therefore would not necessitate a tax to offset the demand. To the extent that a significant part of interest outlays is viewed as a return of capital, borrowing to cover that part is not inconsistent with government's playing a neutral role in aggregate demand.[14]

Unfortunately there is no simple way to assess how recipients of federal interest payments divide the proceeds into income and replacement of capital lost to inflation. Individuals in 1980 directly held only 21 percent of the public debt owned by anyone but the government and the Federal Reserve. The remainder was owned by banks, insurance companies, brokers, state and local governments, nonprofit institutions, and so on. Each of these institutions, not to mention the individuals, probably differs in the degree to which it has adjusted to the inflationary environment that makes ordinary accounting procedures obsolete. To the extent that a nonprofit organization (a university, for example) tries to keep the real value of its capital (endowment) intact, only a small part of its receipts of interest on government bonds will be used to purchase goods and services. At the opposite pole, an elderly widow clipping bond coupons is unlikely to distinguish between income and the inflation premium components. Until we learn more about how interest income affects spending, the implications of an increase (decrease) in interest rates resulting from accelerating (decelerating) inflation for the govern-

14. In the 1970s, therefore, an index of the tightness of fiscal policy is somewhere between the ratio of federal receipts to (a) program outlays and (b) program outlays plus net interest (see table 5-6).

ment's efforts to maintain noninflationary growth in aggregate demand must be regarded as an open question.[15] (The effect of borrowing to cover interest is the same on capital markets as borrowing for any other purpose. It squeezes out some other borrower.)

The Burden of the Debt

Most people seldom worry about the burden of the public debt. President Reagan recently tried to dramatize its size by pointing out that if the debt, now approaching $1 trillion, consisted of one thousand dollar bills the stack would be sixty-seven miles high.

Table 5-10 presents some pertinent measures of the public debt and related items. First, a significant share of all federal debt is held in federal government accounts such as trust funds and by the Federal Reserve System. The only part of the debt bearing interest payments for which the government needs to raise taxes or borrowing is that held by "private investors" (which include state, local, and foreign governments).[16] Debt held by private investors was $594 billion at the end of fiscal 1980. As noted earlier, the government has been acquiring loan assets rapidly in recent years, and part of the growing public debt has been to finance such lending. If loan assets held by the government are subtracted to give a net debt position of the government,[17] it was $430 billion in the hole by the end of 1980.

One reason to worry about the debt is that Americans eventually have to pay taxes to service the debt and would like to limit the portion of their national income that goes into such debt service. From 1960 to 1975 the debt in relation to national income fell sharply. The ratio rose in the next five years, largely because of substantial

15. This discussion is most applicable to the case where debt is short term and premiums for current inflation are part of the nominal interest rate. For long-term debt, spending decisions would be affected by the transfer of wealth from bondholders to the government whenever interest rates rise.

16. Interest paid on debt held by federal trust funds involves offsetting entries in the budget: interest paid is counted as an outlay of the U.S. Treasury and as a negative outlay of the trust fund. Interest paid to the Federal Reserve is counted as a federal outlay; but when the Federal Reserve returns the interest to the Treasury in the form of deposits of earnings, it is recorded as a budget receipt. In neither case is the federal deficit affected by the payment.

17. The government owns many other assets besides loans (fuel, tanks, cash accounts), and it has many other liabilities (implicit deficit in social security accounts, for example). This measure is thus a limited part of the federal balance sheet. It should be noted that many of the loan assets held by the government would probably be valued by the market at less than face value.

Table 5-10. Public Debt and Loan Assets of the Federal Government, End of Selected Fiscal Years, 1960–80

Billions of dollars unless otherwise specified

Item	1960	1970	1975	1980
Gross federal debt	290.9	382.6	544.1	914.3
Held by federal government accounts	53.7	97.7	147.2	199.2
Held by Federal Reserve System	26.5	57.7	85.0	120.8
Held by private investors	210.7	227.2	311.9	594.3
Direct loans outstanding	27.4	51.1	74.1	163.9
On-budget	27.4	51.1	59.7	91.7
Off-budget	0.0	0.0	14.4	72.3
Debt held by private investors minus direct loans outstanding	183.3	176.1	237.8	430.4
Addendum				
Debt in constant dollars[a]				
Held by private investors	536.8	441.0	447.9	594.3
Held by private investors minus direct loans outstanding	467.3	341.9	341.5	430.4
Debt as percent of GNP				
Held by private investors	42.2	23.4	21.1	23.1
Held by private investors minus direct loans outstanding	36.7	18.2	16.1	16.8

Sources: Office of Management and Budget, "Federal Government Finances," December 1980 edition, pp. 56–57; *The Budget of the United States Government, Fiscal Year 1982*, p. 611; *Special Analyses, Budget of the United States Government, Fiscal Year 1982*, pp. 113 and 150; OMB, "Federal Credit Programs: Historica Data, 1950–1980," table 2; and unpublished data from the Office of Management and Budget. Figures are rounded.

a. Deflated by GNP deflator with fiscal year 1980 = 100.

deficits in the 1976 and 1980 recession years and because of the growing deficit attributable to greater federal lending activity. Debt net of loans held by the government in relation to GNP showed a similar pattern of sharp decline to 1975 and an upward drift over the subsequent five years (table 5-10).

An alternative measure of the state of the federal balance sheet is the public debt (held by private investors) expressed in constant dollars. By deflating the debt by the price level, this measure recognizes that when a debtor's liabilities are fixed in money terms a capital gain accrues to the debtor when prices rise unexpectedly. The capital gain is due to his liability being smaller in terms of the real goods and services owed. This real gain to the government as debtor is equal to the loss suffered by bondholders as the real value of their bonds declines. Thus maintaining the real value of the debt implies that there is no transfer of real wealth between the government and its creditors. The real debt, expressed in constant dollars, fell by 18 percent in the 1960–70 period, held steady from 1970 to 1975, and then rose by 33 percent between 1975 and 1980. To put this measure into a current dollar perspective: with the federal debt held by private investors at nearly $600 billion at the end of 1980 and inflation running at about 10 percent, the real public debt will rise if federal borrowing exceeds $60 billion in 1981.[18]

While there is no widely agreed-upon standard for an ideal level of public debt, the notion of aiming for no increase in the ratio of debt to GNP is equivalent to ensuring that future taxpayers will not have a larger share of their income taken by taxes to pay interest than is now the case. (When interest rates are rising or declining, however, the share would vary even if the debt–GNP ratio were held steady.) A constant real debt would mean that the government's liability in terms of real goods and services held steady. Finally, it should be noted that a balanced budget (including off-budget entities) rule implies that the nominal federal debt would be unchanged and that both the debt–GNP ratio and real debt measures would decline with growth and inflation.

Budget Outlook

This review of recent budget history and concepts highlights some of the problems that policymakers face in the 1980s. Although it is hard to make the case that federal spending "hemorrhaged" in the 1970s, it built up considerable momentum and threatens to take an increasing share of GNP. Tax burdens have become unusually heavy and will continue to increase unless tax laws are changed. Greatly enlarged deficits, which will occur if tax relief is granted without curbing expenditure growth, would impinge on business access to capital markets and might raise debt burdens in the future. And they could add inflationary pressure to an already high built-in inflation rate. Although annual budget planners might want to deviate from

18. A similar measure of real net indebtedness could be constructed by computing the real value of the public debt net of loan assets held by the government. Inflation causes the government to suffer a capital loss to the extent that it is a lender. This measure will rise if federal borrowing exceeds $43 billion in 1981.

some of the longer term goals stressed in this section, one lesson of the 1970s is that the long-term goals should not be ignored.

The Reagan Budget Plan

President Reagan's budget revisions proposed some dramatic reversals in recent budget trends: greatly accelerated growth in national defense outlays accompanied by severe reductions in many nondefense programs; a halt in the recent increase in the income tax burden; and a large retrenchment in federal lending and borrowing activity.

The Reagan proposals appear to have been drafted with a heavy emphasis on budgetary and economic targets for fiscal year 1984. Although projections through 1986 accompany the budget revisions, they seem to be extrapolations of tax and spending decisions made through 1984. Accordingly, this analysis will focus on 1984.

Two problems arise in discussing the Reagan plan. The first is that although full details of a multiyear tax reduction were provided, the spending reductions proposed were incomplete. One package of reductions applicable to the 1982 budget was introduced in early 1981 (and these cuts can be projected to later years), but an additional $30 billion in reductions in 1983 and $44 billion in 1984 were unspecified and simply listed as needed to achieve "target outlay" levels. Therefore, in what follows I will refer to the first-stage budget (meaning that only the first stage of spending cuts announced in March 1981 are implemented) and the "target budget" (including the effects of additional reductions yet to be spelled out).

Another problem arises because President Reagan's budget plan is based on a forecast for the economy both very different from his predecessor's and very optimistic in the light of recent history (see table 2-9). The Carter economic assumptions—of a gradual decline in consumer price index inflation to about 8 percent in 1984 (as against Reagan's 5.7 percent) and of slow real economic growth averaging 3.4 percent (as against Reagan's 4.3 percent) from 1981 to 1984—represent a useful alternative by which to assess how the budget might develop if the optimistic assumptions do not work out. Accordingly, President Reagan's program is discussed under its own economic assumptions and then the differences under the Carter estimates are noted.

The Size and Composition of Outlays
under the First-Stage Reductions

Table 5-11 summarizes the Reagan budget proposals through 1984. The proposals are virtually a reversal of developments of the previous ten years. Under the administration's projections, outlays for lending programs, which grew most rapidly in the late 1970s, fall the most. Net interest outlays barely increase. Total outlays, which grew steadily for twenty years at a pace slightly faster than GNP, would grow at a pace only slightly more than half of GNP growth in 1981–84 even if the second stage of future reductions were not made (see first-stage outlays in table 5-11). Total outlays, which grew less than inflation (measured by the implicit price deflator for

Table 5-11. The Reagan Administration's Federal Budget Outlay Projections, by Major Category, Fiscal Years 1980–84

Billions of dollars unless otherwise specified

Category	1980	1981	1982	1983	1984	Annual rate of growth, 1981–84 (percent)
Program outlays	518	588	622	690	745	8.2
Loan outlays	24	27	22	14	12	−23.7
On-budget	9	3[a]	5[a]	3[b]	2[b]	−12.6
Off-budget	15	24	17	11	10	−25.3
Net interest outlays	53	64	68	69	68	2.0
First-stage outlays[c]	580	655	695	762	814	7.5
Future reductions	0	0	0	30	44	. . .
Target outlays	580	655	695	732	770	5.5
Addendum						
GNP	2,568	2,847	3,200	3,598	3,999	12.0
Program outlays as percent of GNP	20.2	20.7	19.4	19.2	18.6	. . .
Future reductions as percent of GNP	0.0	0.0	0.0	0.8	1.1	. . .
Percentage change in GNP deflator	8.5	10.0	8.7	7.3	6.3	7.4[d]

Sources: *The Budget of the United States Government, Fiscal Year 1982*, pp. 3 and 611; *Special Analyses, Budget of the United States Government, Fiscal Year 1982*, p. 150; unpublished data from the Office of Management and Budget; and *Budget Revisions, Fiscal Year 1982*, pp. 3, 13, 24, 27, and 124. Figures are rounded.
a. The Reagan administration proposed cuts in direct loan *obligations* of $2.6 billion in 1981 and 1982. It is assumed here that the reductions will reduce net loan *outlays* by $1 billion in each year.
b. Author's estimate.
c. Excludes off-budget outlays.
d. Rate of growth of GNP deflator.

Table 5-12. The Reagan Administration's Program Outlays, by Major Category, First-Stage Reductions Only, Fiscal Years 1981–84

Billions of dollars unless otherwise specified

Category	1981	1982	1983	1984	Annual rate of growth, 1981–84 (percent)
			Current dollars		
National defense	162.1	188.8	226.0	255.6	16.4
Payments for individuals	317.4	337.3	365.3	391.8	7.3
Social safety net[a]	241.4	262.6	286.1	308.8	8.6
Other entitlements	76.0	74.7	79.2	83.0	3.0
Other grants	54.9	47.2	45.7	44.3	−6.9
Other operations	53.6	48.7	52.8	52.9	−0.4
Program outlays	588.0	622.0	689.8	744.6	8.2
			Constant 1972 dollars		
National defense	77.8	83.0	92.6	98.4	8.1
Payments for individuals	146.3	142.5	144.8	147.0	0.2
Social safety net[a]	111.2	110.9	113.4	115.8	1.4
Other entitlements	35.1	31.6	31.4	31.1	−4.0
Other grants	27.1	21.3	19.1	17.2	−14.1
Other operations	27.1	23.0	23.3	21.9	−6.9
Program outlays	278.3	269.8	279.8	284.5	0.7
			Percent of GNP in current dollars		
National defense	5.7	5.9	6.3	6.4	...
Payments for individuals	11.1	10.5	10.2	9.8	...
Social safety net[a]	8.5	8.2	8.0	7.7	...
Other entitlements	2.7	2.3	2.2	2.1	...
Other grants	1.9	1.5	1.3	1.1	...
Other operations	1.9	1.5	1.5	1.3	...
Program outlays	20.7	19.4	19.2	18.6	...

Sources: Unpublished data from the Office of Management and Budget; *Budget Revisions, Fiscal Year 1982*, p. 124; OMB, "Federal Government Finances," March 1981 edition, p. 75; and table 5-11.

a. Includes old age, survivors, and disability insurance, railroad retirement, medicare, basic unemployment benefits, supplemental security income, aid to families with dependent children, and veterans' income security and health care.

GNP) in only five of the previous twenty years, would rise less than inflation in every year from 1981 to 1984 under the target outlay plan.

Changes in program outlays after the budget changes announced in early 1981 (but before future reductions) are shown in table 5-12. Payments for individuals have been divided into two components. One is the "social safety net," which the administration defined as entitlement programs for the "truly needy." These programs—including social security, medicare, supplemental security income (aid to the elderly, blind, and disabled), "basic" unemployment insurance, aid to families with dependent children and other smaller welfare programs, and most veterans' programs—were generally exempt from the budget reductions announced early in 1981. The other components, including many income-tested programs that aid poor people—such as medicaid, food stamps, and housing assistance—are listed as "other entitlements."

The first thing to note about President Reagan's first-stage budget is that it proposes a reduction in the relative size of government programs from 20.7 percent of GNP in 1981 to 18.6 percent by 1984. Sharp though this reduction is, it would bring the relative size of the federal government back down only to where it was as recently as 1970–74, the Nixon era (see table 5-3).[19]

Total outlays for programs are scheduled to rise by $157 billion from 1981 to 1984. Of this increase, national defense outlays account for $94 billion and outlays for the protected social safety net programs account for $67 billion. All other programs, therefore, are reduced drastically, after taking inflation into account.

The differences in inflation-corrected spending in the various program categories are dramatic. National defense outlays in the three years ending in 1984 rise by 8.1 percent a year after correcting for inflation. By contrast, real defense expenditures rose about 14 percent a year in the three-year Vietnam buildup. However, in calculating real defense expenditures, separate corrections are made for personnel costs (about half of total defense spending) and for investment-type expenditures (hardware, construction, research and development). The real increase in the former is projected to be about 1 to 2 percent a year, implying that in the investment accounts the annual increase is close to 15 percent a year. Such increases are unprecedented for a period in which no war is being fought.

Payments for individuals, which exhibited such rapid growth through the mid-1970s, are held to no real growth in the Reagan projections (table 5-12). The social safety net programs (about 75 percent of the benefit payments category in 1981) advance at a

19. Unified outlays (including net interest and on-budget loans) in relation to GNP would fall to 20.4 percent under the first-stage cuts and to 19.3 percent under target outlays in 1984. The former corresponds to the share in the early 1970s and the latter to the share in the middle 1960s.

1.4 percent real rate, largely accounted for by demographic and rising-earnings factors in the social security program. The remaining transfer payment programs are slashed sharply in 1982 and then held constant in real terms for the remainder of the period. These reductions in medicaid, food stamps, subsidized housing, and the like are discussed in chapter 3.

Other grants—which include payments to state and local governments for highways, mass transit, social services, education, training, and employment—is the broad category most severely hit by President Reagan's proposals. The rate of reduction in constant dollar spending in these programs is 14.1 percent a year from 1981 to 1984. (If I may take a cue from President Reagan's depiction of the national debt, what a real rate of decline of 14.1 percent a year for three years means is that 7'4" Ralph Sampson, the center for the University of Virginia basketball team in 1981, would shrink to 4'8" by 1984, short even for a junior high school team.) The reductions in the grant programs are especially sharp in 1982 (dropping more than 20 percent in constant dollars in that year alone) and then are frozen in nominal dollars in 1983 and 1984 (resulting in further real erosion as inflation continues). In short, changes in this grouping of programs will result in a dramatic shift in the federal and state-local relationship.[20]

The residual category of other operations, which had maintained a steady 2 percent share of GNP throughout the 1970s (table 5-3), also shrinks under the Reagan proposals. The budgetary reductions in this area—which include sharp reductions in federal employees' salaries relative to private salaries, employment cuts in most agencies, and scores of service cutbacks from the National Aquarium to

---

20. No projections for total federal, state, and local spending are included in this section, because with the abrupt changes proposed by the administration it is difficult to make a guess at state and local spending outcomes. If governments merely reduced their spending by the amount of the reduced federal grants, the size of total government in relation to GNP would fall along with the federal ratio. But if lower-level governments tried to maintain some services previously supported by the federal government, the total government share would decline more slowly. In that instance either borrowing or taxation at the state and local level would rise, partially offsetting federal improvements in those measures. To the extent that past research —which analyzed what happened on the way up, not down—on this subject is valid, one would expect significant maintenance of service levels at first, financed largely by borrowing (or smaller surpluses), followed eventually by an erosion of service levels, with whatever is left financed by state and local taxes.

Amtrak to the postal service—amount to about 7 percent a year (in constant dollars) from 1981 to 1984. (If Ralph Sampson shrank at that rate, by 1984 he would be 5'11" tall, probably the shortest player in the National Basketball Association.) These overhead and direct service expenditures would fall to their lowest real level since the early 1960s.

A convenient and interesting way to sum up what the program budget of the federal government would look like by 1984 if the first stage of spending reductions were enacted is to compare the distribution of 1984 outlays with the distribution in 1970–74 (as already noted, the ratio of program outlays to GNP in the two periods is about the same—18.6 percent):

	Share of program outlays (percent)		
	1970–74	1980	1984
National defense	37	26	34
Payments for individuals	42	52	53
Other grants	10	11	6
Other operations	11	10	7

The restoration of national defense to about the same relative importance it had in federal spending in 1970–74 takes place in just a few years, and the growth of social safety net programs allows benefit payments for individuals to continue to grow as a fraction of the budget. Thus, in contrast to the early 1970s, the 1984 budget severely tightens grants and service programs to achieve the same relative size of government. There is little relation between the sources of growing expenditures in the 1970s and the program outlay components selected for major reductions. Most of the rapidly growing category of payments for individuals was exempt from cutbacks by inclusion in the social safety net. By contrast, grants and other operations that contributed little to the growing size of government in the 1970s (table 5-3) receive the largest cuts under President Reagan's first-stage program.

Achieving Target Outlay Levels

According to the administration, to achieve its overall target level of outlays in 1984, an additional $44 billion in spending reductions must be identified and enforced. If such cuts were made in program outlays, their share of GNP would shrink to 17.5 percent and program outlays in real terms would be smaller in 1984 than in 1981 or 1982. The size of the federal government would shrink in real terms. One has to go back to the early 1960s to find a comparably small share of GNP devoted to federal government programs. At no time in the last thirty years has the real size of government declined over three consecutive years. Attaining the target outlay level would result in the much smaller federal government that the Reagan administration clearly believes is desirable.

Could an additional $44 billion of reductions in program outlays be found by 1984? There appear to be four possibilities. One would be to continue reducing service levels in "other operations." Since over half of the expenditures remaining in that category are for pay and benefits of federal employees of nondefense agencies, such cuts would mean eliminating more federal jobs, perhaps by closing the National Zoo or reducing weather services or the number of national park rangers. Other items in this category are the remaining parts of federal support for the arts, humanities, and research, agricultural price supports, postal subsidies, rail subsidies, travel of federal employees, and other overhead expenses. Once, shrinking these would have been regarded as unpopular actions.

Second would be to resort to a little understood budgeteer's gambit. The $53 billion in 1984 outlays for other federal operations that remains after the first stage of proposed reductions is actually composed of gross outlays that are more than $30 billion higher than that figure *minus* over $30 billion in offsetting receipts. These receipts, counted as negative spending, stem mainly from the government's sale of land and products (timber, minerals) and its receipts of interest, rents, and royalties from loans, land leases, and mineral and petroleum development leases. Even in its early 1981 budget revisions, the Reagan administration proposed substantial increases in these negative outlays, the most notable being an acceleration of the rate of drilling for oil and gas on the outer continental shelf, which, it was estimated, would bring $3 billion more in rents and royalty payments to the government (which equals $3 billion less in outlays) in 1984 than under Carter's budget. The possibilities here are limitless, given all the land, minerals, and physical assets that the government owns. So the budget could be cut by accelerating activities that result in offsetting budgetary receipts; the more timber development you allow, the less need there is to close the National Zoo or cut funds for poets. Whatever the merit of accelerating mineral development and the like is, although it reduces federal spending, it hardly constitutes a contribution to a smaller government share of real resources.

A third route to second-stage budget reduction would be to decentralize government even further and tighten up even more on entitlements. Even after the first-stage cuts, there are $127 billion in 1984 outlays in the other grant and other entitlement programs that are not included in the social safety net (table 5-12, top panel). Among the areas that the Reagan administration listed as under study for further reductions are medicaid financing reform, tightening federal pensions, elimination of overlapping or redundant subsidies and benefits, and efficient sharing of the provision of services by the federal government and state and local governments.

The final way to cut $44 billion in program spending in 1984 would be to reopen the two untouchable categories in the administration's initial budget plan: national defense and the social safety net. Alternative budget strategies in these areas are discussed in chapters 3 and 4. Suffice it to say here that the focus of such budget reductions would be on less expensive hardware in the military, less indexing in the safety net, and some form of expenditure controls in medicare. It is hard to imagine that the projected $564 billion in 1984 outlays for national defense and the social safety net would remain unscathed in these further budget reductions.

Taxes, Fiscal Balance, and the Burden of Taxation

The Reagan administration proposes a business tax reduction amounting to $30 billion by fiscal year 1984 and an across-the-board reduction in individual income tax rates (Kemp-Roth) that would decrease receipts by $118 billion in fiscal year 1984. The details of these tax proposals are given in chapter 2.

If the entire tax package was enacted as proposed and only the first stage of budget reductions was passed, the 1984 budget would become slightly more restrictive than in the late 1970s. Federal receipts would reach 104 percent of program outlays and 95 percent of program outlays plus net interest in 1984, compared to 100 and 91 percent, respectively, in 1980. Under these assumptions the federal deficit would be $44 billion, or 1.1 percent of GNP, down 1 percentage point from the average during 1977–80. This fiscal plan would be highly reminiscent of the 1970–74 period.[21]

It is only when the proposed second stage of spending reductions enters the picture that the fiscal balance turns much more restrictive than at any time in the 1970s. With these additional reductions, which amount to 1 percent of GNP, the overall fiscal plan resembles that of the late 1950s. As in that earlier period, by 1984 under the reduced target outlay plan the federal budget would come into balance.

Whether the economy would grow as rapidly as the administration predicts, given the tighter fiscal balance of the target outlay plan, is a matter of some dispute. All parties seem agreed that for the economy to recover rapidly private business investment would have to respond strongly to the tax incentives and hoped-for improvement in confidence and expectations for the future. Also, the Federal Reserve would have to cooperate in allowing such a business expansion. These matters are discussed in chapter 2.

The burden of federal taxes is reduced by President Reagan's program, though not drastically (table 5-13). In relation to GNP, total receipts in 1984 fall to 19.3 percent, about the same level as in 1977–78 (table 5-6), but down from 21.1 percent in 1981. Individual income taxes as a percentage of personal income fall to 10.6, one percentage point below the level in 1980. This level of income taxation is about the same as in the prosperous years of the 1970s (see table 5-6), but the combined burden of individual income and payroll taxes after the Kemp-Roth tax reductions will be higher than it was in most of the 1970s.

The administration has emphasized the effect of the tax reduction in stimulating personal saving, work effort, and entrepreneurship. This supply-side approach emphasizes not so much the overall level of taxes in relation to income, but rather the marginal rate that the taxpayer pays on the next dollar of earnings. The Kemp-Roth tax reduction plan would by 1984 cut this marginal rate for every tax bracket by about 30 percent. Thus a family with taxable income of $27,250 in 1980 was squarely in the middle of the 32 percent tax bracket. In 1984, under Kemp-Roth, taxable income of $27,250 on a

21. In 1970–74 federal receipts were 103 percent of program outlays and 95 percent of program outlays plus net interest; the deficit as a percent of GNP averaged 1.2 (see table 5-6).

Table 5-13. Ratio of Federal Receipts under the Reagan Administration's Budget to Outlays and Gross National Product, Fiscal Years 1980–84

Item	1980	1981	1982	1983	1984
Receipts as percent of program outlays[a]	100	102	105	103–107	104–110
Receipts as percent of program outlays plus net interest[a]	91	92	94	93–97	95–100
Receipts as percent of GNP	20.3	21.1	20.4	19.7	19.3
Addendum					
Individual income taxes as percent of personal income	11.6	11.9	11.1	10.7	10.6
Individual income taxes plus employee social security taxes as percent of personal income	14.7	15.2	14.5	14.1	14.0

Sources: *The Budget of the United States Government, Fiscal Year 1982*, p. 3; *Budget Revisions, Fiscal Year 1982*, pp. 11, 13, 15, and 122; Office of Tax Analysis, "Individual Income Tax Liability and Employee Social Security Contributions as a Percent of Income," revised; Office of Management and Budget, "Federal Government Finances," March 1981 edition, p. 8; and tables 5-2, 5-6, and 5-11.

a. For 1983 and 1984 the lower percentage assumes that only first-stage budget cuts are passed; the higher percentage reflects further cuts as well.

joint return would be in the middle of the 21 percent tax bracket. However, since incomes tend to rise in inflationary times, if the family's taxable income rose at a rate equal to the Reagan administration's projections of consumer price inflation from 1980 to 1984 (that is, if it rose to $36,700), it would be taxed at a marginal rate of 32 percent, exactly the same marginal rate as prevailed in 1980. (With no tax cut at all, the family's marginal rate would rise to 43 percent for the same example.) It is only at the higher incomes ($50,000 and over for joint returns), where tax brackets are wide and where a 30 percent rate cut amounts to a larger percentage point cut, that the Reagan administration's tax reduction plan would significantly lower marginal tax rates from those of the past. Thus any increase in work, saving, or entrepreneurship would have to come from a relatively small segment of the population. There are no reliable recent studies that allow confident predictions of responses to changes in marginal taxes by these top earners. On the other hand, if tax rates were not adjusted at all, the bracket creep described previously would continue, especially in low and middle income ranges, with possibly significant effects on saving and labor supply.

In large measure, therefore, Kemp-Roth is a holding action. With no change in income tax laws, inflation and real growth will push more and more income into higher tax brackets; Kemp-Roth offsets this bracket creep and provides a modest overall reduction in tax burdens. The overall tax burden comes down fairly sharply in 1982, and then declines slowly until 1984, when budget outlays are brought into balance with receipts. The distinguishing feature of the tax reduction plan is that it concentrates more of the reductions in upper brackets than the typical tax cut of the past decade.

Lending and Investment

There is no doubt where the Reagan administration stands on federally assisted lending programs. On virtually every lending front, the administration's proposals involve retrenchment of lending activity. The elimination of several lending agencies, such as the Economic Development Administration and the National Consumer Cooperative Bank, was proposed. Several direct loan programs that are heavily subsidized, such as the 5 percent loans of the Rural Electrification Administration, are to be switched to loan guarantee programs, presumably carrying market rates of interest. The REA and the Student Loan Marketing Association would lose access to the off-budget Federal Financing Bank, thereby eliminating their "back door" entry to U.S. Treasury financing. Another proposal is that the direct loan and guarantee activity of a host of agencies be cut back sharply: the Export-Import Bank, the Farmers Home Administration, the Small Business Administration, the Government National Mortgage Association, and the Federal Housing Administration are among the major reductions. In several instances, guaranteed student loans being the best known, the administration proposed significant reductions in interest subsidies and less generous eligibility criteria.

The impact of these changes on the budget proper in the initial years is modest. In 1981 and 1982 direct loan outlays of on-budget agencies would be down about $1 billion in each year. For the off-budget federal entities (primarily the Federal Financing Bank), the reduction in outlays is more significant, amounting to $5 billion, $7 billion, and $9 billion for the three years 1982–84. In addition, an indeterminate amount of interest subsidy spending was removed from the program outlay lines of the budget. These reductions, which may be significant in the future, are reflected in the estimates shown in table 5-11.

The real significance of these loan program reductions lies in their effect on who gets credit. As rural telephone and electric companies, consumer cooperatives, college students, and exporters lose access to subsidized loans, they presumably will find it harder to compete with other borrowers for the available capital. It is clearly the administration's hope and presumption that the borrowers who win out over the discouraged federally assisted borrowers will use their capital to invest in productivity-raising, energy-saving, or fuel-development activities. This presumption is based on a belief that a less regulated, freer capital market will be better able to sort out worthy, high-payoff projects than the more governmentally influenced markets of the past decade.

The last word on federal credit activities has probably not been heard from the Reagan administration. New direct loan obligations in fiscal 1982 are still $50 billion, even after all of the proposed reductions. It may in fact prove tempting to the administration to reduce direct lending activity below the level of repayments on past direct loans. This would result in negative outlays for the loan items in the unified budget and would help to "balance the budget." Acceleration of collections on loan repayments or sales of loan assets to the public would similarly lower budget outlays and the deficit. With $164 billion in outstanding loans at the end of fiscal 1980, any of these methods of reducing the outstanding balance (lower new loan activity, higher repayments, or sale of loans) would enable the Treasury Department to borrow less. Although these activities would make federal financing look better—the public debt and the deficit would be smaller—their economic and financial market effect would be limited. One dollar less in public debt and one dollar less in federal loan assets would leave the balance sheets of the government and the private sector in the same position as before the change. So although there are many good reasons to reduce federal lending activity—such as less interference in private markets or reduced subsidies—helping to balance the budget should not be one of them.

Borrowing and the Debt

Federal borrowing to finance the budget deficit and the deficit of the off-budget entities is projected to be severely curtailed under the administration's budget proposals and economic assumptions. The upper panel of table 5-14 shows the Reagan administration's projection of a declining volume of federal borrowing, from $71 billion in

Table 5-14. Federal Borrowing, Reagan Budget Plan, under Alternate Economic Assumptions, Fiscal Years 1980–84

Billions of dollars unless otherwise specified

Item	1980	1981	1982	1983	1984
		Reagan economic assumptions			
Unified budget deficit	60	55	45	23a–53	0a–44
Off-budget deficit	14	24	17	11	10
Other means of financing	−3	−8	−2	0	0
Borrowing from the public	71	71	60	34a–64	10a–54
Projected total funds raised in nonfinancial U.S. credit marketsb	348	386	434	488	542
Borrowing as percent of total funds raised in nonfinancial U.S. credit markets	20.4	18.4	13.8	7.0a–13.1	1.8a–10.0
		Carter economic assumptions			
Borrowing from the public	71	73	70	56a–86	37a–81
Projected total funds raised in nonfinancial U.S. credit marketsb	348	385	436	490	548
Borrowing as percent of total funds raised in nonfinancial U.S. credit markets	20.4	19.0	16.1	11.4a–17.6	6.8a–14.8

Sources: *The Budget of the United States Government, Fiscal Year 1982*, pp. 559 and 613; Office of Management and Budget, "Final Economic Assumptions for the 1982 Budget" (December 20, 1980), p. 3; *Budget Revisions, Fiscal Year 1982*, pp. 3, 11, 13, 27, and 29; Board of Governors of the Federal Reserve System, Flow of Funds Accounts (FRS, 1980); table 5-15, below; and author's calculations.

a. Includes budget cuts yet to be specified.
b. Assumed to increase at same rate as fiscal year GNP.

1980 down to $60 billion in 1982 and to $10 billion to $54 billion in 1984 (the smaller borrowing entries for 1983 and 1984 reflect the effect of the second-stage outlay reductions in the target budget). To put these numbers in context, included is an illustrative projection of total funds raised in U.S. credit markets that is based on the assumption that the overall volume in that market rises at the same rate as GNP.[22] Under that assumption federal borrowing from the public would represent about 14 percent of funds raised in 1982 (not very

22. In the 1970s credit markets rose faster than GNP. With the Federal Reserve now committed to a less expansive posture, it seems plausible that the historical relation to GNP will be restored. Note that the base year for these projections is 1980, when credit markets were depressed by a recession and credit controls. The projection for fiscal 1981 reported here is consistent with a commonly used independent forecast for calendar 1981; see Donald E. Woolley and Beverly Lowen, *Credit and Capital Markets, 1981* (New York: Bankers Trust Company, 1981). But the reader is warned that multiyear projections of credit markets are even less reliable than projections of the federal budget.

different from the 1970s average of 15 percent; see table 5-9) and then would decline a little (if the second stage of outlay reductions is not enacted) or quite a lot (if it is). Therefore, if heavy emphasis is placed on a significant reduction in the federal borrowing share, the second-stage budget reductions amounting to $30 billion in 1983 and $44 billion in 1984 become crucial. They must be implemented —or an equivalent amount of tax reduction must be forgone—if the window for private business borrowing is to be opened in 1983–84. Even if federal borrowing goes down, the outlook for business investment is uncertain. The administration made no proposals to reduce the tax advantages of homeownership or consumer borrowing. A number of the curbs on federal lending activity may discourage speculative activity in housing and so may the announced firmness of Federal Reserve control over growth in monetary aggregates. Nonetheless, it is an open question whether reduction in federal borrowing alone will actually raise business investment rather than housing investment or consumer borrowing. The possibility that reducing federal grants to state and local governments might raise their borrowing has already been noted.

The foregoing analysis is based on the new administration's economic forecast. However, if the economy does not grow as rapidly and inflation and interest rates do not recede as much as this forecast assumes, outlays and receipts will change. Table 5-15 shows the impact on President Reagan's budget program of an alternative set of economic assumptions—those used for President Carter's final budget. The footnotes to the table describe the origin of the numbers.

The Reagan administration's program for reduced federal borrowing is less feasible under the alternative economic assumptions. Because the higher inflation rates, lower economic growth, and higher interest rates of the Carter economic assumptions all trigger considerably higher budget outlays and only slightly higher receipts, deficits and borrowing would rise by $10 billion in 1982, $22 billion in 1983, and $27 billion in 1984.[23] When these projections of

23. A Congressional Budget Office study of the Reagan administration's budget that incorporates both a less optimistic economic outlook and an alternative set of spending rate factors concludes that deficits would exceed the administration's projections by $22 billion, $36 billion, and $50 billion in 1982, 1983, and 1984, respectively. See *An Analysis of President Reagan's Budget Revisions for Fiscal Year 1982*, staff working paper prepared for the House Committee on Appropriations (Government Printing Office, 1981), p. xxiii.

Table 5-15. Effects of Changed Economic Assumptions[a] on the Reagan Administration's Estimates of Outlays, Receipts, and Deficits, Fiscal Years 1981–84
Billions of dollars

Category	Increase			
	1981	1982	1983	1984
Unified outlays	3	14	26	38
Program outlays	*	6	15	25
National defense[b]	*	1	3	5
Payments for individuals[c]	*	5	12	20
Net interest	3	8	11	13
Effect of higher rates[d]	3	7	8	9
Effect of higher debt[e]	*	1	3	4
Receipts[f]	1	4	4	11
Deficit	2	10	22	27

Sources: *The Budget of the United States Government, Fiscal Year 1982*, pp. 3–5; unpublished data from the Office of Management and Budget; *Budget Revisions, Fiscal Year 1982*, pp. 15 and 122; and OMB, "Final Economic Assumptions for the 1982 Budget," pp. 3 and 10.
   * $500 million or less.
   a. The economic assumptions are those listed in Carter's 1982 budget. See table 2-9.
   b. Author's estimates based on the assumption that one-half of defense outlays are indexed to the GNP deflator.
   c. Based on unpublished OMB data that adjust the following accounts for inflation and real growth: major retirement programs, medicare and medicaid, and other major income security programs. No adjustment is made here for changes in employee salaries under alternate economic assumptions.
   d. Based on unpublished OMB data.
   e. Author's estimates of net interest costs of the increased deficits in 1981–84 under alternative economic assumptions.
   f. Receipts were adjusted by taking the difference in fiscal year GNP between the Carter and Reagan economic assumptions and applying a marginal tax rate of 25 percent.

borrowing are compared with projections of funds raised in credit markets (this time the projections are based on Carter's assumed GNP path), the result is a federal share over the 1982–84 period that will be greater than in the 1970s unless all the second-stage spending cuts are made (or unless taxes are reduced less than the administration has proposed). While no one knows exactly which set of economic assumptions is most likely to be realized, these estimates suggest that if one stresses the opening up of capital markets to more private business borrowing, President Reagan's budget package may need both full implementation and a fully realized economic forecast.

The impact of President Reagan's program on the burden of the debt is illustrated in table 5-16. (This table assumes enactment of the whole Reagan package, including second-stage budget cuts.)

Table 5-16. Federal Debt under the Reagan Administration's Budget, Fiscal Years 1980–84

Billions of dollars unless otherwise specified

Item	1980	1981	1982	1983	1984
Federal debt held by public[a]	715	786	846	880	890
Federal Reserve System[b]	121	128	134	141	147
Private investors	594	658	712	739	743
Direct loans outstanding	164	191	213	227	239
On-budget	92	95	100	103	105
Off-budget	72	96	113	124	134
Federal debt held by private investors minus direct loans outstanding	430	467	499	512	504
Addendum					
Debt as percent of GNP					
Held by private investors	23.1	23.1	22.2	20.5	18.6
Held by private investors minus direct loans outstanding	16.8	16.4	15.6	14.2	12.6
Debt in constant dollars					
Held by private investors[c]	594	598	595	576	544
Held by private investors under alternate economic assumptions[d]	594	598	598	588	566

Sources: *The Budget of the United States Government, Fiscal Year 1982*, p. 611; *Special Analyses, Budget of the United States Government, Fiscal Year 1982*, pp. 113 and 150; Office of Management and Budget, "Final Economic Assumptions for the 1982 Budget," p. 3, and unpublished data; *Budget Revisions, Fiscal Year 1982*, pp. 13, 15, and 29; and tables 5-10, 5-14, and 5-15.

a. Debt held by the public is gross debt minus debt held by government accounts. The estimates assume President Reagan's target outlay estimates are reached and that after 1982 means of financing other than taxes and borrowing from the public equal zero.

b. Author's estimates, assuming that Federal Reserve holdings rise at 6 percent, 5 percent, 5 percent, and 4 percent in 1981, 1982, 1983, and 1984, respectively. By contrast, in the 1970s the annual rate was 7.5 percent.

c. Deflated by implicit price deflator for GNP in President Reagan's budget revisions, with fiscal 1980 = 100.

d. Deflated by implicit price deflator for GNP in President Carter's January 1981 budget, with fiscal 1980 = 100.

The debt held by the public (including the Federal Reserve) would grow more slowly than GNP. Even if the Federal Reserve System bought government securities at a much slower pace than in the 1970s,[24] the debt held by private investors would shrink as a percent of GNP. The net debt—that is, the debt held by private investors minus direct loan assets of the government—would rise by 17 percent from 1980 to 1984, one-fifth the rate of increase of the previous five years.

24. See table 5-16, note b.

All of these results are, of course, the product of the economic assumptions on which the budget is based. As noted, alternative economic assumptions would lead to higher deficits, cumulating to $61 billion by 1984. But even these deficits would not change the broad picture of a reduced burden of the debt. If the extra deficits are added to those projected under the Reagan plan, the real federal debt held by private investors declines by about 5 percent from its peak in 1981 (table 5-16, bottom line). If preventing the real debt from rising were the only constraint on federal financing, cumulative deficits in the three years ending in 1984 could amount to $45 billion above those projected under the Reagan plan even if the less optimistic economic outlook turns out to be the right one. Such added deficits would, however, almost certainly impinge on capital market objectives.

The sensitivity of the federal budget to economic assumptions makes it all the more important that summary measures of the state of federal finances be put in a proper context. If the Reagan economic forecast is wrong and more stagflation is what occurs, both spending and deficits will rise above the projections. But nominal GNP might rise as well, so that viewing federal spending or the public debt in relation to GNP would cause less concern than a simple examination of nominal values. The one summary measure that is often used as a standard for federal fiscal health—a balanced budget, zero deficit—is the only one not amenable to being put in the perspective of the economy's scale. As a result, the advantage of a balanced budget over, say, a $40 billion deficit (1 percent of GNP) in 1984 is often made to seem the obvious, and only responsible, choice. But, in fact, the only responsible way to assess alternative budget plans is to work back through their implications for fiscal balance, tax burdens, capital markets, and debt. Given a set of values and priorities in each of these realms, a responsible budget can be found, but it is not obvious.

The Reagan Plan in Historical Context

The Reagan administration hopes its budget proposals will increase the share of national resources devoted to strengthened national defense and raise productivity through an enlarged capital

stock. To achieve these goals, the administration had to choose between two strategies. It could have proceeded gradually by identifying structural flaws in government spending and educating the public
and Congress on the need for major reforms. This approach, however, suffers from the political disability that it exposes each proposed reduction to special interest lobbying and allows the opposition to mobilize. For political reasons, therefore, the administration
has chosen a strategy designed to make simultaneously a broad range
of cuts that would be politically vulnerable if attempted one by one.
Speedy implementation of this comprehensive program is bound to
lead to unintended or unexpected results as the interaction of the
changes is felt by people and state and local governments.

Under any administration a shift of resources to defense and investment would have required some reductions in federal assistance
to state and local governments, in benefit programs for individuals,
or in federal services. These reductions became larger when the
Reagan administration decided to support a significant across-the-
board tax reduction to avert the continued upward ratcheting of
marginal tax rates and to encourage greater personal saving. The
decision to exempt major entitlement programs from cuts concentrated the reductions in a limited number of programs, which were
severely pared. The Reagan administration's political philosophy of
decentralization, free markets, and less obtrusive government helped
identify the programs to reduce; its judgment about important political constituencies also had a role to play in allocating the budgetary
pain.

Since political philosophies and allegiances to constituencies in
Congress may differ from those of the administration, the two
branches are likely to disagree over specific program reductions. But
it would be unfortunate to gloss over the decisions on reallocating
national output that set the scale for the magnitude of the budget
changes in the first place. While there is little doubt that both expert
and public opinion favor the shifts toward more defense spending
and increased investment, not all the questions and trade-offs to
achieve those ends have been explored.

The administration's budget proposals are nothing if not single-
minded and ambitious in their attempt to boost defense and investment. Business saving is to be increased by the depreciation reforms;

government saving is to be provided by the reduced deficit; personal saving is to be stimulated by Kemp-Roth; the quality of business investment is to be improved by reduced federal interference in lending activities.

These objectives can be met in different ways. Incentives for business investment need not be concentrated exclusively on controversial depreciation liberalization but could be combined with liberalized investment tax credits, incentives for research and development, or larger reductions in taxes on property income than on earnings. Personal saving could be stimulated by broadened eligibility rules for individual retirement accounts, which allow people a tax break on retirement savings. Capital markets could be made more accessible to business investment if tax incentives that encourage consumer and state and local government borrowing and home mortgages were reduced. Encouragement of work effort (another intended effect of Kemp-Roth) could be accomplished by reduced taxation of the wages of the second earner in a family. These alternatives to the administration's tax proposals would probably yield better results per dollar of revenue loss, but they are more complicated than the simple call for three years of 10 percent across-the-board personal tax cuts and a "clean" business tax cut.

Debate over these alternatives (or other similar alternative strategies in the national defense area) would take time. And it might require that the reallocation of resources to the new uses be approached step by step by gradually slowing nondefense spending (and carefully assessing the ability of people and governments to adjust to the changes), gradually raising defense spending, and phasing in general tax reductions as seemed warranted. Moreover, since the gains from enhanced weapon systems and business investment will be realized only over a long period of time, the losses from not doing everything the administration proposes in 1982 would not be great.

The chief drawback of gradualism is political. Despite its advantages in principle, it risks losing the sense of urgency about redirecting resources. As programs are carefully examined before being cut, special interests will arise to testify that some destitute person would be hurt by a program reduction. Once a tax bill is opened up to anything but a "clean" across-the-board rate cut, all kinds of pet tax incentive schemes emerge. Too much debate over defense spending could lead to endless deliberation about the merits of an all-volunteer military force or about various military strategies. There is some truth to the argument that a gradual approach to re-allocating resources increases the risk that action will not be decisive and that too many compromises will be struck.

It may be that the only way to turn budget priorities around is to do it swiftly and sharply. But it would be a shame if hastily developed policies, designed to capitalize on a propitious prevailing mood, had to be passed because only they are compatible with our political system's ability to bring about changes.

CHAPTER SIX

A Change in Direction

A. JAMES REICHLEY

RONALD REAGAN has brought to the presidency an unusually coherent social philosophy. Coherence may have certain dangers—particularly if the views on which it is based turn out to be largely mistaken. But commitment to a broadly consistent set of beliefs about human nature and society provides a guide through which to interpret events and a foundation on which to build specific programs and policies. These, at the least, should make it easier for the administration to impose discipline and continuity on its policymaking processes.

Reagan's social outlook apparently is shared by his major department heads and advisers and is widely held among the new Republican majority in the Senate. Even the House of Representatives, where the Democrats remain in control, and the Supreme Court, which bears the ideological imprints of earlier administrations, seem inclined to move toward the more conservative direction endorsed by a majority of voters in November 1980.

Commentators have disputed the extent to which the 1980 election represented a mandate for conservatism. Only about 54 percent of the eligible voters cast ballots, the lowest turnout since 1948. But a *New York Times*/CBS News poll taken shortly after the election in-

I am grateful to several colleagues for helpful comments, particularly Martha Derthick, Robert Hartman, Herbert Kaufman, and James Sundquist, and to Diane Hodges, Radmila Nikolic, and Thomas Somuah for administrative and secretarial assistance.

dicated that if all the nonvoters had participated, Reagan would still have won by a large margin. Among those who voted, dissatisfaction with President Carter and unhappiness over economic troubles and foreign reverses were certainly influential factors. An exit poll on election day showed that the single most important reason given by voters for choosing Reagan (37 percent) was the feeling that it was "time for a change." It would be hard to maintain, however, that most of those who supported Reagan did not realize that the change for which they were voting was a movement toward conservatism. Few leaders in American public life since the Second World War have been as resolute as Reagan in identifying with a political ideology. Moreover, most of the new Republican senators ran campaigns that emphasized their conservatism, and many defeated highly visible liberals. In the fall of 1980, before the election, the University of Michigan Center for Policy Studies reported that its data "for the first time . . . revealed a significant shift to the right." Among respondents in the center's national study, 45 percent identified themselves as conservatives—a record—and only 21 percent as liberals.[1] The Democrats' continued control of the House of Representatives, by a reduced majority, is probably largely due to the fact that contests for the House have in recent years been the federal elections least affected by ideology.

The new administration, therefore, entered office with a better than usual chance for putting its program into effect. The institutional sluggishness of Congress, the normal recalcitrance of politicians, the bureaucracy's powers to delay and obstruct, the current tendency of much of the press to adopt an adversary stance toward any president—as well as the immensity and seeming intractability of many national problems—remain as formidable barriers against the administration's achievement of its goals. But Reagan holds more political leverage than any president since Lyndon Johnson in 1965. If conservatism now fails, conservatives can hardly claim that it has not been given a fair chance.

The questions, then, are: What are the beliefs and values on which the new administration's policies will be based? How closely do these conform to reality? Do they provide practical means for dealing with

---

1. Arthur H. Miller, "Liberal-Conservative Ideology in the 1980 Election," *Economic Outlook USA,* vol. 7 (Autumn 1980), p. 86.

current national problems? In this chapter I seek to answer the first of these questions, and offer some comments and hunches on the second and third.

Taft and Goldwater Republicans

Reaganism, as is well known, grew out of the movement led by Senator Barry Goldwater that in 1964 temporarily took control of the Republican party. But what is the origin of Goldwaterism? Some political scientists and journalists have traced it to the old Taft wing of the Republican party that at every national convention from 1940 through 1952 struggled against the moderate or progressive forces marshaled behind Wendell Willkie, Thomas Dewey, and Dwight Eisenhower; or even beyond that to the regular Republicans who supported William Howard Taft against the progressives led by Theodore Roosevelt in the epic confrontation that divided the Republican party in 1912. Most of what remained of the Taft wing did indeed support Goldwater in 1964, partly because former Taft supporters, like Senate minority leader Everett Dirksen of Illinois, saw an opportunity to take revenge at last against the eastern establishment that had humbled them so often at earlier Republican conventions. But the real dynamism of the Goldwater movement came from outside the traditional geographic, political, or ideological strongholds of Taft Republicanism.

The Taft Republicans were based mainly in the Middle West (though they had some auxiliaries in New England, upstate New York and Pennsylvania, the border states, and the Rocky Mountain West). Their leaders were almost all white Protestants, generally of the more evangelical denominations. They shared a number of policy views with their chief intraparty rivals, the Dewey and Eisenhower moderates: firm belief in the market as the best means for making most economic decisions, concern about the growing power of organized labor, preference for keeping as much governmental authority as possible at the state and local levels, and adherence to the Republican party's traditional support for the constitutional rights of black Americans.

They differed from the moderates on three main issues. In foreign policy, most of them were isolationists supporting Robert Taft's view that neither the interests nor the responsibilities of the United

States called for extensive entanglements abroad; while the moderates, particularly after the Second World War, were strong internationalists. In economic policy, the Taft Republicans regarded themselves as defenders of the interests of Main Street small business against the encroaching power of Wall Street big business, which they identified with the moderates. In what has since come to be called social policy, they were more inclined than the moderates to use government to regulate personal morals, as had been tried most ambitiously in the experiment with national prohibition. Beyond these issue positions, the Taft Republicans represented an underlying spirit of longing for a simpler time (perhaps largely imaginary), a distrust of the twentieth century and many of its innovations, a dislike for big cities, a suspicion of theory, and a Burkean predisposition to stick to the known and tested except where change was clearly necessary—and then to yield to change only gradually.

The Goldwater supporters who took over the Republican party in 1964 drew on some of the same attitudes and traditions that characterized Taft Republicanism. In large part, however, they expressed new interests and new concerns that were developing in national politics during the 1950s and the early 1960s. Their chief bases of political strength were in the "sun belt" states of the South and Southwest. Among their leaders and intellectual spokesmen were Catholics, Jews, and white southerners, all groups traditionally aligned with the Democrats. Many of them were ardent modernizers in the sense that they thrived on technological change and pressed for the maximum in economic growth; and some practiced distinctly nontraditional life-styles associated with expensive sports cars, jet airplanes, and rock music. They shared the Taft Republicans' dislike and distrust for Wall Street and the eastern establishment; but most often these hostilities grew from attachments to new urban centers, such as Los Angeles or Houston, rather than from loyalty to rural or small-town values.

In foreign policy, the Goldwater Republicans' fear of world communism and their tendency to blame almost all international troubles on the machinations of the Soviet Union led them to favor a global military and economic role for the United States, although they joined the Taft Republicans in challenging the value of most foreign aid that was not tied to explicit political objectives. Some of them, particularly those in the South, had switched from the Democratic to the Republican party for the purpose of combating governmentally imposed racial integration. These, feeling no obligation to the Republican tradition supporting civil rights, insisted that the federal government's role in desegregation be held to a minimum. In economic policy, the Goldwater Republicans subscribed to the strict libertarianism recommended by Milton Friedman and the Chicago school and looked with scorn on the fairly eclectic and pragmatic application of free-market principles that had satisfied both the Taft conservatives and the Eisenhower moderates.

Behind these positions in particular policy areas lay in many cases a view of life that was deeply moralistic (good guys against bad guys), and a conviction that both traditional forms of authority and traditional economic and political freedoms were being dangerously eroded by practices of the welfare state that had grown up under the New Deal. (The world view of many liberals of the period was similarly moralistic, though with the roles of good guys and bad guys of course reversed.)

The Making of a Conservative

Ronald Reagan's own involvement with the Goldwater movement came at the end of an ideological journey that had taken him from New Deal liberalism to a role as evangelist for free-market capitalism along what he called "the mashed potato circuit."

Reagan has traced the beginning of his disenchantment with liberalism to his participation, as president of the Screen Actors Guild in the latter part of the 1940s, in the fight against communist influence in the movie industry. Many Hollywood liberals, he found, were prepared to accept the communists as allies, and even to defend Stalin's totalitarian regime in the Soviet Union. Differing with part of the liberal community on this issue, he began to question other liberal attitudes and beliefs. In 1948 he campaigned for Harry Truman, but it seems to have been Truman the cold warrior rather than Truman the social democrat who chiefly appealed to him.

When Reagan's movie career began to run down in the 1950s, he switched to television and became host of General Electric's television theater. Under GE's sponsorship he began touring the country as an after-dinner speaker. The speech he gave gradually evolved into an effective sermon, filled with punchy one-liners and arresting statistics that extolled the achievements of the free enterprise system and warned of the dangers and inefficiencies stemming from "big government."

After he moved to conservatism, Reagan continued to include quotations from liberal exemplars like Thomas Paine and Thomas Jefferson in his speeches. But the liberalism on which he drew was the eighteenth century liberalism of don't-tread-on-me economic and political individualism, rather than the contemporary liberalism of governmental activism and social protest, which modern liberals claim carries on the underlying values of Jefferson and Paine. His favorite twentieth century presidents, Reagan would later say, were Dwight Eisenhower and Calvin Coolidge.[2]

Unlike some libertarian conservatives, particularly those with roots in the West, Reagan did not couple attacks on big government with hostility toward the power of the eastern business establishment. Early in his campaign for the presidency in 1976, John Sears, his campaign manager at that time, kept trying to persuade him to include big business along with big government and big labor as political targets. Although Reagan took a few pokes at big business, he never seemed comfortable with antibusiness rhetoric. His criticisms of business have usually been limited to gibes at those businessmen who help "feed the crocodile" of big government in hopes that "the crocodile will eat them last."

Reagan first attracted national political attention through the televised speech that he gave on behalf of Barry Goldwater one week before the 1964 election. Some of Goldwater's managers, and reportedly Goldwater himself, tried to dissuade Reagan from giving the speech because he insisted on suggesting that "voluntary features" might be introduced into the social security system—a subject on which Goldwater had already been burned. But it was a huge success; it raised more than a million dollars and boosted the morale of the Goldwater legions as they marched toward certain electoral disaster.

2. *U.S. News and World Report*, May 5, 1980, p. 34. On Inauguration Day, 1981, Reagan became the first president in more than a decade to eliminate the bipartisan mix among the three portraits of former presidents that hang in the White House cabinet room. Richard Nixon's choices for these places of honor were Abraham Lincoln, Theodore Roosevelt, and Woodrow Wilson. Gerald Ford kept Lincoln, but replaced Roosevelt and Wilson with Eisenhower and Truman. Under Jimmy Carter, Lincoln and Truman remained, but Eisenhower gave way to Jefferson. Reagan's selections were Eisenhower, Coolidge, and again Lincoln—apparently almost everybody's hero.

In 1966, as public support for Lyndon Johnson and his Great Society program dwindled, Reagan was elected governor of California. His arrival in Sacramento, where liberal Democrats or moderate Republicans had governed for more than two decades, caused something close to hysteria among California's liberal interest groups. During his eight years as governor, however, the interest groups discovered that Reagan's rhetorical bark was considerably more severe than his economizing bite. Faced with a $200 million deficit left by the preceding Democratic administration, he at first talked of making drastic cuts in state services to balance the budget. But he finally dealt with the problem by calling for a record increase in state tax rates. Later these higher rates, applied to an expanding economy, provided huge revenue increases that enabled him to finance both tax rebates and a substantial growth of state services. State organizations devoted to causes like mental health and conservation found that Republican businessmen and philanthropists on their boards of directors gave them channels to the governor. At the end of Reagan's second term virtually all state services were more generously funded in real dollars, as well as generally better managed, than they had been when he took office.

None of this is to say that Reagan was not a conservative governor. His highly visible reliance for guidance on a circle of friends from the business community and his appointment of conservative businessmen and lawyers to state offices gave both large and small businessmen confidence that the state government was in friendly hands—perhaps a factor in the renewed vitality of the state's economy, which had begun to falter in the 1960s. His welfare reform plan, while only modestly reducing the number of persons on the state's relief rolls, made the system more acceptable to most taxpayers by strengthening procedures to detect fraud and establishing the principle that able-bodied welfare recipients could be made to work on public projects for their grants. (In practice, few persons on welfare were required to work.)

In 1973 Reagan campaigned for an amendment to the California constitution that would have placed fixed limits on state tax rates and expenditures. The amendment referendum, which was vigorously opposed by public employee unions and liberal interest groups, was defeated. But it helped lay the ideological groundwork for the taxpayers' revolt that five years later produced the more drastic Proposition 13 to cut sharply California's local property taxes. (Reagan endorsed Proposition 13, but did not take a leading role in the campaign that preceded its approval.)

Supply-side Economics

Reagan clearly believes that his nomination for president in 1980 and subsequent election were vindication and fulfillment of the conservative crusade that began in 1964. In an interview in spring 1980 Reagan said that Goldwater was "warning the people what would happen if we continued down the road of government interventionism." The message failed to get through in 1964 because "the opposition—and I'm sorry to say it was the Republican opposition in the primaries and not the Democrats—was successful in portraying [Goldwater] as a dangerous radical."

Does the Reagan administration embody the same principles and beliefs that Goldwater stood for in 1964? The answer is, in general, yes. Reagan's inaugural address emphasized most of the major Goldwater themes: reduction of federal taxes and regulation, elimination of federal deficits, return of power to the states, renewal of national pride, and a tougher attitude toward "those who are potential adversaries."

There have, however, been some changes and refinements in the conservative program. These reflect both adjustments to meet altered conditions and developments in conservative thought. (When Goldwater ran for president, the expression "conservative thought" would have been considered by many to be a contradiction in terms. By 1980 even many liberals conceded that conservatives were generating a substantial supply of fresh ideas.)

The administration takes its philosophic direction in economic policy from the doctrine that the least possible government intervention, consistent with a stable currency and protection of the public health and safety, will produce the most desirable levels of economic efficiency and growth. Ideas flowing from the new supply-side school of economists are particularly influential.

When Reagan sought the Republican presidential nomination against Gerald Ford in 1976, he took the traditional conservative position that the only way to break the momentum of inflation was by causing a temporary slowdown in the economy. "To cure inflation," he said, "there will have to be a period of economic dislocation." Reagan's chief criticism of Ford's economic policy was that the incumbent president's proposed cuts in federal expenditures did not go deep enough. Reagan's own proposal was that federal domestic spending be cut by $90 billion, then about one-third of the nondefense budget.

Between 1976 and the 1978 congressional elections Reagan was persuaded by Congressman Jack Kemp, a Republican representing a suburban district around Buffalo, that the key to curing inflation is not so much reducing federal expenditures as cutting federal tax rates.[3] Conservatives had always favored cutting taxes as well as spending. But the traditional conservative view was that the cuts in spending should come first in order to balance the federal budget. If taxes were reduced without corresponding cuts in spending, conservatives argued, additional dollars would be poured into consumption, which would inevitably drive up inflation. This was the issue over which Ford fought with the Democratic Congress in 1975 and 1976: tax cuts, Ford maintained, must be matched "dollar for dollar" by cuts in spending.

It was this attitude against which Kemp revolted when he, together with Senator William Roth, a Republican from Delaware, introduced the Kemp-Roth tax reduction bill in July 1977. The departures proposed in the Kemp-Roth bill were based on the theories of supply-side economics, which were then beginning to attract attention.

Supply-side economics, though an offshoot of the free-market ideology, derives less from the robust empiricism of Locke, Hume, and Adam Smith, than from the elegant deductive rationalism of the nineteenth century French school of classical economists, particularly Jean Baptiste Say and Leon Walras. The supply-siders claim that the fundamental premise on which their policies are based is Say's law: supply creates its own demand.

The inference that supply-siders draw from Say's law is that the market, if permitted to operate without government interference, will naturally establish equilibrium between supply and demand at full employment. The truth of this proposition *over the long run* has been accepted by Marx, Keynes, and most other economic theorists.

---

3. Kemp once served on Reagan's staff, during the off-season while he was playing as a quarterback in the National Football League.

Marxist and modern liberal economists, however, have argued that under conditions of depression or recession, achievement of equilibrium through the unassisted operation of the market entails so much human suffering that the theory breaks down in practice, which leads to massive government intervention and perhaps ultimately to revolution. In the twentieth century, probably the most important difference between conservative and liberal economists has been on the issue of how much suffering is acceptable to promote economic efficiency—a dilemma that some (not all) of the supply-siders claim to have escaped.

The supply-siders' argument that high taxes debilitate the economy was a favorite topic with Say. "Taxation pushed to the extreme," he wrote, "has the lamentable effect of impoverishing the individual without enriching the state." Taxes act as a drain on the economy, Say argued, because "taxes paid to the government by the subject are not refunded by its expenditures—[government] never can replace the value [taken] because it produces no value whatever."[4]

The Keynesian revolution in economics in the 1930s seemed for a time to have made Say's law almost irrelevant. Government, Keynes claimed, could create demand virtually at will, without waiting for the operation of market forces. John Kenneth Galbraith was able to write in *The New Industrial State,* first published in 1967, that Say's law was "one of the familiar antiquities of economics," which "no longer commands belief."

Conservative economists, businessmen, and politicians, however, always insisted that continuous "fine-tuning" of demand by government sooner or later undermines economic stability. In the 1970s rising inflation, falling productivity, and recurring recession convinced many people that the conservatives had a point.

At first the chief beneficiaries among economic theorists of the reaction against Keynesianism were Milton Friedman and his monetarist school. Economic stability, the monetarists claim, can be maintained by strictly limiting the growth of the money supply to the rate of the actual growth of the economy. Monetarist doctrine holds that when inflation has risen as a result of excessive monetary expansion, as at present, a period of forced economic penance is the only effec-

---

4. Jean Baptiste Say, *A Treatise on Political Economy,* translated from the 4th edition by C. R. Prinsep (London: Grigg Elliott, 1827), pp. 412 and 378.

tive cure. The monetarist remedy for inflation, however, in addition to some theoretical problems, has the drawback of causing severe economic hardship in its early stages, which leads to loss of popularity for the government that applies it—as the experience of the Thatcher government in the United Kingdom has shown.

The supply-side economists claim to offer a third way, which transcends the conflict between the Keynesians and the monetarists. But in their approach to inflation, the supply-siders rely heavily on monetary restraint. A number of the supply-siders, including some now influential within the Reagan administration, go even further than the orthodox monetarists in arguing that the best way to regulate the supply of money is to tie the value of the currency to the price of a real commodity, preferably gold. "Under a price rule [pegging the currency to gold]," Paul Craig Roberts, a supply-sider whom Reagan has appointed assistant secretary of the treasury for economic affairs, has written, "it is harder for government to 'oversupply' money, either inadvertently or on purpose."

Supply-siders who doubt that return to the gold standard is currently feasible insist that monetary policy at least "eschew all consideration of extraneous economic variables like short-term interest rates, housing market conditions, business cycle fluctuations, etc., and . . . concentrate instead on one exclusive task: bringing the growth of Federal Reserve credit and bank reserves to a prudent rate and stabilization of the international and domestic purchasing power of the dollar"—in the words used by David Stockman and Jack Kemp in their celebrated "manifesto" submitted to Reagan a few weeks after the 1980 election.

Belief that inflation can be defeated through monetary discipline has a liberating effect on the supply-siders when they turn to fiscal policy. They use this freedom not like the Keynesians, to stimulate demand, but rather to propose a range of tax-cut incentives which, they claim, will dramatically increase the growth of productivity. "Supply-side economics," Norman Ture, another supply-sider appointed under secretary of the treasury for tax policy by Reagan, has written, "rejects the whole [Keynesian] demand-side approach. . . . Tax cuts alone cannot increase real disposable income and spending. Any such increase will only occur if the tax cuts first affect the incentives to supply labor and capital, resulting in an increase in use of these production inputs, more real output, and hence more real income." Ture calls on policymakers to "recognize that taxes should affect the economy through incentives instead of through rivers of money."[5]

This belief in the effectiveness of economic incentives helped produce Congressman Kemp's proposal, endorsed during the campaign by Reagan, for designating some depressed big-city neighborhoods as "enterprise zones" in which new industries would be encouraged to locate through both special tax concessions and relaxation of some government regulations. It also led, by another track, to the Kemp-Roth tax reduction bill.

Avoiding an Economic Dunkirk

The original Kemp-Roth bill, introduced in 1977, called for cutting all individual income tax rates by an average of 30 percent over a three-year period and reducing the corporate tax rate from 48 to 45 percent. It contained no provision for an accompanying reduction in spending.

Much of the rationale for the Kemp-Roth bill was provided by Arthur Laffer, a young economist at the University of Southern California, to whom Kemp had been introduced by Jude Wanniski, an editorial writer with the *Wall Street Journal* and an ardent proselytizer for supply-side ideas. Using the now-famous Laffer curve, Laffer argued that because tax *revenues* will be zero at tax *rates* of both zero and 100 percent, there must be an optimum rate of taxation beyond which revenues will decline. If rates have been raised beyond this optimum point, a reduction in rates will provide incentives for increased work and investment, which will cause the economy to grow. This in turn will produce an expanded tax base and a resulting increase in government revenues. The tax cut therefore will pay for itself—and then some.

This chain of events actually transpired, Kemp and the supply-side economists claim, at least twice in American history: during the 1920s when Republican administrations whose economic policies were dominated by Secretary of the Treasury Andrew Mellon achieved a series of tax cuts; and again in the early 1960s when

5. Norman B. Ture, "The Department of the Treasury," in Charles L. Heatherly, ed., *Mandate for Leadership: Policy Management in a Conservative Administration* (Heritage Foundation, 1981), p. 650.

President Kennedy, acting on the advice of Walter Heller, pushed through a large reduction in tax rates. On both occasions tax revenues rose. According to the supply-siders, this was because the economy responded to the cut in rates. When critics pointed out that both the Mellon and the Kennedy tax cuts were passed in noninflationary economies with plenty of slack to respond to demand stimulus, Kemp replied that the Kemp-Roth bill was anti-inflationary because it would increase "incentives for work, saving, and investment."

Along with this economic argument, Kemp added the political argument that dedication to balancing the budget had brought the Republicans a steady series of electoral defeats since the 1930s. "As Republicans," he said, "we must rid ourselves of the perceived political idolatry of balanced budgets. Republicans must not be bookkeepers for Democratic deficits." He was joined in this counsel by Irving Kristol, one of the founders of the "neo-conservative" school of social commentators (a group of former liberals and leftists, based mainly in New York City, who have grown disenchanted with some aspects of the welfare state). "When in office," Kristol wrote, "liberals . . . will always spend generously, regardless of budgetary considerations, until the public permits the conservatives an interregnum in which to clean up the mess—but with the liberals retaining their status as the activist party, the party of the 'natural majority.' The neo-conservatives have decided that two can play at this game—and must, since it is the only game in town. . . . They vigorously advocate [increased defense spending and] tax cuts, with the budget remaining a secondary consideration."

Critics of the Kemp-Roth bill, among both liberals and orthodox conservatives, contend that the trouble with the Laffer curve is that, while it is theoretically valid as an abstraction, the practical question for policy is whether current tax rates in the United States are really so high that they constitute major disincentives, not only for saving and investment, but also for work. Theoretical and empirical evidence for this proposition is at best ambiguous.[6] If tax rates are reduced under the impression that resulting supply-side incentives will produce massive increases in productivity, and this turns out not to happen, revenues will probably decline rather than increase, at least in the short run.

6. For the most recent evidence, see Henry J. Aaron and Joseph A. Pechman, *How Taxes Affect Economic Behavior* (Brookings Institution, 1981).

Some supporters of the bill concede that the proposed cut in rates would not lead directly to a gain in revenues, but insist that the plan is nevertheless fiscally feasible. "Revenue reflow" resulting from Kemp-Roth tax rate reductions, Norman Ture has written, "would fall short of replacing the revenues lost by reductions. Nonetheless, the additional saving undertaken in response to the rate reductions would be sufficient to finance the incremental government deficit as well as substantial gains in capital formation." In other words, the Kemp-Roth bill would probably increase the deficit, but its stimulative impact on the private economy, according to this argument, would generate enough additional savings to finance the deficit out of private capital without inflationary effects.

Another flaw of Kemp-Roth, according to some of its critics, is that it is not really a supply-side tax cut at all because, according to Kemp's own figures, only about 30 percent of the reduction would go to people with incomes over $50,000 a year, who provide the largest part of saving by individuals. The main effect of the bill, therefore, would be to increase consumption rather than to raise saving and investment. As a result, demand would increase faster than supply, adding further fuel to inflation.

The supply-siders' reply to this charge is that, even if it were politically feasible to concentrate tax cuts on income that is most likely to go directly into investment, it would still be economically undesirable, because current tax rates weigh down not only on investors but on the whole productive vitality of the economy. The United States, Paul Craig Roberts has written, is in danger of becoming a "transfer society" in which "economic rewards lie in political action" rather than in "productive activity." Lowering marginal tax rates will increase incentives for income earners at all levels, thereby restoring the competitive drives and optimism that move the economy.

Members of the establishment of orthodox conservative economists—men who served in recent Republican administrations, like Herbert Stein (chairman of the Council of Economic Advisers under Nixon), George Shultz (secretary of the treasury under Nixon), Alan Greenspan (chairman of the Council of Economic Advisers under Ford), and Charls Walker (deputy secretary of the treasury under Nixon)—were at first almost unanimously critical of Kemp-Roth on the ground that it would probably increase inflation. As the 1980 presidential election approached, however, they were faced with an embarrassment: Reagan, the almost certain Republican nominee after his victory in the New Hampshire primary in March, was committed to Kemp-Roth. If the orthodox conservatives wished to become close counselors of their party's candidate, and perhaps future president, they had two choices: either they would have to ease him away from Kemp-Roth, which they recognized would not be easy, at least until after the election; or they would have to sign on as supporters of Kemp-Roth themselves. A third possible choice, that of advising the candidate from a distance, without endorsing his particular policy positions, was taken by Stein. But the others wanted to be more directly involved.

Changes in the economy in 1980 made it relatively easy for the orthodox conservatives to go along with a form of Kemp-Roth, provided it was accompanied by a promise to cut federal spending. "When I was preparing to testify before the Ways and Means Committee in February [1980]," Walker has said, "I realized that the rise in inflation had tremendously changed the revenue outlook for the federal government. Inflation was pushing more and more taxpayers into the higher income brackets, so that existing tax rates were producing huge increases in federal revenues. That made it possible for George Shultz and Alan Greenspan and Charley Walker to go for an immediate tax cut, and still move toward a balanced budget."[7]

While joining the call for a tax cut, some of the orthodox conservatives continued to counsel against complete commitment to Kemp-Roth. They argued that the tax-cut package should be stretched over five years, or that Reagan should limit his commitment to only the first year's installment.

By the time of the Republican national convention in Detroit in July, Shultz, Greenspan, and Walker had taken positions in Reagan's inner circle of economic advisers. Laffer, who had earlier played a prominent role, was slipping toward the periphery. Even Kemp, vainly pursuing the nomination for vice president, seemed to be losing ground.

The convention, however, despite Reagan's selection of George Bush over Kemp as his running mate, was on the whole a triumph for

---

7. The second version of the Kemp-Roth bill, introduced in 1979, called for limiting spending as a percentage of gross national product, beginning at 21 percent in 1980 and falling to 18 percent by 1983. This addition was made at the suggestion of Senator Robert Dole of Kansas, who in early 1981 became chairman of the Senate Finance Committee.

the supply-siders. The Republican platform firmly endorsed Kemp-Roth and promised "the restoration of a dependable monetary standard"—which the supply-siders said meant gold. Reagan told the convention (and the television audience) in his acceptance speech: "I have long advocated a 30 percent reduction in income tax rates over a period of three years. . . . A phased reduction of tax rates would go a long way toward easing the heavy burden on the American people. But we should not stop here. Within the context of economic conditions and appropriate budget priorities during each fiscal year of my presidency, I would strive to go further."

The conflict over the nature of the Republican economic program continued into September. It was finally settled, for the duration of the campaign, by Reagan's speech on economic policy to the International Business Council in Chicago on September 9. Both the supply-siders and the orthodox conservatives contributed to this speech and were able to make their favorite points. The candidate reiterated his intention of calling for a 30 percent "across-the-board, three-year reduction in personal income tax rates." But he also promised, following the advice of Shultz, Greenspan, and Walker, to make deep cuts in federal spending—beginning with a cut of 2 percent from the currently projected level for fiscal 1981, and rising to "7 percent of what otherwise would have been spent" in fiscal 1985. In addition, he promised, somewhat confusingly, to pursue the goal of achieving "spending reductions of 10 percent by fiscal year 1984." By implementing even the lower level of cuts, Reagan claimed, the budget, after providing for full implementation of Kemp-Roth, acceleration of business depreciation allowances (Walker's particular project), and substantial increases in defense spending, would be brought into balance by fiscal 1983. All this could be done, the candidate maintained, without "altering or taking back necessary entitlements already granted to the American people"—the critical word obviously being "necessary."

A surge of government outlays during the fall, caused mainly by effects of the 1980 recession and continued high inflation, brought the supply-siders and the orthodox conservatives into agreement on the need for truly drastic cuts in federal spending as soon as the new administration took office. George Shultz hit upon the expression that the budget was "hemorrhaging," a cry immediately taken up by all Republicans. The chief remaining difference between the two camps was the issue of whether it would still be possible to go ahead with the full Kemp-Roth package.

A few weeks after the election, Kemp and Congressman David Stockman of Michigan, who was to be director of the Office of Management and Budget in the new administration, sent the president-elect a memorandum, soon publicized as the Stockman manifesto, grimly predicting that "an economic Dunkirk" might lie ahead. The federal budget, the memorandum said, had become an "automatic coast-to-coast soup line." Recommended cures were "severe rescission of entitlements and new obligation authority in the federal spending pipeline," and "a dramatic, substantial rescission of the regulatory burden." But "dilution of the tax cut program to limit short-run revenue losses," the memorandum maintained, would be "counterproductive." Kemp and Stockman recommended going ahead immediately with "the calendar year 1981 and 1982 installments of Kemp-Roth, reduction of the top income tax rate on unearned income to 50 percent, further reduction in [tax rates on] capital gains, and a substantial reform of corporate depreciation."

During the weeks between the election and the inauguration, the persons selected to serve on Reagan's top economic team gave mixed signals. Donald Regan, the new secretary of the treasury, came from the New York financial community, which has viewed Kemp-Roth with considerable skepticism. After his appointment, Regan endorsed the need for a tax cut, but hedged on the wisdom of going ahead immediately with Kemp-Roth. Stockman, though a confirmed supply-sider, indicated willingness to compromise on the timing and extent of the tax cut. The appointment of Ture and Roberts to sub-cabinet posts at the Treasury, on the other hand, assured that there would be strong advocacy within the administration for major, immediate cuts. "Delaying the tax cuts 'because the deficit is too large,' " Roberts wrote in the *Wall Street Journal* on the eve of taking office, "is a way of sending a signal that the administration doesn't have confidence in its own policy." Murray Weidenbaum, the new chairman of the Council of Economic Advisers, has been best known in recent years for his advocacy of deregulation; although in the early 1970s, while serving at the Treasury during the Nixon administration, he was an early and influential proponent of some kind of "incomes policy" to combat inflationary wage increases.

Some of Reagan's associates warned that the administration must identify its program with the needs of the whole nation rather than merely with the affluent. Drew Lewis, who was to be the new secretary of transportation, said shortly before the inauguration: "The Republicans are still very much the minority party. If we don't have programs for the cities and help workers find jobs, we are going to lose the support of the blue-collar workers and minorities who voted for Reagan in 1980." The president himself sought in his inaugural speech to reassure those who need help from government: "How can we love our country and not love our countrymen? And loving them reach out a hand when they fall, heal them when they are sick, and provide opportunity to make them self-sufficient so they will be equal in fact and not just in theory."

The administration's economic program, presented by Reagan to Congress in a speech on February 18 and in a revised budget message on March 10, called for enactment of the full 30 percent Kemp-Roth tax cut over three years, with the effective date on the first installment deferred to July 1, and more than $48 billion in budget cuts for fiscal 1982. Bringing down inflation no longer appeared as painless as Reagan had suggested during the campaign. Administration leaders still expressed confidence that the cut in taxes would yield gains in productivity. But the administration's first objective was to reduce the rise in prices. To achieve this goal, it turned to the traditional conservative remedy of cutting federal spending.[8] George Bush, the new vice president, said: "The administration must show that its approach is demonstrably different. There will be no instant renaissance, but economic expectations have got to be changed." Or as James Baker, Reagan's White House chief of staff, put it: "The important thing is to get the numbers on inflation moving in the right direction. We must show our determination to cut, even if it means cutting some programs that we may eventually want to put back."

The Old Federalism

Besides striving to reduce the impact of government on the national economy, the Reagan administration has set out to decentralize control of government services. In his economic policy message to Con-

8. See chapter 2 for an analysis of the probable economic effects of the administration's proposals.

gress, Reagan proposed consolidating about forty-five federal categorical programs (dealing with narrowly defined purposes) in education into two block grants, which would permit the states and local governments to use the money to suit their own priorities. In social and health services, the administration proposed combining forty categorical programs into four block grants dealing with health services, preventive health services, social services, and hardship assistance. In the area of community development, the urban development action grant would be "integrated" with the community development block grant to curtail "excessive . . . federal intervention in developing, selecting, and monitoring local economic development projects."

The administration supports governmental decentralization in part, as liberals suspect, as a means for holding down public expenditures. Also, however, Reagan's advocacy of decentralization reflects the conservative beliefs that state and local governments are more responsive to the realities of local needs and conditions, and more conducive to preserving or building strong neighborhoods and communities.

Reagan's proposals for decentralization grow out of some of the same ideas that lay behind the "new federalism" policy initiated by President Nixon in August 1969. The Reagan approach, however, goes well beyond anything that was attempted by the Nixon administration. Nixon sweetened proposals for shifts from categorical to block grants for education, urban development, and other domestic services with additions to total federal expenditures in these areas, but Reagan would provide from 20 to 25 percent less for the block grants than now is called for to maintain current program levels. As a result, state and local governments would either have to cut programs or dig into their own resources. In the area of income maintenance for the poor (welfare), which Nixon proposed making primarily a federal program (on the argument that it is essentially a national rather than a local or regional problem), Reagan has indicated plans for shifting federal aid to a block grant basis, which would place increased responsibility on the states and localities.

Pressed by the ceiling imposed by Reagan's overall budget target, the administration did not, at least in its first budget proposals, recommend renewal of revenue sharing for the states, which was eliminated in Carter's last budget. But unlike the Carter administration, which favored giving a large amount of federal aid directly to the cities, the new administration plans to enhance the role of the states. His experience as governor of California convinced Reagan that the states not only are more efficient managers of domestic services than the federal government, but also are better suited than the cities to coordinate programs dealing with problems that overlap local boundaries. (The fact that the states are much more likely than the larger cities to be under Republican direction no doubt has some effect on the administration's position.)

Under Reagan's conception of federalism, the states will hold primary responsibility and control for most domestic programs. "All of us need to be reminded," he said in his inaugural address, "that the federal government did not create the states; the states created the federal government."

Conservative Nationalism

The administration's fight against inflation and budgetary expansion will be made more difficult by its commitment to increase spending for defense. Reagan's determination to strengthen the nation's military forces in part reflects what Vice President Bush has called a "somber" view of the intentions of the Soviet Union. It also grows out of an interpretation of history and a system of political values that differ fundamentally from those that guided the previous administration's international policies.

The principal makers of foreign policy in the Carter administration, except Edmund Muskie, whose tenure was brief, all shared in one form or another the view that the world is in a transitional stage. The transition, according to this view, is from a time when nations made national interest their ultimate test and guide in foreign policy to a new era in which an international concert of democratic governments led by enlightened technocrats will deal with common human problems through a structure of values that Zbigniew Brzezinski has called "rational humanism." Seen from this perspective, the essential role of American foreign policy is to serve as a kind of political midwife, negotiating the birth of a global community dedicated to the service of "human rights." The threat of the Soviet Union in this view is not, as Ronald Reagan has said, that it aims to establish a "one-world socialist or communist state" but rather that, by clinging to a regressive nationalism, it obstructs the creation of that very one world, democratically conceived and organized.

The chief architects of foreign policy in the Reagan administration simply do not agree with this theory of history or accept the political values on which it is based. In the Reagan view of things, the nation-state is and for the foreseeable future will remain the ultimate instrument (though not the source) of political authority, the highest object of civic loyalty, and the collective embodiment of public honor. Reagan's repeated assertions of national pride in his inaugural speech contrasted markedly with Jimmy Carter's avowal four years before: "Our commitment to human rights must be absolute." Reagan appears to share Irving Kristol's belief that the American people want "rather more Theodore Roosevelt, and a lot less of Woodrow Wilson, in their foreign policy." One month before the inauguration, Robert Neumann, director of the new administration's transition team at the State Department, told foreign service officers to expect "a fundamental change in course" toward a policy that would be "avowedly nationalistic," defined as "belief that the basic criteria for American actions ought to be American national interests."

Some administration leaders, notably Secretary of State Alexander Haig, have indicated awareness of the terrible mischief that may be caused by extreme nationalism in a world facing the danger of nuclear war and the reality of growing economic interdependence. In a speech given while he was still commander of the North Atlantic Treaty Organization, Haig warned that the "growing imperative" of interdependence among Western nations is threatened by "a counter-trend of nationalism on the ascendancy." Testifying before the Senate Foreign Relations Committee during his confirmation hearings, he observed that "we face a world in which power in a variety of forms has become diffused over 150 nations," many of which are "willing to foment instability and violence to achieve their objectives." To deal with this situation, Haig recommended not global humanism but a policy based on "consistent United States interests . . . consistently pursued."

The nationalism that motivates the Reagan administration, unlike that of the old Taft Republicans, does not lead to isolationism. The United States, Haig said, should "seek actively to shape events and, in the process, attempt to forge consensus among like-minded peoples." Richard Allen, Reagan's director of the National Security

Council, has written: "While the United States does not assume global responsibility for international peace and stability, no area of the world is beyond the scope of American interest if control or influence by a hostile power threatens American security."

This activist approach to foreign policy is dictated, not only by direct economic and security interests, but also by the belief, old as the republic, that the United States has a special responsibility to uphold Western values. One way to carry out this responsibility is by the example of domestic institutions—by building a "shining city upon a hill," as Reagan likes to say. But, under current conditions, it also requires active intervention in world affairs. "We did not seek leadership of the Free World," Reagan has said, "but there is no one else who can provide it, and without our leadership there will be no peace in the world."

The great antagonist of the role to which the United States has been called, in this view, is international communism, particularly the Soviet Union. Reagan's preoccupation with the threatening power of the Soviet Union has sometimes led him to suggest that he believes all the world's tensions are the products of Russian intrigue. "Let's not delude ourselves," he told Karen Elliott House of the *Wall Street Journal* in the summer of 1980. "The Soviet Union underlies all the unrest that is going on. If they weren't engaged in this game of dominoes, there wouldn't be any hot spots in the world." In more temperate moments, he has refined this idea to the belief that the Soviet Union seeks tensions that, whatever their underlying or original causes may be, lend themselves to use against the United States. "The main axis of American foreign policy over the past 20 years has been that of the U.S.-Soviet relationship," Richard Allen has said. "So it is not at all simplistic to say that U.S.-Soviet relations are crucial." Reagan, according to Allen, "views this relationship as a complex one, yet one that can be reduced to understandable terms in light of the growing imbalance of power in the world and the increasing assertiveness of the Soviet Union."

Reagan does not subscribe to the belief, which he once attributed to Henry Kissinger, that American power is in irreversible decline, and that the best that can now be hoped for is a reasonable bargain with the Russians. Recent administrations, including Republican ones, Reagan has said, have permitted the Russians to build up their military advantage to the point that "our principal adversary, the

Soviet Union, surpasses us in virtually every category of military strength." But this situation must not be regarded as permanent. The Russians, Caspar Weinberger, the new secretary of defense, testified before the Senate Armed Services Committee, have set out to achieve "an imbalance that would make it very difficult, if not impossible, for us to assert our interests or the interests of our allies" anywhere in the world. "Obviously," Weinberger said, "this has to be totally unacceptable." While backing off somewhat from the 1980 Republican platform's promise of a return to "military superiority," Reagan has continued to insist that his administration will "restore the margin of safety for peace in our defense program . . . to meet our needs throughout this critical decade."

Increased defense expenditures, the administration claims, will guard American security and pave the way for genuine disarmament. "By recognizing the ominous sweep of the present trends," Fred Charles Iklé, whom Reagan has appointed under secretary of defense for policy, wrote in an article published by the Hoover Institution in 1980, "chances for meaningful arms control and mutual restraint are much improved."[9]

Over the long term, administration leaders believe, historic trends favor the United States and are adverse to the Soviet Union. "In a historical sense," Haig told the Senate Foreign Relations Committee, "we are witnessing the unraveling and demise of Marxism-Leninism as a wave of the future." (The image of an unraveling wave presumably perplexed Russian translators.) Marxist policies, Haig claimed, are "in a position of historic failure" in terms of "agriculture, economy, the ability to satisfy the public sector." But "for totalitarian systems of that kind," he cautioned, "when faced with that failure and armed so heavily, it raises the temptation for an incumbent leader to engage in external diversions so they can insure their incumbency. So for a decade or more, we are in an extremely dangerous period. We cannot take comfort in Marxist-Leninist failure."

Unlike the Goldwater Republicans in 1964, Reagan and his associates acknowledge that the communist movement is no longer monolithic. Communist forces, Haig has said, are now divided among "three competitive centers of Marxist influence—one in Mos-

---

9. Fred Charles Iklé, "Arms Control and National Defense," in Peter Dunigan and Alvain Robushka, eds., *The United States in the 1980s* (Hoover Institution Press, 1980), p. 438.

cow, one in Peking, and one in the revolutionary Third World." But this division, in Haig's view, may actually have increased the danger that the Soviet Union will "look outward as a diversion from its own problems."

Reagan, despite previous misgivings, since his election has seemed to accept Haig's belief that there is "a compatibility and a convergence in the strategic sense between ourselves and the People's Republic of China." The administration does not, however, appear to place so high a value on the "China card" as did Presidents Nixon and Carter. The People's Republic, Haig said, should be encouraged to "recognize that there is some value in a normalization of its relations with the United States." But American policy toward China should not be carried to the point of heedlessly "poking sticks in the polar bear's cage"—antagonizing the Russians.

With regard to the third world—a term that Haig has called "misleading" and a "myth"—the administration promised to "tailor policy" to fit "the individual circumstances" of nations "as diverse as Brazil and Libya, Indonesia and South Yemen, Cuba and Kuwait." Before the Senate Foreign Relations Committee, Haig spoke critically of the "propensity" of recent administrations "to apply to these emerging states Western standards which resolutely ignore vast differences in their cultural [and] political development, economic vitality, and internal and external security."

The administration appears to hold no great hopes for rapid democratization of most third world countries. Jeane Kirkpatrick, a political science professor at Georgetown University, whom Reagan has appointed U.S. ambassador to the United Nations, wrote in the November 1979 issue of *Commentary:* "In the relatively few places where they exist, democratic governments have come into being slowly, after extended prior experience with more limited forms of participation. . . . Decades, if not centuries, are normally required for people to acquire the necessary disciplines and habits." Professor Kirkpatrick's article, which Reagan let be known he had read and admired, argues that the real choice in many third world countries is between "traditional authoritarian governments" and "revolutionary autocracies." Traditional authoritarian governments, like those of the Shah in Iran and the Somoza regime in Nicaragua, she maintained, are usually "less repressive . . . more susceptible of liberalization, and more compatible with U.S. interests" than their revolutionary replacements. "Revolutionary leaders [who] describe the United States as the scourge of the 20th century, the enemy of freedom-loving people, the perpetrator of imperialism" are not "authentic democrats, or to put it mildly, friends." The United States must learn, she concluded, that "groups which define themselves as enemies should be treated as enemies."

No president, Richard Allen said in summer 1980, would "discard the notion of human rights." But a Reagan administration, he suggested, would "take into consideration the necessary subtleties in expressing one's view of human rights in the conduct of foreign relations, especially with friendly nations."

Speaking more bluntly, Jeane Kirkpatrick, in a television exchange at the end of 1980 with Patricia Derian, assistant secretary of state for human rights in the Carter administration, said: "If we are confronted with the choice between offering assistance to a moderately repressive autocratic government which is also friendly to the United States, and permitting it to be overrun by Cuban-trained, Cuban-armed, Cuban-sponsored insurgency, we would assist the moderate autocracy." (Patricia Derian responded: "What the hell is 'moderately repressive'—that you only torture half of the people, that you only do summary executions now and then? . . . The idea that we somehow must stand closer to dictators—people who are cruel to their people—is absurd.")

George Bush has suggested that the administration's way of exerting pressure on friendly governments accused of human rights violations may be modeled on the way a homeowner deals "with a neighbor who has trash in his front yard—often the best way to get results is, not to shout from the rooftops, but to speak to him quietly."

Reagan's overall model for the conduct of foreign policy appears to be that of the Eisenhower administration, which carried on a forceful worldwide diplomacy on behalf of American interests, and held the line, except in Indochina and Cuba, against the communist tide that had begun to rise after the Second World War. This policy will be much more difficult to carry out, and will be more hazardous than it was in Eisenhower's time. But the administration's nationalist values and assumptions should make it better suited, at least in the short run, than an administration devoted to global humanism would be to deal with other nationalisms, whether of friends, neutrals, or potential adversaries. "Peace," the president has said, "is made by the fact of strength. . . . Peace is lost when such strength disappears, or, just as bad, is seen by an adversary as disappearing."

In the study of American political history, the idea of a strong, activist national government is identified with the tradition of Alexander Hamilton, and that of relatively restrained use of federal authority with the tradition of James Madison. Reagan's belief in a Hamiltonian activist foreign policy may seem in some ways incongruous with his Madisonian commitment to internal decentralization. The two approaches, however, have been variously combined in foreign and domestic policies by past administrations and national political leaders. The four possible combinations of the two policy approaches with the two policy areas may be diagramed as follows, with a representative political leader in each quadrant.

| | | *Foreign Policy* | |
		Activist government	*Restrained government*
Domestic policy	*Activist government*	Henry Jackson	George McGovern
	Restrained government	Ronald Reagan	Robert Taft, Sr.

The administration's combination of a Hamiltonian approach to foreign policy with a Madisonian inclination in domestic policy appears to rise out of three conceptual ideas: first, that the nation is the shield of the republic, defending internal freedom through skilled diplomacy and a strong military establishment; second, that Americans have important common international economic interests which require vigorous representation all over the world; and third, that in addressing the rest of the world, American diversity should be expressed as a moral unity—"the exemplar of freedom," as Reagan said in his inaugural address.

The Moral Issue

Congressman Newt Gingrich of Georgia, a leader among the younger generation of Republicans now holding national office, has said that in the 1980 election: "The moral issue was what put us over the top. The economic issue and the national security issue between them brought us close to a majority. But it was the moral issue that carried us to victory."

What is the moral issue and what are its implications for national policy? Almost all political issues are, of course, moral issues in the sense that they involve normative value judgments as well as questions of fact and technical feasibility. Issues like disarmament, inflation, unemployment, and conservation of natural resources all include intense moral components. As the term is now commonly used in politics, however, it applies to a series of issues and concerns on which "traditional morality" (morality, that is, built around such institutions as the traditional family and traditional forms of religion) is challenged by modern ideas of social fairness or individual freedom of choice. Some of these issues that have figured in recent campaigns are abortion, busing schoolchildren to achieve racial integration, the proposed constitutional amendment to establish "equal rights" for women, the Supreme Court's prohibition of state-sponsored prayer in the public schools, exploitation of sex and violence on television, affirmative action policies to achieve increased representation of women and minorities in all phases of American life, recreational use of drugs, prohibition of discrimination against homosexuals, sex education programs in the public schools, open sale of pornography, and the perceived tendency of many modern institutions to erode the closeness of family life.

The moral issue has been particularly identified with conservative social action groups like the Moral Majority and Christian Voice, which make up the so-called new religious right. The concerns that it represents, however, are felt among a much larger body of voters, including many who do not agree with all of the positions taken by the religious right, or admire the political style of the Moral Majority, but who are disturbed by what they perceive to be the loss of moral direction and consensus in American life.

Such old antagonists as fundamentalist Protestants and strict

Roman Catholics are drawn together by the moral issue. "The ironic thing," Gary Jarmin, chief spokesman for Christian Voice has said, "is that the liberal element of the church has tended to be more ecumenical, but it is our movement that has brought conservative Baptists and Catholics together in a spirit of Christian community." The religious right also seeks allies among blacks and other minorities. "It is true," Jarmin has said, "that some evangelical preachers used to quote the Bible to justify racism. But that time is past. On issues like school prayer and gay rights, we are shoulder to shoulder with black and Hispanic preachers."

The moral issue in its contemporary form first appeared as an important factor in national politics in the 1972 campaign when the Republicans' charge that George McGovern was the candidate of "acid, amnesty [for draft evaders from the Vietnam war], and abortion" contributed to his landslide defeat by Richard Nixon. Four years later Jimmy Carter disassociated himself from McGovern's anti-traditionalist image and won substantial support from morally conservative evangelical Protestants, who regarded him as one of their own. As president, Carter took the traditionalist side on some questions related to the moral issue, and the liberal side on others. He supported the equal rights amendment, but opposed government financing of abortion; he favored affirmative action, but frowned on busing. In the end, he lost the confidence of most evangelical white Protestants, only 34 percent of whom voted for him in 1980 according to the *New York Times*/CBS News exit poll, without arousing much offsetting enthusiasm among liberals.

Ronald Reagan, in contrast, set out from the start of the 1980 campaign to make the moral issue his own. "Traditional Judeo-Christian values, based on the moral teachings of religion," Reagan told a gathering of evangelical Christians in Dallas in August, "are undergoing what is perhaps the most serious challenge in our nation's history." Under a Reagan administration, he said, "traditional moral values" would be "reflected in public policy." The 1980 Republican platform promised support for "a constitutional amendment to restore protection of the right to life for unborn children" (not quite the total prohibition of abortion demanded by the more extreme anti-abortionists), withheld endorsement of the equal rights amendment for the first time since 1940, promised to "restore the right of individuals to participate in voluntary, non-denominational prayer in schools and other public facilities," and pledged legislation to protect "the traditional American family against the ongoing erosion of its base in our society." At the suggestion of Richard Wirthlin, Reagan's pollster and a key policy adviser, family, neighborhood, and work were made theme words for the Republican campaign.

Reagan and his advisers have taken pains to distinguish between "traditional moral values" and the kind of racist attitudes that were espoused by some of Goldwater's more visible supporters, though not Goldwater himself, in 1964. Their opposition to busing and some forms of affirmative action, they maintain, is based not on rejection of the goals of these programs but on the belief that such attempts at "social engineering" are both ineffective and harmful to other values, like the right of children to be educated in their own neighborhoods or communities and reliance on merit to select among applicants for advanced education and employment.

Some items on the traditionalists' moral agenda, such as opposition to the equal rights amendment and busing, fit consistently with the conservatives' general preference for restrained government. But other traditionalist objectives, such as prohibition of abortion and stepped up action against the sale of drugs and pornography, require more government, not less. The return of prayer to the public schools would involve extension of government into an area from which it is now barred.

Why are conservative politicians attracted to moral traditionalism, even when it calls for expansion of governmental authority? Partly for political reasons. Despite some liberalization of social attitudes among the public in recent years, most politicians are convinced that traditional morality still weighs much more heavily than liberal humanism in the voting booths. To put it another way, social conservatives who have usually voted Democratic because of liberal views on economic issues are more likely to be brought to the Republican side by moral issues than are economic conservatives with liberal social inclinations to be switched to the Democrats. Paul Weyrich, director of the conservative Committee for the Survival of a Free Congress, has estimated that the abortion issue by itself accounted for about three percentage points in Reagan's vote in 1980—a statistic that, whatever its actual validity, is regarded as credible within the political community. In several close Senate races in 1980, such as those in New York and Idaho, the abortion issue was widely credited with supplying winning margins for conservative candidates.

There is more, however, than calculation of political interest to the conservatives' commitment to moral traditionalism. "It would be a mistake," Richard Wirthlin has said, "to think that Reagan bases his positions entirely on political considerations. On many issues, Ronald Reagan takes positions simply because he believes they are right." Apart from their views on particular issues, social conservatives find in traditional moral values the very root and structure of the social system—the underlying faith on which domestic order, economic prosperity, and national strength ultimately depend.

The first amendment to the Constitution, Reagan has argued, "was written not to protect the people and their laws from religious values but to protect those values from government tyranny." Governmental laws, he has said, "must be based on a higher law." In this view, the United States is essentially a religious nation, supporting no particular church, but drawing sustenance from and answerable to the moral and ethical principles set forth by the Judeo-Christian tradition, as is symbolized by the participation of clergy in all important government ceremonies and by the motto "In God We Trust" on the nation's coinage. (Reagan's own religious belief, though quietly expressed, is apparently deeply held. "Ronald Reagan is a very religious man," Lyn Nofziger, Reagan's faithful Sancho Panza and political aide, said in 1978. "He is always worrying about what God wants him to do." Nofziger added: "I tell him not to worry. God isn't interested in the United States or he wouldn't give us the presidents he gives us"—a judgment no doubt revised after the 1980 election.)

Reagan's position is, of course, fiercely disputed by many liberals and some economic conservatives. In a pluralist democracy, these critics hold, attempts to impose direction on matters of personal morality are both divisive and unjust. Yet the traditionalists are probably right that a society largely lacking in moral and spiritual ties—in the ability to say, as a society, either yes or no—will become first a jungle and then a desert. The danger is that if such ties are made too tight, individual rights will be violated and respect for legal authority will be weakened, as occurred under prohibition.

During a lecture appearance at the Woodrow Wilson International

Center for Scholars in Washington about three weeks after the 1980 election, Harold Macmillan, former Conservative prime minister of Britain, was asked: "What are the forces, the fundamental forces, that will hold us together and give us hope for the new period that we don't slide into a new dark age?" He answered: "There are only two forces. One is the great spiritual force of religion. The other is what I would call the force of common sense, ordinary decent life, and how people behave reasonably to each other. If you can have both, you're strong." The trick for modern governments is to go as far as they can in honoring the first (shared spiritual and moral values), without infringing on the second (common sense and respect for differences).

In the early weeks of the new administration, some of Reagan's key aides were urging that he downplay social and moral issues until after Congress acts on his economic program. How far the administration will go in promoting legislation on such controversial items as abortion and school prayer remains to be seen. The traditionalists can probably count, however, on at least rhetorical support from the White House's "bully pulpit."

A Reagan Revolution?

In all four of the policy areas discussed in this chapter—economic, intergovernmental, foreign, and social—the Reagan administration seeks to achieve major transformations. The extent of these proposed changes can be exaggerated. Reagan's political style is not revolutionary, and his record in California indicates that he is a pragmatic rather than an autocratic conservative—a Burkean, not a Metternichean. The earlier Republican administrations of Nixon and Ford in a general way shared Reagan's commitments to a market-oriented economy, governmental decentralization, the pursuit of national interest in foreign policy, and moral traditionalism. Reagan has said that he agreed with most of the stated principles of the Nixon and Ford administrations, but that he would seek to apply them more vigorously and consistently. Even the Carter administration was moving in its final years toward some of Reagan's positions, particularly in the area of economic deregulation.

Reagan, however, differs crucially from Nixon and Ford as well as from Carter because he is trying not merely to modify existing trends, but to shift policy into a fundamentally altered ideological frame-work. Whether he will succeed will depend not only on the administration's political skill and on the validity of the social, economic, and geopolitical theories on which its policies are based, but also on whether the time is really ripe for an epoch-making change in national direction.

APPENDIX A

Fiscal Activities outside the Budget

ANDREW S. CARRON

THE fiscal impact of the federal government is not fully revealed by the spending and revenue totals of the official unified budget. "Off-budget" activities can affect the level of demand and the allocation of resources within the economy just as appropriated expenditures do, yet until recently they have received little attention. The increasing size and scope of off-budget programs have raised concerns about their economic impact and the proper methods of accounting and control to be applied. Although improved surveillance mechanisms have been introduced in response to those concerns, the rising importance of these off-budget activities requires a greater degree of integration into the federal budgetary process, if not inclusion in the budget itself.

The most important off-budget activities are programs that make loans to the public for specified investment and assistance projects. These comprise direct lending by federal agencies and federal guarantees of loans made by private issuers. Also included are lending activities of the government-sponsored enterprises—private corporations originally established with federal backing, which facilitate the functioning of credit markets in certain sectors—and off-budget federal entities, which are federal agencies but whose activities are excluded from the budget by law.[1] As table A-1 shows, outlays of

1. The government-sponsored enterprises are the Student Loan Marketing Association, the Federal National Mortgage Association, the three components of the Farm Credit Administration, and the Federal Home Loan Bank system (which includes the Federal Home Loan Mortgage Corporation).

Table A-1. Outlays for the Budget, Off-Budget Federal Entities, and Government-Sponsored Enterprises, Selected Fiscal Years, 1960–80

Billions of dollars

Fiscal year	Total budget	Off-budget federal entities	Total federal government	Government-sponsored enterprises
1960	92.2	...	92.2	0.4
1965	118.4	...	118.4	1.2
1970	196.6	...	196.6	9.6
1975	326.2	8.1	334.2	7.0
1976	366.4	7.3	373.7	4.6
1977	402.7	8.7	411.4	10.2
1978	450.8	10.4	461.2	25.6
1979	493.6	12.5	506.1	27.1
1980	579.6	14.2	593.9	26.4

Source: *The Budget of the United States Government, Fiscal Year 1982*, p. 327.

off-budget federal entities and government-sponsored enterprises have risen sharply in recent years.

While lending is the most prominent of the off-budget activities, other government actions also affect private allocation decisions even though they also do not involve spending or taxing. Government regulation of private enterprise, for example, can redirect some of society's resources. Requirements for utility companies to provide particular services or regulations mandating the installation of pollution control devices can have effects comparable to those achievable through federal taxation and appropriations. Assessing the allocative effect of regulation presents major analytical problems, however, and thus lies beyond the scope of this review. In the following the focus of the discussion is on the allocative and distributional effects of federal lending and guarantee programs.

Federal Lending Programs

The core of federal credit programs is the guarantee by the federal government that it will pay interest and principal on a loan that goes into default.[2] Generally such a guarantee is sufficient induce-

2. Some off-budget lending, such as mortgages issued under the auspices of the Federal Housing Administration, are "insured" loans rather than "guaranteed." The agency collects a small fee upon origination of the loan to operate an insurance

ment for private lenders to advance the desired sums. But in some instances the amounts forthcoming have been deemed insufficient to meet perceived social needs, and the federal government has acted as both lender and guarantor. When those funds are appropriated by Congress to particular agencies, the loans made from such appropriations appear in budget outlays. Subsequent repayments of principal are counted as offsets to loan outlays in future years, and interest received is treated as an offset against future expenses. This method, called direct on-budget lending, predominated until the mid-1970s. Such loans are tallied separately from loan guarantees, although functionally they are very similar.

By statute, however, when the agencies themselves borrow funds for relending rather than receive them through appropriations, the amounts do not appear in the budget. Yet this off-budget direct lending clearly increases the total amount of financing that the federal government must undertake. The fiscal impact of off-budget direct loans—now the more prevalent type—is indistinguishable from those made on-budget.

Although some federal agencies that engage in off-budget lending are empowered to borrow from the public, most funds are now raised through the Federal Financing Bank. This federal entity was established in 1973 to consolidate and reduce the cost of agency borrowing. The bank borrows from the Treasury to purchase assets of guaranteed loans from agencies and to make direct loans that are negotiated and guaranteed by agencies. The bank matches the amounts and maturities of its borrowing and lending and adds one-eighth of a percentage point on funds advanced for administrative expenses. These lending activities of the Federal Financing Bank, like those of the off-budget agencies it serves, are not included in the unified budget totals.

The government-sponsored enterprises borrow from the public to obtain funds for lending. While repayment is not guaranteed explicitly by the government, these entities can borrow at nearly the government rate because their loan portfolios are well secured and often contain government-guaranteed loans, and because of the wide-

---

fund. Yet the federal government remains liable for losses that exceed the amount in the fund. So except for the shift that the fee imparts to the incentive structure, there is little difference between government-insured and government-guaranteed private loans.

spread belief that the federal government would not allow these agencies to default. Although privately owned and self-supporting, these off-budget enterprises are restricted in the scope of their activities and enjoy certain tax and borrowing privileges. They are today more akin to regulated industries than to agencies of the federal government, but their special status argues for some review of their credit-market activities.

Table A-2 shows the extent to which total federal lending has grown: from $8.7 billion in fiscal 1965 to $80.8 billion in fiscal 1980. The share that is off-budget has grown from 75 to 88 percent during that period. To put these figures in perspective, compare the amount of federal lending with the total amount of credit advanced in the economy. Until the mid-1970s, lending under federal auspices averaged about 15 percent of the total funds advanced in U.S. credit markets. In 1980, however, the share was 23.2 percent. For fiscal 1981, the amount is estimated at $98.8 billion in the Carter budget, and for fiscal 1982 the budget projects $109.8 billion in loans under federal auspices, with the off-budget share rising to 94 percent. Most funds will be advanced by private lenders under federal guarantees

Table A-2. Net Change in Lending under Federal Auspices and Relation to Total Funds Advanced in U.S. Credit Markets, Selected Fiscal Years, 1965–82

Amounts in billions of dollars

Item	1965	1970	1975	1980	1981 estimate[a]	1982 estimate[a]
On-budget direct loans	2.2	3.0	5.8	9.5	3.9	6.1
Off-budget loans						
Direct loans[b]	. . .	. . .	7.0	14.7	23.2	18.5
Guaranteed private loans	5.2	8.0	8.7	32.4	51.3	56.9
Government-sponsored enterprise loans	1.4	5.2	5.6	24.1	20.3	28.3
Total loans[c]	8.7	16.1	27.1	80.8	98.8	109.8
Loans as a percentage of total funds advanced in U.S. credit markets[d]	12.2	16.9	14.9	23.2	e	e

Sources: U.S. Office of Management and Budget, "Federal Credit Programs: Historical Data 1950–80" (OMB, Fiscal Analysis Branch, October 7, 1980), table 1; Board of Governors of the Federal Reserve System, *Flow of Funds Accounts, 1946–1975* (December 1976), pp. 8, 9; and *Special Analyses, Budget of the United States Government, Fiscal Year 1982*, p. 144.

a. Estimates do not reflect reductions proposed by the Reagan administration.

b. Primarily loans guaranteed by federal agencies and purchased or made by the Federal Financing Bank. On-budget agencies that were off-budget in earlier years are excluded from this category in all years.

c. Columns may not add to totals due to rounding.

d. Nonfinancial sectors, including equities.

e. Not estimated.

or by the government-sponsored enterprises. Additional borrowing through the Federal Financing Bank or directly by the Treasury will be required for less than one-fourth of the new loans.

The Reagan administration has proposed a substantial decrease in federal credit activity. New direct loan obligations, both on-budget and off-budget, and new loan guarantee commitments are to be cut by $13.6 billion in fiscal 1981 and by $21.0 billion in fiscal 1982. Savings in budget outlays will be much smaller in the first few years, reflecting commitments for loans and guarantees made under previous budgets. For fiscal 1982, the administration has projected outlay reductions of at least $0.3 billion in on-budget loans and $4.7 billion in off-budget direct loans.

Uses of Federal Loan Guarantees

Events in recent years have focused attention on federal assistance to private corporations and cities. Loan guarantees were approved for Lockheed Aircraft Corporation, Chrysler Corporation, and New York City. Yet the majority of federally guaranteed lending continues to be directed toward the traditional sectors of housing, agriculture, and community development.

Mortgage loans insured by the Federal Housing Administration or guaranteed by the Veterans Administration and Farmers Home Administration will account for over half of the net increase in new loan guarantees in fiscal 1982. One of the fastest growing components of off-budget lending has been the college student loan program. Legislation proposed by the Carter administration would result in a substantial reduction in such lending; the Reagan administration plans to eliminate access to federal funds for student loans, which can be expected to reduce the volume of activity even further. Loans to other countries for the purchase of U.S. military equipment are guaranteed by the Department of Defense and constitute another important component of off-budget lending.

Federal Lending in the Budget

In determining the proper treatment of loans in the budget, two considerations are important: whether to include a particular loan in the budget and how to redistribute income through lending programs.

Although off-budget direct loans are not included in the budget, as mentioned earlier, direct loans made by on-budget agencies are included. This practice is certainly inconsistent, inasmuch as the fiscal impact of the two activities is identical for a given end use. But the argument for equal treatment does not necessarily resolve the issue. In terms of federal borrowing requirements, increased lending can add to the deficit in the same way that increased government purchases can. Yet from the wider perspective of the entire credit market, the use of the borrowed funds does matter. One possible result is that borrowing that would otherwise still take place is shifted from private to public sources, and the economic impact is limited to a reduction in the risk and liquidity components of the interest rate, which may be offset by fees or restrictions placed on the loans. The other possibility is that federal borrowing for relending (whether on-budget or off-budget) changes the types of programs that are funded. These alternative outcomes for direct loans also apply to guarantees of private loans. So an appropriate treatment of federal lending would involve identifying programs that resemble allocations in the private sector and programs that alter private resource choices.

This is not to deny the possibility that programs that bring about allocational changes may improve efficiency without imposing costs on any sector of the economy. Mortgage loans insured by the Federal Housing Administration and other agencies may have these characteristics. Government programs initially increased housing production by promoting lender acceptance of new loan terms. Today the guarantees do little more than facilitate the packaging of loans into pools for resale on the secondary market. For unsubsidized, average-risk mortgages, federal and private insurance compete on an equal basis.

The redistribution of income through lending programs is the second important fiscal consideration. A direct on-budget loan or a federal guarantee, with or without access to off-budget Treasury borrowing, results in a lower interest rate. (Tax and liquidity advantages of Treasury issuances may lead borrowers to prefer government financing to the private market even with a guarantee.) The value of the lower interest cost may accrue to the government if it imposes fees that are in excess of its own borrowing costs, or accrue to the private lender or borrower. In cases in which a proposed loan contains a substantial element of default risk, private lenders will accept a lower interest rate (risk premium) if the loan is backed with a federal guarantee—assuming the government accepts the risk without imposing a fee sufficient to cover its expected losses. Certain loans, especially large ones made to a few borrowers, may have such a large default risk that private lenders are unable to bear the risk or request a prohibitive risk premium. In this case the federal loan or guarantee almost surely results in loans that otherwise would not be made. A choice by the government to accept such risks requires a judgment on equity or national security grounds that resources should be reallocated to projects with a lower risk-adjusted return on investment. These are examples of hidden subsidies; the government is, in effect, paying the insurance premium, although it does not appear in the budget until a default occurs. Additional subsidies are provided in a number of programs operating with loans made by both the private sector and the federal government. When the ultimate borrowers pay interest rates that are below the federal rates for off-budget loans, the subsidy appears explicitly as a line item in the budget. Interest subsidies for on-budget direct loans, however, are not reported and are reflected only in the excess of outlays over offsetting receipts in an agency's account.

Government-Sponsored Enterprises

The primary function of these enterprises is to improve capital market liquidity. The Federal National Mortgage Association developed a secondary market for mortgages; the Federal Home Loan Bank established a system of raising funds for savings and loan associations in times of tight money; the Student Loan Marketing Association created a new market for loans to students and their parents. The potential fiscal effect of the government-sponsored enterprises is limited to their contribution to the ability of on-budget agencies to carry out their credit functions. For example, if the mortgage agencies and the Federal Home Loan Bank make more funds available for mortgages, the number and cost of loans originated under various federal housing programs will be affected. The role of these agencies in the economy suggests that their budget impact is little different from that of any large private financial institution, and it seems appropriate to treat them as independent (off-budget) firms.

Control of Off-Budget Fiscal Activities

Although the activities of the off-budget agencies and government-sponsored enterprises remain outside the budget, surveillance and control of these activities have increased since the mid-1970s. The activities of several previously off-budget entities, including the Export-Import Bank and the Pension Benefit Guaranty Corporation, have been incorporated into the budget. The annual budget documents have also become more comprehensive in their treatment of activities that remain off-budget. Beginning with the 1981 budget, the Carter administration proposed annual limitations on new off-budget loans and loan guarantees. Congress has been asked to use appropriations legislation to control both on-budget and off-budget activities. The activities of the Federal Financing Bank are now recorded in the budget together with the agency functions the bank supports rather than as a separate entry for all bank lending. There is now a "credit budget" that shows the status of all activities associated with federal direct loans and loan guarantees. Attempts have been made to identify and quantify the subsidies and resource allocation decisions inherent in off-budget activities.

This work still has a long way to go. As the federal budget for fiscal 1982 (pp. 55–56) states: "The lack of a mechanism to integrate fully credit assistance with other resource allocation decisions creates perverse incentives. . . . Federal credit assistance may appear preferable to other forms of Federal assistance, since it largely escapes the review associated with activities that contribute to the current budget deficit." Accordingly, the Carter administration proposed the formation of a special commission to study the problem and recommend improvements to the credit-control system.

With the government constantly pressed on the one hand to cut the budget and on the other to render assistance, off-budget financing provides an expedient. The costs of programs supported in this manner are not reflected in spending totals, nor do they raise tax burdens. Rather, their costs are hidden in the resource shifts that occur when off-budget projects are moved ahead of other private sector claims in the credit markets.

Recent government changes in federal credit reporting have brought a greater awareness of off-budget activities. Putting a statutory cap on loans and guarantees through the appropriations process is clearly a useful step. Yet the measures taken to date are inadequate.

All these credit programs have a pure loan aspect, which reflects the government's role as financial intermediary, and a distributional aspect, to the extent interest subsidies exist. There is a strong case for treating the pure loan component consistently, whether on-budget or off-budget. An argument for making all loans off-budget is that loans by themselves do not have the same fiscal impact as do outlays for government purchases or income transfers. The large subsidies inherent in low-interest loans (below federal borrowing costs) would appear explicitly as items in the budget. Thus only the distributional component, as reflected in the interest subsidies, would be on-budget. In this way, the costs of federal credit programs would appear in the budget in true proportion to other federal outlays.

Once the pure loan aspect has been removed from the budget, with any distributional interest subsidies coming through the appropriations process on-budget, the case for direct lending by the government is weakened. With an accurate credit budget, statutory credit limitations, and an awareness of the cost of interest subsidies, loan guarantees can take the place of most direct loan programs. Shifting such lending to the private sector would clarify and improve resource allocation decisions. The Reagan administration has in fact proposed to do this in several programs, including the Student Loan Marketing Association. After many years of growth in these programs under a system of incomplete controls, the next several years may see reductions in federal credit as Congress and the president begin to address the problems inherent in off-budget activities.

APPENDIX B

Tax Expenditures

JOSEPH J. MINARIK

TAX EXPENDITURES are preferential departures from identical treatment of all types of income under either the individual or corporate income taxes. The term was coined to emphasize the similarity between a direct government expenditure for some public purpose and a concession in the tax law designed to induce or subsidize private action toward the same end. The major difference between the two is that direct expenditures are shown in the budget as outlays, while tax expenditures reduce measured receipts. The Congressional Budget Act of 1974 requires a listing of tax expenditures in each budget and directs all congressional committees to identify changes made in those budgets by new legislation.

The 1974 act defines tax expenditures as "revenue losses attributable to provisions of the federal tax laws which allow a special exclusion, exemption, or deduction from gross income or which provide a special credit, a preferential rate of tax, or a deferral of tax liability." For this purpose, "gross income" is generally regarded as being as close to economic income as practical measurement permits. (Thus capital gains are included in full, but imputed incomes such as rental values of owned homes are not because they are difficult to measure.) The personal exemption, standard deduction, and rate schedules are considered part of the usual income tax structure and thus are not tax expenditures.

J. Edward Shephard and Timothy A. Cohn provided research assistance.

271

Tax expenditures in fiscal 1982 are estimated at $266.7 billion. If they were replaced by direct expenditures of the same value to taxpayers, both outlays and receipts would be raised by $266.7 billion; thus current services outlays in 1982 would be $1,002.9 billion instead of the $736.2 billion reported in the budget, and receipts would be $973.2 billion, so that the deficit would remain at $29.7 billion (table B-1).[1] (Total tax expenditures are the sum of the revenue effects of the individual items, each computed separately and assuming no other changes in the tax laws. They probably understate the total revenue effects because individuals are pushed into higher brackets if all or a group of tax expenditures are removed simultaneously.)

The major tax expenditures are (1) personal deductions under the individual income tax (for state and local income, sales and property taxes, charitable contributions, medical expenses, and interest paid); (2) exclusions from taxable income (state and local government bond interest, employee benefits, and transfer payments such as social security, unemployment compensation, and welfare); (3) preferential treatment of long-term capital gains; and (4) tax credits and accelerated depreciation for investment. A list of the major tax expenditures is given in table B-2.

Tax expenditures have grown much faster than direct outlays over the past two fiscal years. This is largely because inflation has pushed taxpayers into higher marginal tax rate brackets; the cost of the tax

Table B-1. Effect of Tax Expenditures on the Federal Current Services Budget, Fiscal 1982[a]

Billions of dollars

Item	Outlays	Receipts	Deficit
1982 current service budget	736.2	706.5	−29.7
Tax expenditures[b]	266.7	266.7	...
Revised total	1,002.9	973.2	−29.7

Sources: *The Budget of the United States Government, Fiscal Year 1982*, p. 8; and *Special Analyses, Budget of the United States Government, Fiscal Year 1982*, pp. 12, 226–30.
a. Current services outlays and receipts are the amount the government would spend and collect if all programs were continued at the January 1, 1981, level with no policy changes.
b. See text for explanation.

1. Current services outlays and receipts are the amounts the government would spend and collect if all programs were continued at the January 1, 1981, level with no policy changes.

Table B-2. Major Tax Expenditures, Fiscal 1982
Millions of dollars

Tax expenditure	Individuals	Corporations	Total
Deductibility of state and local nonbusiness taxes	33,980	...	33,980
Deductibility of charitable contributions	11,505	885	12,390
Deductibility of mortgage interest and interest on consumer credit	31,335	...	31,335
Deductibility of medical expenses	4,080	...	4,080
Deductibility of casualty losses	895	...	895
Exemptions for elderly and blind and tax credit for the elderly	2,655	...	2,655
Exemption for parents of students aged nineteen and over	1,055	...	1,055
Exclusion of employer contributions to pension, health, and welfare plans[a]	49,010	...	49,010
Exclusion and deferral of interest payments[b]	8,980	7,495	16,475
Exclusion of benefits and allowances to armed forces personnel	1,715	...	1,715
Exclusion of transfer payments	24,370	...	24,370
Dividend exclusion	3,170	...	3,170
Earned income credit	755	...	755
Residential, conservation, and new technology energy credits	640	730	1,370
Job credits	30	175	205
Credit for child and dependent care expenses	1,175	...	1,175
Tax credits or exclusions for income from abroad	665	1,095	1,760
Preferential treatment of capital gains	26,975[c]	1,600	28,575[c]
Maximum tax on personal service income	2,105	...	2,105
Investment tax credit[d]	3,555	18,340	21,895
Asset depreciation range[e]	770	3,980	4,750
Excess of first-year depreciation and depreciation on buildings and rental housing in excess of straight line	635	285	920
Excess of percentage over cost depletion and expensing of exploration and development costs	2,795	3,400	6,195
Expensing of construction period interest and taxes	160	615	775
Expensing of research and development expenditures	45	2,230	2,275
Deferral of income of domestic international sales corporations and controlled foreign corporations	...	2,350	2,350

Table B-2 (*continued*)

Tax expenditure	Individuals	Corporations	Total
Excess bad debt reserves of financial institutions	. . .	470	470
Reduced rates on first $100,000 of corporate income	. . .	7,590	7,590
Other	1,370	1,060	2,430
Total	214,425	52,300	266,725

Source: *Special Analyses, Budget of the United States Government, Fiscal Year 1982*, pp. 12, 226–30.
a. Includes contributions to individual retirement accounts and prepaid legal services and Keogh plans for the self-employed.
b. Includes exclusion of interest on state and local government debt and life insurance savings and deferral of interest on federal savings bonds.
c. Includes revenue effect of deferral of tax on capital gains transferred by gift or at death.
d. Includes credit for rehabilitation of structures.
e. Includes expensing of certain capital outlays.

expenditures is estimated as though the exclusions and deductions were abolished and the resulting additional taxable income were taxed at those higher rates. However, some tax expenditures have grown more rapidly because they are more widely used; an example is the exclusion of interest on state and local industrial development bonds, owner-occupied housing bonds, and student loan bonds, which has more than doubled in revenue cost in two years (see chapter 3).

The inclusion of estimates of tax expenditures in the budget encourages the administration and Congress to consider them in budget decisions. The total of tax expenditures is 36 percent as large as that of budget outlays (see table B-3), and in recent years has grown faster. For some budget functions, tax expenditures (for example, aid for housing and aid to state and local governments) exceed direct outlays. The distributional effects of tax expenditures are often quite different from those of direct expenditures; for example, the deductibility of mortgage interest is of little benefit to the poor, whereas outlays for rent subsidies do help them.

There is a continual tug-of-war between the proponents of tax expenditures and the budget and tax experts who resist the proliferation of special tax provisions because they complicate the tax laws and are frequently less efficient than direct expenditures.[2] Congressional appropriations committees prefer direct outlays, and the tax committees prefer tax expenditures. The budget committees, recognizing

2. For illustrations of inefficient tax expenditures, see chapter 3.

Table B-3. Estimated Federal Current Services Outlays and Tax Expenditures, by Function, Fiscal 1982[a]

Amounts in billions of dollars

	Current services outlays[b]	Tax expenditures	
Budget function		*Amount*	*Percent of outlays*
National defense	177.8	1.9	1.1
International affairs	11.9	3.0	25.2
General science, space, and technology	7.3	2.3	31.5
Energy	11.8	7.3	61.9
Natural resources and environment	13.8	2.2	15.9
Agriculture	4.8	1.6	33.3
Commerce and housing credit	5.1	115.1	2,256.9
Transportation	21.9	*	0.2
Community and regional development	9.2	0.3	3.3
Education, training, employment, and social services	35.0	17.0	48.6
Health	75.5	23.3	30.9
Income security	259.3	60.0	23.1
Veterans' benefits and services	24.4	1.8	7.4
Administration of justice	4.8	...	...
Interest (includes interest from trust fund)	75.2	0.3	0.4
General government	5.2	0.1	1.9
General purpose fiscal assistance	6.5	30.6	470.8
Total[c]	749.7	266.7	35.6

Sources: *The Budget of the United States Government, Fiscal Year 1982*, table 13, pp. 578–88; and *Special Analyses, Budget of the United States Government, Fiscal Year 1982*, pp. 12, 226–30. Figures are rounded.

* Denotes less than $50 million.

a. Current services outlays and receipts are the amounts the government would spend and collect if all programs were continued at the January 1, 1981, level with no policy changes.

b. Excluding undistributed offsetting receipts and allowances.

c. See table B-1, note a.

both the similarities of and the differences between the two approaches, are trying to focus the attention of Congress on the merits of individual proposals rather than on the choice of the committee that originates the legislation. The budget process can be truly effective only when tax expenditures are recognized as being similar in many ways to direct expenditures.